D0721711

This is an important new critical analysis of Derrida's theory of writing, based upon close readings of key texts ranging from his stringent critique of structuralist criticism to his sympathetic and dialogical analysis of Freud's scriptural models. It reveals a dimension of Derrida's thinking which has been largely neglected by standard literary critical interpretations and appropriations of 'deconstruction'. Recognizing the importance of recent philosophical re-evaluations of Derrida's work, the author suggests an alternative perspective on his theory of writing with reference to aspects of contemporary natural science and systems theory. In addition, he shows how Derrida's philosophy of system and writing rejoins an atomist and materialist tradition repressed by centuries of idealist metaphysics. This study casts new light on an exacting set of intellectual issues facing philosophy and critical theory today.

CAMBRIDGE STUDIES IN FRENCH

General editor: Malcolm Bowie (*All Souls College, Oxford*)
Editorial board: R. Howard Bloch (*University of California, Berkeley*),
Ross Chambers (*University of Michigan*), Antoine Compagnon
(*Columbia University*), Peter France (*University of Edinburgh*),
Toril Moi (*Duke University*), Naomi Schor (*Duke University*)

A complete list of books in the series
is given at the end of the volume.

SYSTEM AND WRITING IN THE PHILOSOPHY OF JACQUES DERRIDA

CHRISTOPHER JOHNSON

University of Keele

CAMBRIDGE
UNIVERSITY PRESS

Published by the Press Syndicate of the University of Cambridge
The Pitt Building, Trumpington Street, Cambridge CB2 1RP
40 West 20th Street, New York, NY 10011-4211, USA
10 Stamford Road, Oakleigh, Victoria 3166, Australia

© Cambridge University Press 1993

First published 1993

Printed in Great Britain at the University Press, Cambridge

A catalogue record for this book is available from the British Library

Library of Congress cataloguing in publication data

Johnson, Christopher, 1958–
System and writing in the philosophy of Jacques Derrida /
Christopher Johnson.
p.   cm.   – (Cambridge studies in French; 40)
Includes bibliographical references and index.
ISBN 0 521 41492 X
1. Derrida, Jacques – Contributions in philosophy of writing.
2. Writing – Philosophy.   3. System theory.   I. Title.   II. Series.
P85.D47J64 1993
194 – dc20   92-16567 CIP

ISBN 0 521 41492 X hardback
ISBN 0 521 44852 2 paperback

UP

For Cecily

La 'métaphore' scripturale intervient donc chaque fois que la différence et la relation sont irréductibles, chaque fois que l'altérité introduit la détermination et met un système en circulation.

(*La dissémination*, p. 189)

(The scriptural 'metaphor' thus [comes into play] every time difference and relation are irreducible, every time otherness introduces determination and puts a system in circulation.)

(*Dissemination*, p. 163)

Contents

Acknowledgements

I would like to thank Trinity College, Cambridge, for granting me the time, space and material support essential to the production of this book. I thank also Malcolm Bowie for his kind advice and encouragement. Special thanks are extended to Marian Jeanneret, who supervised the thesis on which this book is based, and who has been an invaluable source of inspiration, insight and moral support.

Abbreviations

WORKS BY DERRIDA

CP   *La carte postale, de Socrate à Freud et au-delà*
D1   *La dissémination*
E1   'Economimesis'
EC   'Entre Crochets'
ED   *L'écriture et la différence*
F1   'Fors. Les mots anglés de Nicolas Abraham et Maria Torok'
GL1   *Glas* (page references will follow the system used in Leavey's *Glassary*, *a* and *b* denoting the left- and right-hand columns of the text, *i* the insets in both columns)
GR1   *De la grammatologie*
J   'Ja, ou le faux bond'
LI1   'Limited Inc., a, b, c'
M1   *Marges – de la philosophie*
MC   'Mes chances. Au rendez-vous de quelques stéréophonies épicuriennes'
ME1   *Mémoires – pour Paul de Man*
OA   *L'oreille de l'autre*
OT   *Otobiographies. L'enseignement de Nietzsche et la politique du nom propre*
P1   *Positions*
PA   *Parages* (*a* and *b* refer to the upper and lower texts respectively)
PS   *Psyché. Inventions de l'autre*
SCH   *Schibboleth. Pour Paul Celan*
VP   *La vérité en peinture*

TRANSLATIONS

D2	*Dissemination*
DE	'Desistance'
E2	'Economimesis'
EO	*The Ear of the Other: Otobiography, Transference, Translation*
F2	'*Fors*: The Anglish Words of Nicolas Abraham and Maria Torok'
GL2	*Glas*
GR2	*Of Grammatology*
LI2	'Limited Inc.'
LO	'Living On'
M2	*Margins of Philosophy*
ME2	*Memoires for Paul de Man*
P2	*Positions*
PC	*The Post Card. From Socrates to Freud and Beyond*
TB	'Des Tours de Babel'
TC	*Taking Chances: Derrida, Psychoanalysis and Literature*
TP	*The Truth in Painting*
WD	*Writing and Difference*

Introduction
From language to writing: the interdisciplinary matrix

It is generally accepted that there was a significant reorientation in French philosophical thought during the 1950s and 1960s, characterized by a shift of attention from the problem of the subject in history to the analysis of structure and language. Such a development reflected an increasing reaction against the intellectual and doctrinal hegemony of Hegel (or a *certain* Hegel, in his Kojèvian, Marxist or existentialist mediations), who had been a decisive reference for the historicist and humanist philosophy of the pre- and post-war periods.[1] The philosopher of the new French thought was unquestionably Heidegger, a Heidegger re-read and retrieved from the narrowly existentialist and humanist gloss, while in the 'sciences humaines', structuralism was beginning to exercise a parallel and equally powerful influence. Together, and in spite of their evident differences, Heidegger and structuralism can be said to be responsible for the 'linguistic' turn in French philosophy during this period. Already in his 'Letter on Humanism', published in 1947, Heidegger was distancing himself from Sartre's existential humanism and turning to the study of language, the 'house of Being'.[2] A few years later, in his inaugural lecture at the Collège de France in 1953, Merleau-Ponty suggested that Saussure's theory of the sign might offer to philosophy the possibility of escaping the eternal dichotomy of subject and object.[3] At the same time, Lévi-Strauss was proposing that the linguistic model could be applied to the analysis of myth and kinship structure, while Lacan incorporated Saussurean linguistics into his re-reading of Freud.[4] By the early 1960s, the linguistic paradigm had effectively displaced the philosophy of the subject in history.

The word 'langage' was applied not simply to verbal communication, to the realm of the immediately anthropological,
but to any complex or system: everything was, or was structured
like, a language.

This episode in French intellectual history has been well-
documented and discussed in standard critical accounts of the
period, but less attention is normally given to the renewed
dialogue with science implicit in the structuralist programme. A
strong characteristic of the departing humanist-existentialist
philosophy was the general lack of such a dialogue, no doubt
due in part to existentialism's rejection of the neo-Kantian
epistemology of its immediate predecessors: a philosophy of the
concrete and of the *vécu* had no need of a transcendental
idealism predicated on the example of scientific thought.[5] Very
much in contrast to this – but also in a spirit quite different to
that of Heidegger's work – were the aspirations of structuralism
to an objective and scientific status beyond philosophy and
ideology, a methodological efficacy in the study of man
comparable to that of the exact sciences. Despite the manifest
limitations of such a programme, one of the results of the
structuralist reorientation was the opening up of French
philosophy to a greater degree of interdisciplinary exchange,
both within but also beyond the so-called 'sciences humaines'.
The pursuit of interdisciplinary knowledge was seen as one way
out of the intellectual impasse in which French philosophy of
the pre- and post-war years now appeared to find itself, an
opening of new perspectives and possibilities. Though such
'interdisciplinarity' was in practice frequently restricted to the
application of the linguistic (Saussurean) model mentioned
above, the efforts of thinkers such as Serres and Piaget were
sufficient reminder of the more general origins and implications
of the structural paradigm. Piaget's survey of structuralism, for
example, points to the multi- and cross-disciplinary origins of
the concept of structure, of which linguistic structuralism is but
one particular region or instance.[6] From the perspective of the
history and philosophy of science, Serres defines the new
paradigm as 'neo-Leibnizian', by which he means that the
concept of the code and the basic operations of permutation and

combination have come to constitute the predominant methodology across the spectrum of the exact and human sciences. According to Serres, historically and chronologically this change of paradigm dates from the late nineteenth century, but it receives decisive and widespread validation during and after the Second World War, with the emergence of the new sciences of information theory, molecular biology and cybernetics.[7] Whereas the dominant concept of the nineteenth century was energy, formalized in the three laws of thermodynamics, in this century it is information. In a discussion of François Jacob's *La logique du vivant* and the philosophical implications of the new biology, Serres writes: 'Les sciences contemporaines sont ... formalistes, analytiques, référées, chacune, à un alphabet d'éléments, grammaticales, signalétiques ... Leur air de famille est si prononcé qu'on se prend de nouveau à rêver d'une *mathesis universalis*' ('The sciences of today are formalistic, analytical, grammatical, semiological, each of them based on an alphabet of elements ... Their affinities are so apparent that we are once again beginning to dream of the possibility of a *mathesis universalis*').[8] Following the discovery of the biochemical basis of heredity, encoded in DNA, life itself can no longer be regarded as irreducible essence, but rather as the product of molecular combination, the rules of which are open to decipherment: 'Ce que la biochimie a découvert, ce n'est pas le mystérieux noumène, c'est, tout simplement, la *caractéristique universelle* ... Elle désigne, comme les autres savoirs, une philosophie globale des éléments marqués' ('What biochemistry has discovered is not the mysterious noumenon, but quite simply a *universal science of the character*. Like the other sciences, it points towards a general philosophy of marked elements').[9] Jacob's account of the fundamental advances made in the life sciences in recent years is, as Serres points out, expressed in Leibnizian language, and repeatedly returns to the metaphor of the textual and the *lisible*: the logic of life is scriptural.[10]

It can be seen from Serres' description of the new Leibnizianism, and from the specific example of biology, that it was not simply the metaphor or model of language that had become a generalized feature of contemporary discourse, but more precisely the analogy of the script. In fact, during the 1960s there is what might be called a minor epistemic shift occurring within structuralism – or between structuralism and 'post-structuralism' – with respect to the linguistic analogy, involving a change in emphasis from 'language' to the more specific notion of 'writing'. As Derrida remarks in *De la grammatologie*, 'Depuis quelque temps, en effet, ici et là, par un geste et selon des motifs profondément nécessaires … on disait "langage" pour action, mouvement, pensée, réflexion, conscience, in-conscient, expérience, affectivité, etc. On tend maintenant à dire "écriture" pour tout cela et pour autre chose' ('For some time now, as a matter of fact, here and there, by a gesture and for motives that are profoundly necessary … one says "lan-guage" for action, movement, thought, reflection, conscious-ness, unconsciousness, experience, affectivity, etc. Now we tend to say "writing" for all that and more').[11]

Of course, Derrida's own work was itself a major influence in the dissemination of the idea of 'écriture', which is thematized in the programmatic texts of 1967, *De la grammatologie* and *L'écriture et la différence*, and which becomes, along with the afferent notions of 'trace', 'inscription', 'différence', and their later variations and mutations, perhaps the most enduring element of his philosophy. The influence of Derrida's reference to 'écriture' should not, however, be overstated. As he himself recognizes, it is as much a symptom as it is a cause. No less than with the reference to 'langage' under structuralism, it is impossible to abstract this new development, the introduction of the concept of writing, from a wider, interdisciplinary context. He continues: 'le biologiste parle aujourd'hui d'écri-ture et de *pro-gramme* à propos des processus les plus élémentaires de l'information dans la cellule vivante. Enfin, qu'il ait ou non des limites essentielles, tout le champ couvert par le *programme* cybernétique sera champ d'écriture' (*GR*1, p. 19) ('the con-temporary biologist speaks of writing and *pro-gram* in relation to the most elementary processes of information within the living cell. And finally, whether it has essential limits or not, the entire field covered by the cybernetic *program* would be the field of writing' (*GR*2, p. 9)). Derrida therefore locates his own conception of writing in a context more general than that of philosophy proper. As he says later in *De la grammatologie* apropos of the trace, 'dans tous les champs scientifiques, et notamment dans celui de la biologie, cette notion paraît aujourd'hui maîtresse et irréductible' (*GR*1, p. 103) ('in all scientific fields, notably in biology, this notion seems currently to be dominant and irreducible' (*GR*2, p. 70)).

The more programmatic and expository of Derrida's texts of this period (*De la grammatologie* and the interviews of *Positions* in particular) give the impression, therefore, that the move from language to writing is a necessary and inevitable one: it is not the initiative or inspiration of one individual thinker (Derrida), but the effect of a more general transformation of the modern episteme. This is recognized by Jean Hyppolite (who had taught Derrida in the 1950s) in the discussion following Derrida's paper 'Le système, le signe et le jeu dans le discours des sciences humaines', given at Johns Hopkins University in 1966, where he says that 'the language we are speaking today, *a propos* of language, is spoken about genotypes, and about information theory'.[12] For Jean-Joseph Goux, Derrida's grammatology, with its emphasis on a certain materiality of the sign, is directly influenced by recent advances in the information sciences:

L'opération scripturale et grammatique, qui pose par ailleurs la question même de la *technique*, du rapport général de la machine au vivant, n'est plus directement décriée. La réalité matérielle du signifiant, ce que la cybernétique nomme volontiers le 'support' d'une 'sémantique', n'est plus l'objet, sous cette forme, d'une dévaluation philosophique ... Le sens, l'information, pour une nouvelle pensée techniciste, n'a plus rien, nous le savons, d'essentiel. Le sens n'est rien d'autre, peut-on lire chez les cybernéticiens, que l'ensemble d'actions qu'il déclenche et contrôle de machine à machine. Et c'est certainement, Derrida y fait des allusions, ce nouveau stade, encore germinal, des pratiques de l'information, cette irruption bouleversante dans l'histoire du gramme ... qui rend possible, entre autres déterminations historiques, cette nouvelle interrogation grammatologique.[13]

(The scriptural and graphical operation, which, moreover, raises the very question of technology, of the general relation between the living and the machine, is no longer an object of disparagement. There is no longer a philosophical downgrading of the material reality of the signifier, what cybernetic theory readily refers to as the 'support' of a 'semantics' … As we know, for the new technicist thought, meaning or information have no intrinsic essentiality. According to the cyberneticians, meaning is nothing more than the ensemble of actions it both activates and regulates from machine to machine. It is clearly this new phase of information technology, still in its early stages, which Derrida alludes to, this revolutionary event in the history of the gram that, among other historical determinants, has made possible the new grammatological enquiry.)

This epistemic shift towards the scriptural and the informational is also, inevitably and inseparably, a socio-cultural phenomenon. Not only have the sciences made a significant step in the direction of a new Leibnizianism, as Serres calls it, but they are also implicated, both as cause and effect, in the more general technological evolution of modern society, most strikingly in the domain of information and communication technology. Derrida refers to this cultural substratum in a number of texts, from 'Freud et la scène de l'écriture' in *L'écriture et la différence* through to *La carte postale* and *Mémoires*, and it is essential to his perception of the urgently contemporary relevance of a philosophy of the trace.[14] His diagnosis of a certain 'end' of (logocentric) metaphysics, of which the grammatological turn is a symptom, depends upon the total social fact of this qualititative as well as quantitative evolution of Western technological culture.

It remains that Derrida makes no systematic use in his work of the developing conceptual and methodological matrix of the disciplines mentioned above. Even in what has been seen as the most declarative of his texts in this respect, *De la grammatologie*, the substance of Derrida's references to, for example, biology or cybernetics is more of the order of allusion and evocation than of active engagement. The passage devoted to 'Le programme' in the first chapter of *De la grammatologie* is brief and summary, while the third chapter, 'De la grammatologie comme science positive', reveals itself to be a history or genealogy of the philosophy of writing rather than (as the title might suggest) an interdisciplinary exploration of the place and scope of grammatology. In a sense this omission is inevitable, given Derrida's own training and disciplinary specialization (philosophy), but also given the essentially critical orientation of his writing, which is based on close and continuous textual analysis rather than on the application of what would be extraneous concepts or methodologies, with the uncritical acceptance of their self-evidence this would entail. In this sense his work is less confidently interdisciplinary – with hindsight, one could argue, prudently so – than that of some of his more syncretic contemporaries of the 1960s and 1970s.

This is not to say that one should attempt to discount or minimize the importance of Derrida's references to the 'extraphilosophical' sphere of modern science. His citation of two sciences in particular, biology and cybernetics, is symptomatic and not simply a passing gesture to the intellectual fashion of the moment, for what these two disciplines offer to philosophical reflection, as Goux intimates above, is obviously of considerable relevance to Derrida's theory of writing. Though this theory emerges most frequently through a process of dialogue with different 'moments' in the history of Western thought, and remains for the most part resolutely within 'philosophy' proper, the theory itself, as I shall attempt to reconstruct it, nevertheless shows some remarkable parallels with the discourse of modern biology, cybernetics and systems theory. The intertext of the vocabulary of these disciplines is clearly visible in Derrida's work, especially at the level of what might be described as his 'bio-genetic' metaphors, discernible in a number of important texts from *La dissémination* onwards. If structuralism is one, intermediate source of such a vocabulary, there is also a sense in which Derrida's appropriation of this vocabulary is profoundly *un*structuralist; for it is clear that structuralism, despite its proclaimed adherence to interdisciplinary knowledge, in fact practised only a restricted form of interdisciplinarity, mainly confined to the 'closed-system' models of linguistics and mathematics. These models are perfectly suited to the structuralist ideal of the homeostatic system, as Anthony Wilden indicates, but they omit to account for the forces of interaction and change, both within and between systems.[15] Derrida's conception of writing, on the other hand, has a greater affinity with the metamorphic and adaptational ('open-system') models found in systems theory, models which were never properly assimilated and applied by structuralist theory.[16]

The reading of the concepts of system and writing in the following chapters will attempt to place Derrida's work squarely in the interdisciplinary context described above. This aspect of his work has in general received little attention, and certainly no detailed analysis. Too often the emphasis has rested on what might be termed Derrida's special theory of writing, the preliminary critique or deconstruction of the phono- and logocentric subordination of writing, found in the 'classic' texts of the period 1967–72. This has most often been the case in literary critical interpretations and appropriations of the theory of writing. Such readings have involved, on the one hand, a privileging of the notions of 'texte' and 'écriture' – a fore-grounding of the formal, material and productive dimension of the written text – and, on the other, the treatment of literature as 'jeu', with its notorious English (mis)translation of 'free play'.[17] The problem with this reading of Derrida is that it deals with only one side of the equation, ignoring the important second moment of his theory of writing. At the same time as Derrida deconstructs the traditional hierarchy of speech and writing, he proposes and asserts something else; following the first moment of deconstruction, or rather implicit in its very movement, is the formulation of a general theory of 'writing' as a fundamental structure of phenomena. This general theory of writing is a constant theme of the 'classic' texts mentioned above, and, as I have said, is probably the most enduring concept in Derrida's work. To suggest that Derrida is proposing or asserting something, or that he is formulating a specific 'theory' or 'concept', is perhaps contrary to a certain orthodox interpretation of his work which would have it that his 'disseminatory' style precludes such reductive analysis or explanation. While the formal dimension of Derrida's texts should not be neglected (on the contrary, the following readings of Derrida will pay close attention to this dimension), one possible response to those who claim the irreducibility of Derrida's work would be that his disseminatory style is itself a theory. Derrida says in *La dissémination* that the programme or law is non-formalizable 'pour des raisons formalisables' (*D*1, p. 60) ('for reasons that *can* be formalized' (*D*2, p. 52)), and the same might be said of his own writing.

It is this aspect of Derrida's thinking, one might assume, that would be of capital interest to philosophers, but the fate of Derrida's philosophy in Britain and the United States has been an equivocal one, to say the least. Though the literary critical conscription of 'écriture' has no doubt been of specific strategic use within the field of literary criticism itself, an unfortunate corollary of this conscription has been a refusal on the part of many philosophers to regard Derrida's work as serious philosophy. The fact of Derrida's own often difficult style, combined with the modality of the initial assimilation of his work into academic institutions in Britain and the United States (via literary studies), has led to a number of misinterpretations of his philosophy. It has been variously construed as destructive criticism, a philosophy of nihilism, or a theory of infinite polysemy, and Derrida's reputation with philosophers has accordingly suffered. Irene Harvey writes of the 'sense of illegitimacy' that has been attached to Derrida's texts:

This 'sense of illegitimacy' and the general unwillingness to take his work seriously have been founded I believe more on his stylistic manner of exposition than the actual content of his work. In addition, the rapidity with which 'deconstruction' has been embraced by the literary critical community – either as ally or foe – has certainly been a deterrent, or perhaps an excuse, for the philosophic community to avoid having to deal with Derrida.

This situation is, however, in the process of change, and a re-evaluation of the possibility that Derrida might indeed be a philosopher, and even perhaps the most significant of our time, is under way. This re-evaluation is most prominent within the philosophic circles involved in or having a legacy from phenomenology, and of those, specifically the philosophers concerned with Husserl and Heidegger.[18]

The kind of revisionism that Harvey refers to here is obviously to be welcomed. Derrida's work *is* philosophy, and an extremely rigorous philosophy, both in its respect for the achievements of

traditional philosophical discourse and in its close and considered textual analyses. On the other hand, the conversion to a
more sober estimation of Derrida's place in a particular
philosophical tradition can also produce a certain marginali-
zation of the more problematically textual aspects of his writing.
Thus for Christopher Norris a text such as *Glas* 'defeats the best
efforts of descriptive analysis or summary' and lies 'at one
extreme of Derrida's project'.[19] Norris' own defence and
illustration of the 'rigour' of Derrida's philosophy is clearly
justifiable as a corrective to the many misperceptions and
misappropriations of his work, but it can also on occasion lead
to a somewhat limiting exclusion of the letter of his text. The
lesson one learns from Derrida's readings of others is that
philosophy is text as well as concept, or rather, that text and
concept are inseparable, given their double articulation and
mutual contamination. This would apply as much to Derrida's
own texts as to the texts of those he reads, to his 'classical' as well
as his stylistically more extreme texts.

   The purpose of my reading of Derrida will therefore be
twofold: to provide a structural analysis of Derrida's general
theory of writing from text to text; at the same time to examine
the language in which this theory is articulated. Having
established the main formal and conceptual parameters of the
theory, I shall compare Derrida's scriptural model with some of
the principal concepts of systems theory. The goal of this
comparison will not be to *explain* Derrida's philosophy from the
external standpoint of another discipline, nor to suggest any
direct or specific channel of influence from the one to the other;
it will be rather to draw attention to significant parallels
between the two discourses, and to investigate how these might
extend our understanding of Derrida's work. As I have already
suggested, this is also a recontextualization of Derrida's philosophy, or a contextualization supplementary to recent philosophical re-evaluations. In addition to the presentation of
Derrida as legitimate heir to a certain (continental) philosophical tradition, it points to the interaction of Derrida's
philosophy with a wider contemporary episteme, and, within
that episteme, the singular and special case of the life sciences.

An interesting corollary of this recontextualization will be its visible links with the 'atomist' or 'materialist' side of Derrida's philosophy, a side that has perhaps been more in evidence in recent texts, but which forms an important strand of Derrida's thought from *La dissémination* onwards. In certain respects, the reference to atomist philosophy in these texts represents a kind of 'short-circuiting' of the mainstream Western philosophical tradition, opening a fascinating dialogue with the semi-repressed other of that tradition.[20]

This introduction began with a discussion of the importance of the linguistic paradigm in the definition of structuralism, and it is with structuralism, or one of Derrida's encounters with structuralism, that I shall begin the first chapter.

CHAPTER I

The passion of inscription
('Force et signification')

L'écriture, passion de l'origine, cela doit s'entendre aussi par la voie du génitif subjectif. C'est l'origine elle-même qui est passionnée, passive et passée d'être écrite. Ce qui veut dire inscrite.

(ED, p. 431)

(Writing, passion of the origin, must also be understood through the subjective genitive. It is the origin itself which is impassioned, passive, and past, in that it is written. Which means inscribed.)

(WD, pp. 295–6)

The first chapter of *L'écriture et la différence*, 'Force et signification', represents an early engagement on Derrida's part with French structuralism. While concentrating on the particular example of literary structuralism, many of the arguments of 'Force et signification' are applicable to structuralism in general, anticipating in certain respects the critique of Lévi-Strauss in the later 'Le système, le signe et le jeu dans le discours des sciences humaines'. Derrida's evaluation of structuralist theory and methodology is made clear from the start of 'Force et signification': he considers its recent proliferation in the discourse of the human sciences to have produced a harmful reductionism, referring somewhat disparagingly to the 'invasion *structuraliste*' (*ED*, p. 9) ('structuralist invasion' (*WD*, p. 3)), or 'cette passion structuraliste qui est à la fois une sorte de rage expérimentale et un schématisme proliférant' (*ED*, p. 14) ('this structuralist passion, which is simultaneously a frenzy of experimentation and a proliferation of schematizations' (*WD*, p. 6)). His study focuses for the most part on a text he considers exemplary of the genre, Jean Rousset's *Forme et Signification*, described in its subtitle as an analysis of the structures of literary texts from Corneille to Claudel.[1] The title of Derrida's study, 'Force et signification', can be seen as a parodic correction to the title of Rousset's work, and indeed, Derrida's own argument, as it unfolds in the course of the chapter, will propose 'force' as a necessary condition or complement of Rousset's forms.

Derrida's approach to Rousset's text is not a unilaterally critical one: he begins his commentary with praise for the quality and originality of Rousset's work. Such praise is not unqualified, however, and he immediately expresses reservations, not so much a priori on his part as arising from within Rousset's text, this especially at its most apparently successful moments (*ED*, p. 14; *WD*, p. 6). Derrida firstly criticizes the 'success' of Rousset's reduction of a number of the literary texts he studies to *geometrical* schemas. This reduction is successful in that it appears to give an exhaustive description of the 'structures' or 'formal constants' (Derrida quoting Rousset, *ED*, p. 25; *WD*, p. 13) underlying the texts in question – in this first instance, certain selected plays of Corneille and Marivaux. Derrida, however, indicates how problematic the notion of structure can be. To begin with, structure itself becomes, in Rousset's analysis, the object under study, over and in spite of the text (*ED*, p. 27; *WD*, p. 14). Furthermore, it is taken quite literally to be a spatial entity, intuited as a morphological or geometrical construction. This application of geometrical – and architectural – figures to the domain of the literary text can only be metaphorical, but as Derrida points out, the use of metaphor is never simple nor innocent: 'Mais la métaphore n'est jamais innocente. Elle oriente la recherche et fixe les résultats' (*ED*, p. 30) ('But metaphor is never innocent. It orients research and fixes results' (*WD*, p. 17)). In Rousset's text this results in an analysis so guided and saturated by spatial metaphor that his a priori geometrical structures are applied to, and confused with, the textual contents they are supposed to explain (*ED*, pp. 32, 35; *WD*, pp. 18, 20). The nature of Rousset's method is indeed appropriately expressed in his choice of title, *Forme et Signification*: his own forms (spatial, geometrical) are imposed upon differing textual significations.

Derrida's corrective to Rousset's geometrical and morphological categories is his proposal of what might be called an additional dimension, that of the 'energetics' of a text: 'Dans *Forme et Signification*, le géométrique ou le morphologique n'est corrigé que par une mécanique, jamais par une énergétique' (*ED*, p. 29) ('The geometric or morphological elements of *Forme et Signification* are corrected only by a kind of mechanism, never by energetics' (*WD*, p. 16)). The attribution of, at best, a mechanics or a kinematics to Rousset's method invites comparison with seventeenth-century science and metaphysics, characterized by their recourse to the categories of figure and mechanical movement in their understanding of natural phenomena. Derrida contrasts Descartes and Leibniz in illustration of this. Leibniz criticized Descartes 'd'avoir voulu tout expliquer dans la nature par figures et mouvements, d'avoir ignoré la force en la confondant avec la quantité de mouvement' (*ED*, p. 29) ('of having explained everything in nature with figures and movements, and of ignoring force by confusing it with the quantity of movement' (*WD*, p. 16)). Derrida also relates Rousset's 'geometricism' to the tendency in seventeenth-century rhetoric (following Aristotle) to classify language according to its spatial arrangement in *figures* of discourse (*ED*, pp. 28, 29; *WD*, pp. 16, 17).

Derrida's placing of Rousset's structural method in the context or lineage of seventeenth-century metaphysics, science and rhetoric is not gratuitous, nor is his critique restricted to Rousset alone. Through Rousset, Derrida questions not only the modern structuralist movement (or elements of it), but equally an entire tradition of thought and the metaphors habitually employed in its articulation. Derrida's question is: how is such a tradition of metaphor made possible? and this question initiates reflection upon the function of language and metaphor in general (*ED*, p. 28; *WD*, p. 16).

The use of geometrical schemas in Rousset's analysis of the plays of Corneille and Marivaux is not the only aspect of Rousset's structuralism with which Derrida takes issue. A further aspect emerges in Rousset's analyses of Proust and Claudel. Here Derrida leaves the geometrical metaphor and indicates another modality of Rousset's approach, what he terms Rousset's 'preformism' (*ED*, p. 38; *WD*, p. 22). 'Preformism', in this context, is the idea that the totality of the literary work is contained in germinal form at its beginning, the end of the work being implicit in its origin. This mode of approach is effective because it is in complete harmony with the aesthetics *and* the textual practices of both Proust and Claudel (*ibid.*). In this case, Derrida no longer questions the apriorism of Rousset's method, and considers it totally appropriate to its object. The teleology of totality imposed upon the works of Corneille and Marivaux by Rousset's geometrical schemas is here a preformist teleology inherent in the literary texts themselves, constituting an integral theme of these texts (*ibid.*). However, the successful harmony established between Rousset's method and object of study in this instance also betrays a common metaphysic, that is, the metaphysics of simultaneity (*ED*, p. 41; *WD*, p. 24). Such a method is effective because the structuralism practised by Rousset has a predilection, shared by Proust and Claudel, for a simultaneous apprehension of all the elements of a given configuration. This is something for which the idea of preformism is especially well adapted, since it postulates that the part mirrors and resumes the whole, thus allowing the totality to be permanently present in any of its partial manifestations. For Rousset, as for J.-P. Richard, simultaneity is the truth of any given configuration (*ibid.*). The tense, the temporality of simultaneity, is that of the present, and in relation to this Derrida goes on to compare and associate structuralism with phenomenology, its immediate philosophical predecessor in France. What are habitually presented as opposing systems of thought, the one (structuralism) historically displacing and superseding the other (phenomenology), are therefore shown to share a common descendance, belonging to the same (logocentric) tradition of philosophical thought (*ED*, p. 46; *WD*, p. 27).

In the structuralism of Rousset, Richard and others the obsession with the idea of simultaneity is not unrelated to its fascination with the spatial: 'la recherche du simultané explique cette fascination par l'image spatiale: l'espace n'est-il pas "l'ordre des coexistences" (Leibniz)?' (*ED*, p. 42) ('The search for the simultaneous explains the capacity to be fascinated by the spatial image: is space not "the order of coexistences" (Leibniz)?' (*WD*, pp. 24–5)). Derrida then proceeds to quote Bergson's description of how the analytical operations of the intellect reduce duration to a homogenous spatial dimension, the simultaneous being the point of intersection of time and space. His own corrective to the preference of structuralist analysis for the simultaneous representation would thus appear to be an assertion of the importance of duration and becoming.

Derrida therefore criticizes a certain kind of structuralism which adopts, consciously or unconsciously, a certain kind of geometry and a certain conception of time as the determining framework of its analyses. Though he links these two models (geometrical and temporal) via the example of Leibniz, his correctives to them are made separately, and are respectively 'force' and 'durée'. In fact, these correctives have the effect of promoting the models, as Derrida presents them, by one dimension. 'Dimension' is a suitable word here, since although Derrida criticizes the geometrical model in Rousset's structuralism, he nevertheless (and perhaps necessarily) uses a spatial metaphor to counter and correct it. This metaphor is contained in what Derrida describes as the *flatness* of the structuralism of Rousset, and indeed of structuralism in general, and is expressed in the opening pages of 'Force et signification' in the figure of the panoramagram:

Le panorographe, image même de l'instrument structuraliste, a été inventé en 1824, pour, nous dit Littré, 'obtenir immédiatement, sur une surface plane, le développement de la vue perspective des objets qui entourent l'horizon'. Grâce au schématisme et à une spatialisation plus ou moins avouée, on parcourt *sur plan* et plus librement le champ déserté de ses forces. (*ED*, pp. 12–13)

(The panoramagram, the very image of the structuralist instrument, was invented invented in 1824, as Littré states, in order to 'obtain immediately, on a flat surface, the development of depth vision of objects on the horizon'. Thanks to a more or less openly acknowledged schematization or spatialization, one can glance over the field divested of its forces more freely or diagrammatically.) (*WD*, p. 5)

The immediacy and totality of perception the panoramagram permits anticipates what Derrida will say of the structuralist tendency to privilege the simultaneous (see above). The geometry of the panoramagram is two-dimensional ('surface plane', '*sur plan*'), and it is this image of the 'flatness' of structuralist analysis which will to an extent guide Derrida's critique of it: the complex of form and meaning constituting the literary object is reduced, under the structuralist analysis, to a flat schema in which form takes precedence over content. (The latter is seen by Derrida to be a force, an energy: 'le contenu … est l'énergie vivante du sens', *ED*, p. 13 ('content, which is the living energy of meaning', *WD*, p. 5).)

Derrida's strategic response to the structuralist reduction is to reintroduce force and energy and (with respect to time) duration. Metaphorically, this is achieved by moving upwards one dimension, as I have suggested. The metaphor is consistent: the text, as Derrida conceives it, is ideally three-dimensional. This extra dimension appears to account for the inclusion of force *and* duration: the two are implicated in a dynamized volume. Derrida's staging of the structuralist and post(?)-structuralist positions *vis-à-vis* the text is perhaps best appreciated in the following description: 'Dans cette exigence du plat et de l'horizontal, c'est bien la richesse, l'implication du volume qui est intolérable au structuralisme, tout ce qui de la signification ne peut être étalé dans la simultanéité d'une forme. Mais est-ce un hasard si le livre est d'abord volume?' (*ED*, p. 42) ('In this demand for the flat and horizontal, what is intolerable for structuralism is indeed the richness implied by the volume, every element that cannot be spread out into the simultaneity of a form. But is it by chance that the book is, first and foremost, volume?' (*WD*, p. 25)).[2]

One might hazard the following questions: is Derrida's dimensional metaphor innocent? Does it not in fact guide and condition his commentary? The proposition of a third dimension of force and duration, implicit in the volume of the text, as Derrida envisages it, seems to fall prey to the same

spatializing tendency of which he accuses Rousset. Against this
it could be argued that Derrida's metaphor is a necessary
strategy in the overturning of the uncritical and self-evident
premises of Rousset's structuralism. And in fact, in a form of
profession of faith (or discourse on method), Derrida proposes
that what might appear to be simply diametrical oppositions to
Rousset's practice are the strategic devices necessary to overcome that practice and the tradition it represents. Derrida
accepts that his own discourse is irrevocably situated within a
metaphysical tradition which he can only effectively disrupt
from within, turning the language of that tradition against
itself. This type of manœuvre, or strategy, is typical of the
practice he elsewhere names 'deconstruction'. The argument
reads as follows:

Nous n'opposons pas ici, par un simple mouvement de balancier,
d'équilibration ou de renversement, la durée à l'espace, la qualité à la
quantité, la force à la forme, la *profondeur* du sens ou de la valeur à la
surface des figures [my emphasis]. Bien au contraire. Contre cette
simple alternative, contre le simple choix de l'un des termes ou de l'une
des séries, nous pensons qu'il faut chercher de nouveaux concepts et de
nouveaux modèles, une *économie* échappant à ce système d'oppositions
métaphysiques. Cette économie ne serait pas une énergétique de la
force pure et informe. Les différences considérées seraient *à la fois*
différences de lieux et différences de force. Si nous paraissons ici
opposer une série à l'autre, c'est qu'à l'intérieur du système classique,
nous voulons faire apparaître le privilège non critique accordé, par un
certain structuralisme, à l'autre série. Notre discours appartient
irréductiblement au système des oppositions métaphysiques. On ne
peut annoncer la rupture de cette appartenance que par une *certaine*
organisation, un certain aménagement *stratégique* qui, à l'intérieur du
champ et de ses pouvoirs propres, retournant contre lui ses propres
stratagèmes, produise une *force de dislocation* se propageant à travers tout
le système. (*ED*, p. 34)

(Our intention here is not, through the simple motions of balancing,
equilibration or overturning, to oppose duration to space, quality to
quantity, force to form, the *depth* of meaning or value to the *surface*
of figures. Quite the contrary. To counter this simple alternative, to
counter the simple choice of one of the terms or one of the series against
the other, we maintain that it is necessary to seek new concepts and

new models, an *economy* escaping this system of metaphysical oppositions. This economy would not be an energetics of pure, shapeless
force. The differences examined *simultaneously* would be differences of
site and differences of force. If we appear to oppose one series to the
other, it is because from within the classical system we wish to make
apparent the noncritical privilege naively granted to the other series
by a certain structuralism. Our discourse irreducibly belongs to the
system of metaphysical oppositions. The break with this structure of
belonging can be announced only through a *certain* organization, a
certain *strategic* arrangement which, within the field of metaphysical
opposition, uses the strengths of the field to turn its own stratagems
against it, producing a force of dislocation that spreads itself
throughout the entire system, fissuring it in every direction and
thoroughly *delimiting* it.) (*WD*, pp. 19–20)

It would therefore appear that Derrida's own spatial metaphor
('profondeur' (depth) as opposed to 'surface') is a conscious
and necessary one. But it is necessary also for a reason slightly
different from that of simply providing a strategic counterpart
to Rousset's model and the philosophical tradition in which that
model is situated. The spatial metaphor is also important in
describing how the 'force' and 'duration' which Derrida so
frequently invokes in opposition or addition to Rousset's forms
are contained or *located*. The countering of Rousset's model, as
Derrida acknowledges in the above quotation, does not involve
simply the proposition of its supposed polar opposite. The
extreme positions of *pure* force and *pure* duration are only a
theoretical limit. Such a limit is, properly speaking, untenable,
since pure heterogeneity, pure difference, pure becoming (all
associated by Derrida with force and duration) cannot be
apprehended as such: a degree of admixture with their
theoretical counterparts (homogeneity, identity, simultaneity)
is required for apprehension to become possible. The force and
duration which are neutralized by certain structural analyses
and privileged by Derrida must inhabit a space or form
nevertheless. In Nietzsche's words, it is necessary to '*stamp* the
character of Being upon Becoming'.[3] The idea or figure of the
stamping of an impression is not irrelevant to the present
discussion, as will be discovered shortly.

In addition to the image of the text as volume (a spatial

image), Derrida uses another model, related to the former but perhaps better suited to the spatio-dynamic entity he is describing here. This model is the 'economy', mentioned in the passage quoted above: 'Cette économie ne serait pas une énergétique de la force pure et informe. Les différences considérées seraient *à la fois* différences de lieux et différences de force' (*ED*, p. 34) ('This economy would not be an energetics of pure, shapeless force. The differences examined *simultaneously* would be differences of site and differences of force' (*WD*, pp. 19–20)). The 'economy', as presented here, is obviously not to be understood in the common, restricted sense of the term. Derrida's 'economy' is a way of conceiving the more general, abstract notion of the dynamic interplay, or exchanges, between the elements of any system or complex. The economy harnesses a force without neutralizing it, since force and location in a sense intersect in the economy (differences are both ('à la fois') spatial and dynamic), they cohabit in a necessary double bind.

The setting forth of the models of the textual volume or the economy, as against 'panorographic' structuralism in 'Force et signification', is, however, of a greater complexity than the preceding, abbreviated account might suggest. There is much more of theoretical import expressed in the essay which does not figure directly in Derrida's critique of Rousset's critical theory and practice. Preceding and preparing the critique, following and concluding it, is a line of argument which, while taking Rousset's work as a point of departure, frequently appears to leave it on one side in order to pursue problems and ideas reflecting the preferences and preoccupations of Derrida himself. In these departures from Rousset's text proper, a not insignificant part is played by the figures of *writing* and *inscription*.

It is first necessary to examine briefly the structure of 'Force et signification'. The essay is divided into two sections.[4] The first section (*ED*, pp. 9–27; *WD*, pp. 3–15) deals with the introduction to Rousset's work, which contains the critic's general statements on the theory of textual criticism. The second section (*ED*, pp. 27–49; *WD*, pp. 15–30) is concerned with Rousset's method proper, his critical practice in the essays of *Forme et Signification*. Derrida's first departure from his detailed commentary of Rousset's work occurs in the first section, when he questions the uncritical acceptance by Rousset of certain traditional concepts, employed unanimously by the (then) current school of literary criticism. The last of these concepts criticized by Derrida is the idea that the imagination is the mediatory agent between meaning and the letter, which he traces back to Kant (*ED*, pp. 15–16; *WD*, p. 7). After this, however, the reader is led, via the theme of imagination, into areas apparently quite foreign to both Kant and Rousset. Derrida appears to take leave of Rousset's introduction and embarks upon a description of the nature of literary creation which has little to do with Rousset's brand of structuralism. This description occupies approximately eight pages, and constitutes a form of parenthetic preamble to the critique of Rousset's method in the second section. In the course of this passage, reference to Rousset is minimal and nominal, though the content of the passage doubtless informs and guides Derrida's subsequent criticism of him.

It is not with reference to Rousset, for example, that Derrida begins to speak of the 'excess', the 'absence', the 'vacancy' which precede and are the condition of the text. The principal point of reference here would appear to be Maurice Blanchot (*ED*, p. 17; *WD*, p. 8).[5] Derrida advances that it is *around* this vacuum, this 'absence pure' (absence not of anything specific but of all things) that critical discourse moves. But the pre-textual vacuum cannot itself be the object of such discourse. He proposes that: 'Son objet propre, puisque le rien n'est pas objet, c'est plutôt la façon dont ce rien *lui-même* se détermine en se perdant. C'est le passage à la détermination de l'œuvre comme travestissement de l'origine. Mais celle-ci n'est possible et pensable que sous le travestissement' (*ED*, pp. 17–18) ('Or rather, [its] proper object – since nothing is not an object – is the way in which this nothing *itself* is determined by [losing itself]. It is the [passage] to the determination of the work as the disguising of its origin. But the origin is possible and conceivable only in disguise' (*WD*, p. 8)). As with the 'pure heterogeneity' of force described above, this nothingness or vacuum cannot be apprehended *as such*. But this anticipates the movement of

Derrida's argument: for the present, it is sufficient to remain with the word 'détermination', since in Derrida's text it communicates directly with the idea of inscription. The word 'inscription' itself appears on the following page. After quoting Artaud's description of the painful experience of writing and the feeling of having nothing to say, Derrida says that this feeling is the condition from which all expression proceeds. The verb used is 'surgir' ('Et surgir toute parole', *ED*, p. 18; *WD*, p. 9), which implies a sudden and dynamic apparition of sense. Derrida continues: 'Car la pensée de la chose comme *ce qu*'elle *est* se confond déjà avec l'expérience de la pure parole et celle-ci avec l'expérience *elle-même*. Or la pure parole n'exige-t-elle pas l'inscription un peu à la façon dont l'essence leibnizienne exige l'existence et se presse vers le monde comme la puissance vers l'acte?' (*ED*, p. 18) ('For the thought of the thing as *what* it *is* has already been confused with the experience of pure speech; and this experience has been confused with experience *itself*. Now, does not pure speech require inscription, somewhat in the manner that the Leibnizian essence requires existence and pushes on towards the world, like power towards the act?' (*WD*, p. 9)). Again, that which is *pure* ('pure parole', 'pure speech', the extreme case), pure possibility, pure equivocity, needs ('n'exige-t-elle pas?') a support in which to realize itself, a support which actually constitutes that possibility or equivocity (*ED*, p. 18, note 2; *WD*, p. 9, note 22). In this case, the support is described as the 'inscription', referring to a category more general than the simply empirical operation of graphical inscription in a suitable medium. There is, for example, no indication as to where or in what the inscription is made; its only attribute appears to be that of actualizing the virtuality of 'pure parole'. In its turn, the term 'pure parole' is not restricted to the spoken word, and appears to apply to all forms of expression, spoken, written or otherwise (though Derrida expresses a certain preference for the written, as will be seen). The third important idea in the above quotation is to be found in the words 'se presse' ('pushes on') and 'puissance' ('power'), for 'pure parole' is not a neutral possibility, but is endowed with a force or vector. Hence the appropriateness of the verb 'surgir' (to spring forth) noted above. At the same time, such virtual force is meaningless without its actualization in form. Inscription is the point of articulation between force and form.

A peculiar characteristic of the inscription, as presented by Derrida in this passage, is that it is the instance of pain or anguish:

> Si l'angoisse de l'écriture n'est pas, ne doit pas être un pathos *déterminé*, c'est qu'elle n'est pas essentiellement une modification ou un affect empiriques de l'écrivain, mais la responsabilité de cette *angustia*, de ce passage nécessairement resserré de la parole contre lequel se poussent et s'entr'empêchent les significations possibles. S'entr'empêchent mais s'appellent, se provoquent aussi, imprévisiblement et comme malgré moi, en une sorte de sur-compossibilité autonome des significations, puissance d'équivocité pure, au regard de laquelle la créativité du Dieu classique paraît encore trop pauvre. (*ED*, p. 18)

> (If the anguish of writing is not and must not be a *determined* pathos, it is because this anguish is not an empirical modification or state of the writer, but is the responsibility of *angustia*: the necessarily restricted passageway of speech against which all possible meanings push against one another, preventing each other's emergence. Preventing, but calling upon each other, provoking each other too, unforeseeably and as if despite oneself, in a kind of autonomous [super-compossibility] of meanings, a power of pure equivocality that makes the creativity of the classical God appear all too poor.) (*WD*, p. 9)

The passage from pure compossibility to the inscription of writing is a narrow one (Derrida points to the etymology of the word 'angoisse': the Latin root is *angustia*, 'narrowness', but also 'difficulty', and even 'brevity'). It is because of this anguish and narrowness of passage that one might speak of a *passion* of inscription: the passage is a passion. It will be seen that a whole area of Derrida's work turns, with a certain fascination, around the question of the limen, the threshold, the passage, and its inherent difficulties or violence.

The passional aspect of inscription is of some importance in the understanding of Derrida's presentation of writing and speech. I have interpreted the inscription as being the advent of both spoken and graphical expression upon the vacant space of 'pure parole', but Derrida differentiates between the two and accords a certain preference to the letter rather than to the spoken word. (This is of course a typical gesture in all of Derrida's 'grammatological' texts of this period.) Of the *angustia* of the passage to expression, Derrida writes: 'Parler me fait peur parce que ne disant jamais assez, je dis aussi toujours trop. Et si la nécessité de devenir souffle ou parole étreint le sens – et notre responsabilité du sens – l'écriture étreint et contraint davantage encore la parole' (*ED*, p. 18) ('Speaking frightens me because, by never saying enough, I always say too much. And if the necessity of becoming breath or speech restricts meaning – and our responsibility for it – writing restricts and constrains speech further still' (*WD*, p. 9)).[6] The passion of graphical inscription is considered here to be of a greater intensity than that of speech (from which it derives), and the greater anguish it occasions appears, according to Derrida's logic, to represent a higher value. Such preference is confirmed in the lengthy footnote following this quotation. In this note, Derrida cites Feuerbach's remarks on the function of language as the medium in which the human species realizes itself, suppressing isolation and facilitating interpersonal relations. The passage from Feuerbach concludes that: 'C'est pourquoi l'élément de la parole est l'air, le médium vital le plus spirituel et le plus universel' (*ED*, p. 19, note 1) ('This is why the element of speech is air, the most spiritual and most universal vital medium' (*WD*, p. 9, note 23)). Derrida's rejoinder to this statement contests the valorization of the speech–air dimension of language: 'Mais Feuerbach songeait-il que le langage *éthéré* s'oublie lui-même? Que l'air n'est pas l'élément de l'histoire s'il ne (se) repose sur la terre? La terre lourde, grave et dure. La terre que l'on travaille, que l'on griffe, sur laquelle on écrit. Elément non moins universel où l'on grave le sens afin qu'il dure' (*ED*, p. 19, note 1) ('But did Feuerbach muse upon the fact that [*ethereal*] language forgets itself? That air is not the element in which history develops if it does not rest (itself) on earth? Heavy, serious, solid earth. The earth that is worked upon, scratched, written upon. The no less universal element in which meaning is engraved so that it will last' (*WD*, p. 9, note 23)). The act of speech leaves no permanent mark upon its medium (air), whereas that of graphical inscription endures in a tangible mark. As such, its medium (ultimately the earth) is the condition (the element) of history. The terms in which Derrida describes the earth are notable for their linguistic overdetermination, individual words condensing a number of associated meanings. The heaviness of the earth (it is 'lourde', contrasting with the ethereal lightness of the air) is associated with the following word ('grave') which, apart from its abstract and moral sense, also has the older sense of 'weighty', 'heavy'. But phonetically (and no doubt etymologically) the word also communicates with the verb 'graver', which Derrida subsequently uses to depict the action of inscription upon the earth. The same operation applies to the word 'dure'. The hardness of the earth (it is 'dure') guarantees the durability of the inscription it receives ('élément ... où l'on grave le sens afin qu'il dure'; 'the ... element in which meaning is engraved so that it will last'): the durable endures. Furthermore, the hardness and heaviness of the earth presents a greater resistance to inscription than does the ethereal medium of speech. The earth has to be worked ('La terre que l'on travaille') or scratched, clawed ('que l'on griffe'). It is the scene of passion – of violence. The Hegelian associations of this presentation of inscription as passion and violence, difficulty and constraint, are evident, and Derrida in fact goes on to suggest that 'Hegel nous serait ici d'un plus grand secours' ('Hegel would be of more assistance here'), since, while like Feuerbach he considers the element of air to be a permanent and universal essence, he nevertheless also posits the earth as the subject, origin and destination of that essence.[7]

This leads us to a further point regarding Derrida's reference to Leibniz. On the one hand, this reference is directly relevant to Derrida's argument: Leibniz's theory of compossibles is a useful homology of Derrida's depiction of the vacancy or excess preceding and conditioning the advent – or actualization of the text. What is more, the theory is concerned with the problem of creation, of how there comes to be something rather than nothing, and Derrida is above all interested in the inaugural instance.[8] On the other hand, the *angustia*, the anguish of the narrow passage to the utterance of speech, and a fortiori to the act of writing, is not to be found upon the scene of Leibniz's creation. Though the theory of compossibles may be an adequate homology of the excess of signifying possibilities prior to the determination of inscription, that determination is not wholly analogous to the Leibnizian passage of essent to existent. Derrida reminds us that:

> Dieu, le Dieu de Leibniz ... ne connaissait pas l'angoisse du choix entre les possibles: c'est en acte qu'il pensait les possibles et en disposait comme tels dans son Entendement ou Logos; c'est le 'meilleur' que, dans tous les cas, favorise l'étroitesse d'un passage qui est *Volonté*. Et chaque existence continue d'"exprimer' la totalité de l'Univers. Il n'y a donc pas ici de tragédie du livre. Il n'y a qu'un Livre et c'est le même Livre qui se distribue dans tous les livres. (*ED*, pp. 19–20)

> (God, the God of Leibniz ... did not know the anguish of the choice between various possibilities: he considered possible choices in action and disposed of them as such in his Understanding or Logos; and in any event, the narrowness of a passageway that is *Will* favours the 'best' choice. And each existence continues to 'express' the totality of the Universe. There is, therefore, no tragedy of the book. There is only one Book, and this same Book is distributed throughout all Books.) (*WD*, p. 9)

The 'tragedy' of the book, as Derrida sees it, is that it is not a monadic mirror reflecting and resuming the totality of the Book, as is the case in the Leibnizian universe. The book is irrevocably apart from other books, and has its own, infinite world (*ED*, p. 21; *WD*, p. 10). If one reconsiders Derrida's subsequent criticism of the structuralist metaphysic, it is clear that the idea of harmonious totality it proposes bears evident similarities to the Leibnizian system: there is the serene assumption that the corpus of an œuvre is in a sense already pre-existent in the creator–writer who, in a movement of willed revelation (*ED*, p. 23; *WD*, p. 12), realizes the work in its totality.[9] To this *prescription* (italicized by Derrida, *ED*, p. 22; *WD*, p. 11), Derrida opposes the very act of writing, the decisive moment of *inscription*:

> Ecrire ce n'est pas seulement savoir que par l'écriture, par la pointe du style, il n'est pas nécessaire que le meilleur passe, comme le pensait Leibniz de la création divine, ni que ce passage soit de *volonté*, ni que

le consigné *exprime* infiniment l'univers, lui ressemble et le rassemble toujours. C'est aussi ne pouvoir faire précéder absolument l'écrire par son sens: faire descendre ainsi le sens mais élever du même coup l'inscription.[10] (*ED*, p. 21)

(To write is not only to know that through writing, through the extremities of style, the best will not necessarily transpire, as Leibniz thought it did in divine creation, nor will the transition to what transpires always be *willful*, nor will that which is noted down always infinitely *express* the universe, resembling it and reassembling it. It is also to be incapable of making meaning absolutely precede writing: it is thus to lower meaning while simultaneously elevating inscription.) (*WD*, p. 10)

With this readjustment of Leibniz's cosmology, sense, meaning, concept, the Idea are brought down from heaven above, whilst the earthly (and lowly) graphical inscription is accorded a certain promotion. This displaces the traditional, idealist hierarchy: 'L'antériorité simple de l'Idée ou du "dessein intérieur" au regard d'une œuvre qui l'exprimerait seulement, ce serait donc un préjugé: celui de la critique traditionnelle qu'on appelle *idéaliste*' (*ED*, p. 23) ('Thus, the notion of an Idea or "interior design" as simply anterior to a work which would supposedly be the expression of it, is a prejudice: a prejudice of the traditional criticism called *idealist*' (*WD*, p. 11)). Somewhere between heaven and earth is the spoken expression which is rendered suspect through its collusion, in the history of Western metaphysics, with the Idea, the concept, the intentioned subject, in short, with all that is pre-scriptive. Derrida's example of Jeremiah receiving God's words and in turn dictating their content to the scribe Baruch (*ED*, p. 19; *WD*, p. 9), is a very appropriate representation of the hierarchical schema of Idea-speech-writing, which he here calls into question. The Divine Word is made progressively more incarnate in two instances: firstly, in Jeremiah's voice (the inscription of speech), and subsequently in Baruch's transcription (the inscription of writing). Despite the traditional metaphysico-theological acceptance of the precedence of the Word, or the spoken word over the letter, however, Derrida privileges the latter: it is the moment of human (earthly) responsibility and endeavour, and in one sense is the condition of its supposed determinants (*ibid.*).

However, the reversal which Derrida appears to be proposing in this instance is not an absolute one. His frequent rearrangements of hierarchies are never simply diametrical reversals, but rather lateral displacements of former configurations; hence the habitual caution in the wording of many of his statements. For example, it emerges from the foregoing analysis that the written inscription is given a certain preference over the spoken word, and that the traditional precedence of sense to the act of writing is parenthesized. (These two propositions are related in that Derrida sees a close association in the history of metaphysics between speech and the concept. The voice assures proximity to the self, a minimal departure from the interiority of the concept.)[11] This readjustment does not, however, accord absolute precedence to writing, and speech or concept are not dismissed out of hand. The movement is more subtle than this. In the preceding quotation, Derrida advances that one cannot place sense absolutely before writing, which implies also that there is, nevertheless, some precedence of sense. It is simply that the precedence is not absolute. The simultaneous ('du même coup') bringing down of sense from above and the promotion of inscription enhances this sense of relative, and not absolute, reversal. Neither ascent nor descent are absolute.[12]

The word 'precedence' is of course not only to be understood in its hierarchical sense (implied in the spatial figures of promotion and demotion), but also in a temporal sense. Because writing is, in a certain way, the condition of meaning and of the concept, Derrida considers it to be 'inaugural': 'C'est parce qu'elle est *inaugurale*, au sens jeune de ce mot, que l'écriture est dangereuse et angoissante. Elle ne sait pas où elle va – aucune sagesse ne la garde de cette précipitation essentielle vers le sens qu'elle constitue et qui est d'abord son avenir' (*ED*, p. 22) ('It is because writing is *inaugural*, in the [primal] sense of the word, that it is dangerous and anguishing. It does not know where it is going, no knowledge can keep it from the essential precipitation toward the meaning that it constitutes, and that is, primarily, its future' (*WD*, p. 11)). Once more, the precedence (here temporal) is not without paradox. This is apparent in the wording of the second sentence ('le sens qu'elle [l'écriture] constitue et qui est d'abord son avenir'). Writing constitutes, is the condition of, sense, which, nevertheless, is first the future of that writing. There is a bizarre reciprocity at work here which defies a conventional understanding of causality or temporal succession. Derrida goes on to explain that: 'Le sens n'est ni avant ni après l'acte' (*ED*, p. 22) ('Meaning is neither before nor after the act' (*WD*, p. 11)). The question of temporal precedence is therefore problematized, to the extent that neither the act (of writing) nor sense has absolute priority. In this connection, Derrida refers to an irreducible 'secondarity', a concept to which I shall return at a later point. For the present, one might hazard that this paradoxical 'secondarity' is approximate to the future anterior tense, to which Derrida refers in other discussions on the subject of time. At all events, the movement is a bizarre one, and it is precisely its *strangeness* which Derrida reiterates in 'Force et signification'.[13]

From the preceding analysis, four related propositions may be inferred in which the idea of inscription is of fundamental importance:

1 Inscription is the actualization of the excess of signifying possibilities preceding the text. It is the condition of sense.
2 The passage to inscription is the instance of pain and passion.
3 The traditional hierarchy of Idea-(voice)-writing is displaced, so that the written inscription is accorded a determining, but not absolute, role.
4 The displacement of hierarchical precedence is at the same time a problematizing of the question of temporal precedence. Both sense and the letter are subject to a certain 'secondarity'.

Together, the above propositions provide a model of the genesis and nature of the text, as Derrida describes it in 'Force et signification'. Such a model is radically opposed to the theoretical aprioris of structuralist analysis which does not discourse upon the text as such, but rather proposes structural constants by which it might be mastered. The general locus of Derrida's argument in 'Force et signification' is contained in this move from the text as the object of a philosophy of literature (structuralism and the tradition it represents) to a philosophy of writing as passion, possibility and production.

However, it should be stressed that what I have named Derrida's 'model' of the text is not thoroughly defined by the propositions set forth above. The analysis of Derrida's critique of Rousset's method has already indicated, in a less schematic fashion it is true, the use of the models, or metaphors, of the economy and the textual volume. The ensuing commentary of another important passage of 'Force et signification' will perhaps give a greater understanding of exactly how these various models are related.

The passage discussed above occurs in the final pages of the first part of 'Force et signification'. As has been noted, this passage is a departure from Derrida's critical assessment of Rousset's work itself, a parenthesis or preamble to the main critique of Rousset in the second part of the essay. Following that critique, and concluding the essay, there is a second departure in Derrida's text, a passage of approximately six pages (*ED*, pp. 43–9; *WD*, pp. 26–30).

This second passage expands the scope of Derrida's essay to a more general discussion of the metaphysical dimension of structuralism and the tradition of thought underlying it. Derrida believes that Rousset's 'ultra-structuralism' (Derrida's term) betrays the original spirit and intentions of structuralism (*ED*, p. 43; *WD*, p. 26). Initially, in the areas of biology and linguistics where the use of a specifically structural approach was first in evidence, the intention was to concentrate upon the coherence of one particular level of a given configuration and to disregard any apparent deficiencies which might anticipate a more 'normal', 'ideal' or 'perfect' state. Such a structuralism does not reason on the assumption of a finality that excludes the pathological on the grounds that it is unstructured, hence deficient in the context of an ideal totality (*ED*, p. 44; *WD*, p. 26 – Rousset is doubtless implied here). For such a structuralism, the pathological itself is structured. However, despite the theoretical and methodological rejection of teleological explanation on the part of the structuralism of, for example, linguistics or biology, Derrida argues that in practice all structuralisms assume some form of *telos*, in so far as an organized totality cannot be conceived without proceeding from at least a presumption of its end (*ibid.*). If sense only makes sense in a totality, how can it come to be without the anticipation of an end? Derrida writes: 'S'il y a des structures, elles sont possibles à partir de cette structure fondamentale par laquelle la totalité s'ouvre et se déborde pour *prendre sens* dans l'anticipation d'un telos qu'il faut entendre ici sous sa forme la plus indéterminée' (*ED*, p. 44) ('If there are structures, they are possible only on the basis of the fundamental structure which permits totality to open and overflow itself such that it *takes on meaning* by anticipating a *telos* which here must be understood in its most indeterminate form' (*WD*, p. 26)). Once more, Derrida is speaking of the conditions of possibility of a given system, the conditions of the delimitation and determination of the forces prior to and working within that system. Conditions without which, properly speaking, *nothing* would be perceptible. Like the moment of inscription described above, the 'fundamental structure' designated here is inaugural ('structure fondamentale par laquelle la totalité *s'ouvre* etc.' [my emphasis]). It is not, however, a 'structure' in the architectural or geometrical sense of Rousset's structures, or indeed in the configurational or combinatorial sense of other types of structuralism. It is rather a structuring principle, an abstract law which is the condition of a given system. But the determination of the structuring principle of finality described here must at the same time be indeterminate ('l'anticipation d'un telos qu'il faut entendre ici sous sa forme la plus indéterminée'). By the agent of such a structuring principle, there is not only the inauguration of a given system, but simultaneously the exceeding of the delimitating powers of inauguration ('la totalité s'ouvre *et* se déborde [my emphasis]'). This is the most Derrida can advance in order to escape the teleological trap which he perceives to be endemic to all structuralisms.[14] He recognizes the difficulty of this movement, continuing: 'Cette ouverture est certes ce qui libère le temps et la genèse (se confond même avec eux), mais c'est aussi ce qui risque, en l'informant, d'enfermer le devenir. De faire taire la force sous la forme' (*ED*, p. 44) ('This opening is certainly that which liberates time and genesis (even coincides with them), but it is also that which risks enclosing becoming by giving it a form. That which risks stifling force under form' (*WD*, p. 26)). The problem here is of the same order as that of the location of force, discussed above. Force must inhabit a structure, is not apprehensible as such. At the same time, there is the danger of the neutralization of force through its determination in a structured totality. The passage to determination or inscription (a necessary passage) entails the risk of loss, the risk of a formal blindness to conditioning forces. The predicament is aptly resumed in Derrida's assertion that: 'Dire la force comme origine du phénomène, c'est sans doute ne rien dire. Quand elle est dite, la force est déjà phénomène' (*ED*, p. 45) ('To say that force is the origin of the phenomenon is to say nothing. By its very articulation force becomes a phenomenon' (*WD*, pp. 26–7)). A possible exit from the constraints of this predicament is to be found in the model of the economy. The economy is a means of conceiving the dynamic interplay of force and form without submitting to the untenable position of either extreme. It is equivalent in this instance to the simultaneous movement of inauguration and excess ('la totalité s'ouvre et se déborde'). The moment of inauguration does not determine in a single sweep the integrality of a system (such integral determination would imply the restriction of a definite *telos*), but is itself surpassed in the movement towards an indefinite finality. However, the problem of *how* the economy works, and of the articulation of the economic model with the inaugural inscription, has yet to be elucidated. Its solution, it will be discovered, lies in the paradoxical temporality of the inscription itself.

The error committed by all structuralisms is that they do not practise the economy which Derrida preaches. In their efforts to understand structures, they omit to account for the forces which constitute those structures. Playing upon the ambivalence of the word 'sens' ('sense' or 'meaning', but also 'direction', that is, in this particular case, the fixed orientation of the classical *telos*), Derrida proposes:

Comprendre la structure d'un devenir, la forme d'une force, c'est perdre le sens en le gagnant. Le sens du devenir et de la force, dans leur pure et propre qualité, c'est le repos du commencement et de la fin, la paix d'un spectacle, horizon ou visage. En ce repos et en cette paix, la qualité du devenir et de la force est offusquée par le sens même. Le sens du sens est apollinien par tout ce qui en lui se montre [enter Nietzsche]. (*ED*, pp. 44–5)

(To *comprehend* the structure of a becoming, the form of a force, is to lose meaning by finding it. The meaning of becoming and of force, by virtue of their pure, intrinsic characteristics, is the repose of the beginning and the end, the peacefulness of a spectacle, horizon or face. Within this peace and repose the character of becoming and force is disturbed by meaning itself. The meaning of meaning is Apollonian by virtue of everything within it that can be seen.) (*WD*, p. 26)

One returns here to the metaphor of two-dimensionality which governs Derrida's critique of Rousset's structural method: the serene state of rest preceding or following the agitation of becoming is a horizon, is flat. In temporal terms, the static synchronism of beginning and end reduces and represses the process of duration and becoming, it is posited as their meaning and their destination. The equivocal (force, process, quality) is reduced to the univocal. However, it should not be assumed that in his critique of the structuralist reduction Derrida is arguing against meaning as such ('sens'). He is contesting instead a certain type of intelligibility. The play upon the word 'sens' ('meaning' or 'direction', 'orientation') is essential in the present context. What Derrida in fact contests is the restraint – and loss – of meaning through its submission to the *telos* of integral intelligibility, which is the inevitable *parti pris* of the structural analysis. This is why he can without paradox say 'c'est perdre le sens en le gagnant' ('is to lose meaning by finding it'): one loses meaning as such and gains a directional meaning, animated by the intent of a logical and comprehensible end (thus the introduction of Apollo). The phrase 'le sens du sens' must not be translated as simply 'the meaning of meaning', but should equally be rendered as 'the direction or orientation of meaning'.[15] Form, reason and harmony are never errant.

If the rational discourse of the structuralist is Apollonian in its extreme adherence to form and directional sense, then its necessary other, force and sense unrestrained by structure, is Dionysian (*ED*, p. 47; *WD*, p. 28). But the history of Western metaphysics has unfolded more or less exclusively in the Apollonian tradition. Derrida believes this history to have been founded and dominated by the metaphor of light: it is a 'photology' (*ED*, p. 45; *WD*, p. 27). This photology is characterized by the 'privilège du regard' (*ED*, p. 47) ('the privilege given to vision' (*WD*, p. 28)); it is a 'heliocentric' metaphysic (the epithet 'Apollonian' is therefore doubly appropriate) which subordinates force to the *eidos* ('c'est-à-dire à la forme visible pour l'œil métaphorique', *ED*, p. 45 ('i.e., the form that is visible for the metaphorical eye', *WD*, p. 27)).[16] Within the photological system, force is consigned to the shadow of darkness as the undeclared other of visible form, and such form is blind to its conditions. Structuralism, of course, is part of the metaphysical tradition of photology, as is its more or less direct predecessor in France, phenomenology (*ED*, p. 46; *WD*, p. 27). In a manœuvre similar to that of page 34 (*WD*, pp. 19–20), where his 'economy' proposed an alternative to the deeply-rooted metaphysical opposition of form and force, Derrida suggests a vigilant resistance to the oppositions practised in the language and thought of photology (*ED*, p. 46; *WD*, p. 28). But here again the question must be asked: if Rousset's structural method is governed by a non-innocent geometrical or architectural metaphor, which, in its turn, may be placed in the wider context of the history of the photological metaphor in Western metaphysics from Plato to Husserl, has Derrida no metaphors? Despite his desire to wrest the discourse of philosophy from the reductive oppositions legitimized by the persistence of certain key metaphors, is Derrida's language itself innocent? Already, the metaphor of dimensionality has been apparent in Derrida's critique of Rousset. To the two-dimensional, 'flat' object which the text becomes under structural

analysis, Derrida opposes the model of the voluminous, implicated text (*ED*, p. 42; *WD*, p. 25), comprising the third
dimension of force and differential time (duration). There is,
however, another, related aspect of Derrida's model which has
not yet been properly explored. One might begin with what he
says of the Apollonian philosophy bereft of its poetical beginnings: 'Elle est, pensée à part, le crépuscule des forces, c'est-à-
dire le matin ensoleillé où parlent les images, les formes, les
phénomènes, matin des idées et des idoles, où le relief des forces
devient repos, aplatit sa profondeur dans la lumière et s'étend
dans l'horizontalité' (*ED*, p. 47) ('Conceived apart, it is the
twilight of forces, that is, the sun-splashed morning in which
images, forms and phenomena speak; it is the morning of ideas
and idols in which the relief of forces becomes repose, its depth
flattened in the light as it stretches itself into horizontality'
(*WD*, p. 28)). This continues Derrida's contrast between the
inscrutable depth of volume ('profondeur') and the clarity of
the two-dimensional plane ('lumière', 'horizontalité'). But the
term 'relief des forces' does not simply evoke a topographical
variety as opposed to geometrical monotony: the topography
thus described is also a *moving* topography, one that has become
immobilized and becalmed under the gaze of a certain
(Apollonian) philosophy. Force is 'le mouvement qui déplace
les lignes' (*ED*, p. 47) ('the movement which displaces lines'
(*WD*, p. 28)). Depth and dynamic relief inevitably elicit an
image which is used consistently (though often only implicitly)
throughout 'Force et signification', the image of *liquidity*: force
is a flow.[17] When, for instance, Derrida sets forth the conditions
of the actualization of the word or the letter, the inaugural
passage is comparable to a high-pressure flow through a narrow
aperture. This is suggested by the verbs 'surgir' (to spring
forth), 'se presser' (to push on), 'se pousser' (to push against
one another) (*ED*, p. 18; *WD*, p. 9). The excess of possibilities
over actuality expressed here is presented later in the essay as a
movement of overflow, 'cette structure fondamentale par
laquelle la totalité s'ouvre et se déborde' (*ED*, p. 44) ('the
fundamental structure which permits totality to open and
overflow itself' (*WD*, p. 26)). The figure of flow is, however, not

without direction. The third dimension which force adds to the two dimensions of structural analysis is a vertical one: the flow of force is ascensional.[18]

What goes up, however, must come down. Another facet of the metaphor of fluidity is the necessity of the fall. The liquid column of force cannot forever ascend to infinite heights, for if this were so, it would mean nothing, be nothing. Therefore Derrida speaks of 'dionysie retombée' (*ED*, p. 47) ('fallen Dionysianism' (*WD*, p. 28)), or of the 'fall' of thought into (Apollonian) philosophy: 'C'est, *in historiam*, la chute de la pensée dans la philosophie, par laquelle l'histoire est *entamée*. C'est assez dire que la métaphore de la "chute" mérite ses guillemets' (*ED*, p. 45) ('*In historiam*, it is the fall of thought into philosophy which gets history under way. Which suffices to say that the metaphor of the "fall" merits its quotation marks' (*WD*, p. 27)). It is only through the agent of the fall that history is begun. (It will be seen shortly that the verb 'entamer' relates also to the act of writing or inscription, discussed earlier.) But a fall into what, one may ask? The pure flow of force can be if, and only if, it enlists the aid of its 'other', that is, figuratively speaking, the elemental earth. Quite simply, the hydraulic ascension of force falls to earth. The earth, the hard and heavy earth, was the subject of Derrida's exchange with Feuerbach in the note to page 19 (*WD*, p. 9, note 23), discussed above. The earth was considered by Derrida to be the fundamental medium of history, the element in which it is written and preserved, in contrast to spoken language which disappears once uttered ('le langage *éthéré* s'oublie lui-même' ('[*ethereal*] language forgets itself')). One cannot write on water any more than one can write on air. The essential fall of the liquid ascension of force (in different contexts, 'parole pure', 'pensée', Dionysus) is its inscription in history ('C'est, *in historiam*, la chute de la pensée dans la philosophie, par laquelle l'histoire est *entamée*'). Once again, we return to the scene of inscription, since the verb 'entamer' possesses a semantic ambiguity or duality which is consistently exploited in Derrida's texts. On the one hand, it refers to the act of beginning something, of initiation or inauguration; on the other, it has the related sense of the gesture of incision, of cutting into. The verb therefore contains, within its condensed semantic field, some of the essential attributes of the instance of inscription, as Derrida describes it: the sense of inauguration, of differentiation (incision separates the medium in which it is practised), and of passion (the incisive gesture is associated with a certain cruelty or violence).

It is necessary here to return to the language of Derrida's commentary of Feuerbach, for it is essential to the understanding of the final paragraphs of 'Force et signification'. To recapitulate: the earth is heavy ('lourde' and 'grave'), and it is upon its hard ('dure') surface that one engraves ('que l'on grave') the durable inscription ('afin qu'il dure'). To this system of associations might be added: the force of gravity (*gravitas*, weight) occasions the fall to earth (inscription). What ascends must descend, with force and mass. The closing pages of 'Force et signification' (*ED*, pp. 48–9; *WD*, pp. 29–30) rest heavily upon the association between the homonymous 'grave-grave(r)' and the conceptual relations (gravity, heaviness, descent, inscription) which derive from such verbal play.

The Nietzschean categories of Apollo and Dionysus apply in Derrida's argument to the photology of form and the hydraulics of force respectively. In the final stages of 'Force et signification', this opposition is extended to the difference between the seated and the erect postures. The difference or debate is between Nietzsche and Flaubert. Nietzsche maintains that, just as we must be able to dance with our feet, our ideas and our words, so must we learn to dance with the pen. Writing must be a dance. He vehemently discards Flaubert's contention that 'on ne peut penser et écrire qu'assis' ('one can only think and write sitting down'), asserting with confidence that 'rester assis, c'est là précisément le *péché* contre le Saint-Esprit. Seules les pensées qui vous viennent en marchant ont de la valeur' (*ED*, p. 48) ('A sedentary life is the real sin against the Holy Spirit. Only those thoughts that come when you are walking have any value' (*WD*, p. 29)). For his part, Derrida is inclined to agree with Flaubert that writing cannot be Dionysian throughout, and suspects that Nietzsche too was aware of this: 'Mais Nietzsche se doutait bien que l'écrivain ne serait jamais debout; que l'écriture est d'abord et à jamais quelque chose sur quoi l'on se penche. Mieux encore quand les lettres ne sont plus des chiffres de feu dans le ciel' (*ED*, pp. 48–9) ('But Nietzsche was certain that the writer would never be upright; that writing is first and always something over which one bends. Better still when letters are no longer figures of fire in the heavens' (*WD*, p. 29)).

The formal coherence of Derrida's *mise en scène* of Flaubert and Nietzsche, with respect to the metaphors of his preceding argument, is clear: the erect posture characterizing Nietzsche's (and Zarathustra's) aspiration to the heights is ultimately barren; the reader is reminded of the infinitely fluid ascension of force, which produces nothing. If one cannot write upon the fluid, then neither can fire written upon the ether of the sky – labile element upon labile element – offer any record of the lofty aspiration of the *Übermensch*. The hunched, sedentary posture of writing imitates the necessary fall, the curving earthwards of force (here the 'Saint-Esprit') made incarnate in inscription. The metaphor is continued in Derrida's reference to Zarathustra's lucid apprehension of the necessary hour of descent: 'Me voici entouré de tables brisées et d'autres à demi gravées seulement. Je suis là dans l'attente. Quand viendra mon heure, l'heure de redescendre et de périr' (*ED*, p. 49) ('Here do I sit and wait, old broken tables around me and also new half tables. When cometh mine hour? – The hour of my descent, of my down-going' (*WD*, p. 29)).[19] This can be interpreted: the force of solitary ascent is the cause of the broken and half-inscribed tablets, of the failure of inscription. In order to inscribe the new Table, Zarathustra must descend to the valley. In Derrida's words: 'Il faudra descendre, travailler, se pencher pour graver et porter la Table nouvelle aux vallées, la lire et la faire lire' (*ED*, p. 49) ('It will be necessary to descend, to work, to bend in order to engrave and carry the new Tables to the valleys, in order to read them and have them read' (*WD*, p. 29)). The verbs 'descendre' and 'se pencher' denote the earthward movement of force. 'Travailler' is perhaps to be understood in its most concrete sense, that of working the earth, as in the passage dealing with Feuerbach ('la terre que l'on travaille'). The verb 'graver' inevitably hearkens back to the same passage with its equation of 'grave-grave(r)'. The valley itself is the medium of inscription, the inevitable (but uncertain) destination of force, the lowest point, that is, the earth. Its geography is highly appropriate to Derrida's frequent rendering of writing as indentation or physical relief.[20] A valley is the hollow of the relief of a landscape, or the furrow between elevated terrain. Expressed in the terms of Derrida's geography or topography, the valley is the 'other' of the ascensional mountain. Writing is precisely a descent into the other: 'L'écriture est l'issue comme descente hors de soi en soi du sens … Creusement dans l'autre vers l'autre où le même cherche sa veine et l'or vrai de son phénomène. Submission ou il peut toujours (se) perdre' (*ED*, p. 49) ('Writing is the outlet as the descent of meaning outside itself within itself… Excavation within the other toward the other in which the same seeks its vein and the true gold of its phenomenon. Submission in which the same can always lose (itself)' (*WD*, p. 29)). The digging or cutting into the other ('creusement': inscription is always indention) is a perilous and risky enterprise. Zarathustra's hour of descent is also the hour of his death ('l'heure de redescendre et de périr'). The scene of inscription is regarded by Derrida as fraught with difficulty and danger, *angustia* and passion (*ED*, pp. 18–19, 22; *WD*, pp. 9, 11). Here also, descent into the other exposes to the risk of total perdition. But what is forever the same, has nothing to lose, is nothing before the risk is taken ('mais il n'est rien, il n'est pas (lui-)même avant le risque de (se) perdre', *ED*, p. 49 ('but the same is nothing, is not (it)self before taking the risk of losing (itself)', *WD*, p. 29)). Again, the Hegelian reference is evident: the master only becomes master and only accedes to self-consciousness and self-determination as a result of a violent and perilous confrontation with the other. At the same time, Derrida appears to be inflecting the Hegelian matrix, and to be proposing less a hierarchy of master–slave than an economy (though a conflictual economy) of 'fraternal others': 'Car l'autre fraternel n'est pas *d'abord* dans la paix de ce qu'on appelle l'inter-subjectivité, mais dans le travail et le péril de l'inter-rogation' (*ED*, p. 49) ('For the fraternal other is not first in the peace of what is called intersubjectivity, but in the

work and the peil of inter-rogation' (*WD*, p. 29)).[21] The lone
Zarathustra, as he is presented in the quotation which closes
'Force et signification', looks inquisitively around him for the
'brothers' who will help him to inscribe the new Table, down in
the valley.

The highly organized system of associations described above
is summarized in the impressively dense phrase preceding the
quotation from Nietzsche which ends Derrida's essay: 'L'écriture est le moment de cette Vallée originaire de l'autre dans
l'être. Moment de la profondeur aussi comme déchéance.
Instance et insistance du grave' (*ED*, p. 49) ('Writing is the
moment of the [originary] Valley of the Other within Being.
The moment of depth as decay. Incidence and insistence of
inscription' (*WD*, p. 30)). 'Grave' in three senses: the low
heaviness or gravity of the earth, or valley, to which ascensional
force curves in descent; the indenture of inscription; the
graveness of the moment of risk and peril (the demotional fall of
'déchéance').

There remains finally the question of the *moment* itself, its
problematic temporality. What is the temporal mode of the
'Vallée originaire'? The fact that Derrida says that writing is
the *moment of*, and not simply *is*, the originary valley, is
significant. As previous analysis revealed, the passion of
inscription is inaugural, it is an instance. But it is itself neither
force nor form, Apollo nor Dionysus: it is the condition of their
intersection. Derrida explains the dilemma in the following
manner: 'Il faudrait conclure mais le débat est interminable. Le
différend, la *différence* entre Dionysos et Apollon, entre l'élan et
la structure, ne s'efface pas dans l'histoire car elle n'est pas *dans*
l'histoire. Elle est aussi, en un sens insolite, une structure
originaire: l'ouverture de l'histoire, l'historicité elle-même. La
différence n'appartient simplement ni à l'histoire ni à la structure'
(*ED*, p. 47) ('We should conclude, but the debate is interminable. The divergence, the *difference* between Dionysus and
Apollo, between [élan] and structure, cannot be erased in
history, for it is not *in* history. It too, in an unexpected sense, is
an [originary] structure: the opening of history, historicity
itself. *Difference* does not simpy belong either to history or to

structure' (*WD*, p. 28)). The term 'différence', suitably italicized, does not simply mean the distinction between, or the opposition of, Apollo and Dionysus, form and force; more exactly, it designates the differentiating principle which operates at their juncture ('entre'), which makes possible that juncture and is the origin (the inauguration) of it. Again, this 'originary structure' is not a structure in the structuralist sense. Like the 'fundamental structure' described by Derrida on page 44 (*WD*, p. 26), it is a structuring principle, a principle which does not properly figure *in* history, since it is, in an unusual sense ('en un sens insolite') the structure that determines history. The idea of 'strangeness' has already been encountered above: for example, the paradox of sense being neither before nor after the critical (decisive, incisive) act of inscription (*ED*, p. 22; *WD*, p. 11); the 'strange movement' by which force, as the origin of a phenomenon, can be apprehended only as phenomenon and never as force (*ED*, p. 44; *WD*, p. 26). Whenever it is a question of order, precedence or temporal sequence, Derrida habitually evokes this 'strange movement' and its difficulties. Inscription is, in fact, a movement, an act, rather than a properly material or substantial entity, and its temporality is accordingly difficult to define.[22] What is more, the originary moment of inscription is not simply a unitary movement or act. It is not the empirical origin of a totality: indeed, as Derrida reminds us, difference (the movement of inscription *is* the movement of difference, of differentiation) is not *in* history, but is historicity itself, its very process (*ED*, p. 47; *WD*, p. 28). At the risk of being paradoxical, it could be said that the moment of inscription is always: it continues to work within a constituted system. Force, once fallen to earth, is not frozen in a single moment of inscription. This would entail certain death, the integral annulment of force, which is precisely the ultimate risk and peril of descent. Life is the survival of force, its continued circulation within an 'economy'. There is an instance, but also an insistence of the fall to inscription, 'instance et insistance du grave' (*ED*, p. 49; *WD*, p. 30). For Derrida, it is important to emphasize not simply the conditioning precedence of force to the phenomenon (a precedence which, however, cannot be apprehended as such), but equally the insistent continuation of that force within it. In the following two chapters it will be seen that this insistence, or continuation, is characterized by a certain mode of *repetition*.

My analysis of 'Force et signification' began with Derrida's critique of the geometrical metaphors informing Rousset's structural analyses of texts in *Forme et Signification*. For Derrida, these geometrical metaphors are closely related to the structuralist obsession with visible form (symptomatic of the 'photological' reflex of the Western philosophical tradition) and the temporal mode of simultaneity (the present tense possessing an unusual privilege in that tradition). The result of this privileging of form and simultaneity is the reduction and neutralization of force and duration, the repressed 'other' of Apollonian philosophy. In itself, this critique of a specific example of literary structuralism (but by implication of structuralism in general) does not differ significantly from the standard critique of structuralism as formulated from a number of philosophical or ideological viewpoints during the 1960s. In essence, the standard critique is directed at what are considered to be the theoretical and methodological limitations of structuralism, namely, its tendency towards synchronism, reductive closure and the hypostatization or reification of structure (the structure being intuited as an almost tangible property of the system). Derrida's own engagement with structuralism includes these elements of the standard critique, but its force and originality derives rather from the manner in which the very *discourse* of structuralism, the models and metaphors it mobilizes in the construction of this discourse, are exposed and questioned in their self-evidence. In addition to this, and perhaps more importantly, Derrida proposes counter-models and counter-metaphors in what is a form of strategic response to structuralist theory. In 'Force et signification', he does not simply disassemble the conceptual edifice of structuralism, he also elaborates a model of the text which stands in contrast to the structuralist model and contests the tradition it represents. Derrida's model, itself by no means neutral in its use of metaphor, includes the third (vertical, hydraulic) dimension of force and duration: the text is represented as a dynamic volume.

However, form is not rejected out of hand, for it is the necessary support for the apprehension of force, the necessary 'other' of force. In fact, force and form must be thought together in an 'economy' which escapes the meaningless or fixed formulation of either extreme. The condition of this intersection of force and form, their successful economy, resides in a certain type of writing or inscription which both brings together and differentiates between their divergent tendencies. It is only with such determination as writing permits that the system or economy can function or be. Inscription – an inscription that is necessarily passion and violence – is the condition of possibility of the system of the text. The following chapter will generalize and extend these points by considering Derrida's model in a wider context.

CHAPTER 2

Infinity, inscription, the economy

Un *système* n'est ni fini ni infini. Une totalité structurale
échappe en son jeu à cette alternative. Elle échappe à
l'archéologique et à l'eschatologique et les inscrit en elle-
même.

(*ED*, p. 180)

(A *system* is neither finite nor infinite. A structural totality
escapes this alternative in its functioning. It escapes the
archaeological and the eschatological and inscribes them
in itself.)

(*WD*, p. 123)

The model of writing that emerges from Derrida's critique of
literary structuralism in 'Force et signification' is not peculiar
to that text alone. Despite the thematic diversity of the book,
what is striking for the reader of *L'écriture et la différence*, as she or
he moves from chapter to chapter, is the relative homogeneity of
Derrida's approach to the texts and authors he selects for
commentary, a certain insistence of interpretation. Thus it
might be possible to formalize Derrida's model of writing, as it
is deployed in the texts of *L'écriture et la différence*, to isolate its
significant or distinctive features. Reasoning from the points
gathered in chapter 1, it could be said that Derrida's model
consists of three 'moments', which, however, are not moments
in a chronological or sequential sense, nor in the sense of
their being necessarily distinct from one another. These three
moments are *infinity, inscription, the economy*.

INFINITY

Already in 'Force et signification' there was reference to a certain kind of infinity. The text, in contrast to the 'flat' structuralist model, was described as a volume, characterized by 'l'implication infinie', 'mouvement, infini, labilité et instabilité du sens' (*ED*, p. 42) ('infinite implication', 'movement, inifinity, lability, and instability of meaning' (*WD*, p. 25)). In addition, the dimensions of force and duration, reduced and neutralized in the structural analysis, were described in terms of hypothetical extremes or limits, with the repeated use of the epithet 'pure' ('puissance d'equivocité pure', 'pure hétérogénéité qualitative', *ED*, pp. 18, 36 ('power of pure equivocality', 'pure qualitative heterogeneity', *WD*, pp. 9, 21)), thereby suggesting their infinitization. Finally, the plethora of signifying possibilities attendant upon the moment of determination or inscription was described as 'une sorte de surcompossibilité autonome des significations' (*ED*, p. 18) ('a kind of autonomous [super-compossibility] of meanings' (*WD*, p. 9)), again evoking, via the allusion to Leibniz, a form of infinity. However, to borrow an expression frequently employed in Derrida's writing, it might be said that the 'infinity' described in 'Force et signification' is a *certain* (type of) infinity. It is not, for example, equivalent to the classical philosophical definition which would distinguish between a potential and an actual infinity, refuting the existence of the latter; nor would it follow Descartes in seeing the argument for the existence of God as requiring the actual rather than the potential infinite. This difference becomes more apparent if one turns to other texts of *L'écriture et la différence*, though typically, nowhere in these texts is a *concept* of infinity actually defined.

In 'Cogito et histoire de la folie', the second chapter of *L'écriture et la différence*, Derrida's 'certain' infinity is defined firstly in terms of *excess*, the key words here being 'hyperbole' and 'démesure'. In what is otherwise a generally sympathetic reading of Foucault's *Histoire de la folie*, Derrida expresses his disagreement with Foucault as to where to situate what the latter names the 'coup de force' by which Descartes achieves the exclusion of madness from the domain of reason. Foucault situates this exclusion in the first of Descartes' *Méditations métaphysiques* (*ED*, p. 71; *WD*, p. 45). In contrast, Derrida, after a close reading of both Foucault and Descartes, concludes that in effect there is no exclusion of madness in Descartes' text, and that if, as Foucault claims, a 'coup de force' does take place, then it comes at a later stage in the *Méditations*, namely in the moment immediately following the *cogito* (*ED*, pp. 86, 91; *WD*, pp. 55–6, 58). The point of interest here is that Derrida's criticism of Descartes does not bear upon the *cogito* itself, but rather on the 'moment' directly succeeding it; he follows Descartes in what is essentially his 'passage à la limite' to the 'zero-point' (Derrida's term, *ED*, p. 86; *WD*, p. 56) of the *cogito*. After the passage through natural doubt (in which Derrida demonstrates that madness is only a regional, intermittent case of a total falsification of the senses, occasioned, for example, by the state of dreaming) and hyperbolic (metaphysical) doubt, Descartes accedes to the *cogito* which holds true *even if* one is mad (*ED*, p. 86; *WD*, p. 55), and which therefore includes both reason *and* madness. Again, Derrida appears to be speaking, with but beyond Descartes, of the conditions of possibility of a particular system, and his vocabulary here is primarily one of excess, a vocabulary which is not to be found in the text of the *Méditations* itself. Because the *cogito* is the zero-point from which both sense and non-sense are derived, it exceeds any actual worldly totality; it is, to quote Derrida: 'pré-compréhension de la totalité infinie et indéterminée … cet excès du possible, du droit et du sens sur le réel … excès inouï et singulier … excès vers le non-déterminé, vers le Rien ou l'Infini … excès débordant la totalité de ce que l'on peut penser' (*ED*, p. 87) ('precomprehension of the infinite and undetermined totality … this margin of the possible, the principled, and the meaningful, which exceeds all that is real … a singular and unprecedented excess – an excess in the direction of the nondetermined, Nothingness or Infinity, an excess which overflows the totality of that which can be thought' (*WD*, pp. 56–7)). Derrida adopts the Cartesian term 'hyperbole', and by way of Glaucon's remark to Socrates in Plato's *Republic*, combines it with the idea of the malevolent demon in the phrase 'hyperbole démonique'. In addition to this, he plays upon the terms 'mesure' and 'démesure' with respect to the measurement of height. In consequence, the passage reads as an extremely dense, closely-knit sequence of associated terms, as is apparent in the phrase: 'Elle [l'hyperbole démonique] implique, à supposer qu'elle soit dérèglement et démesure, le dérèglement et la démesure fondamentale de l'hyperbole qui ouvre et fonde le monde comme tel en l'excédant' (*ED*, p. 87) ('Assuming that it is deranged and excessive, [the demonic hyperbole] implies the fundamental derangement and excessiveness of the hyperbole which opens and founds the world as such by exceeding it' (*WD*, p. 57)). Once again, the concern here is with fundamentals, with that which founds and opens a totality, but simultaneously exceeds that totality. But the *cogito* itself is not the bold hyperbole which inaugurates the totality; it is not the moment of determination, as in fact Foucault believes it to be. Derrida stresses the non-determination of the infinite excess here described. The zero-point of the *cogito* is: 'un point originaire qui n'appartient plus au couple d'une raison et d'une déraison *déterminées*, à leur opposition ou à leur alternative' (*ED*, p. 86) ('an [originary] point which no longer belongs to either a *determined* reason or a *determined* unreason, no longer belongs to them as opposition or alternative' (*WD*, p. 56)). The 'determination' which Derrida italicizes in this phrase would appear to be structurally equivalent to the notion of inscription discussed in chapter 1 above.

If we now turn to 'Violence et métaphysique', Derrida's extended dialogue with the philosophy of Emmanuel Levinas, one finds a similar treatment of the category of the infinite. The persistent preoccupation of Levinas' philosophy is with the suppression, by a whole philosophical tradition, of what he names the 'Other'. One essential attribute of this 'Other' ('l'autre') is that it is infinite in a manner resistant to the delimitating violence of the philosophical concept, which is defined by the quality of sameness ('le même'). In the following passage, Derrida describes the 'movement' (his term) of desire in Levinas' philosophy ('respect et connaissance de l'autre

comme autre', *ED*, p. 138 ('respect and knowledge of the other
as other', *WD*, p. 92)), as contrasted with the finite operations
of intentionality or need: 'Le désir au contraire se laisse appeler
par l'extériorité absolument irréductible de l'autre auquel il
doit rester infiniment inadéquat. Il n'est égal qu'à la démesure.
Aucune totalité jamais ne se fermera sur lui. La métaphysique
du désir est donc métaphysique de la séparation infinie' (*ED*,
p. 138) ('Desire, on the contrary, permits itself to be appealed
to by the absolutely irreducible exteriority of the other to which
it must remain infinitely inadequate. Desire is equal only to
excess. No totality will ever encompass it. Thus, the metaphysics
of desire is a metaphysics of infinite separation' (*WD*, p. 93)). As
in 'Cogito et histoire de la folie', here too there is the idea and
vocabulary of 'démesure'. This particular figure is continued
on the following page, where the invisibility of the 'infiniment
autre' ('infinitely other') is presented thus: 'Inaccessible,
l'invisible est le très-haut... Si haute qu'elle soit, la hauteur est
toujours accessible; le très-haut, lui, est plus haut que la
hauteur. Aucun accroissement ne saurait le mesurer. Il n'appartient pas à l'espace, il n'est pas du monde' (*ED*, p. 139)
('Inaccessible, the invisible is the most high... No matter how
high it is, height is always inaccessible; the most high, however,
is higher than height. No addition of more height will ever
measure it. It does not belong to space, it is not of this world'
(*WD*, p. 93)). This *strange* notion of the infinite ('l'étrange idée
de l'Infini', *ED*, p. 146; *WD*, p. 98) is not reducible to, for
example, God, the classical figure of a positive infinity, of
presence and plenitude (*ED*, p. 168; *WD*, p. 114). Nor is it the
infinity constituted by the Cartesian *cogito* according to Husserl
(*ED*, p. 157; *WD*, p. 106). Levinas believes that Husserl
misinterpreted the third of Descartes' *Méditations*, which in fact
(Levinas claims) presents a *cogito* already made possible by an
infinity which extends beyond it, and therefore unable to
constitute infinity as object (*ED*, p. 157; *WD*, p. 106). It is clear
that while this interpretation is not equivalent to Derrida's re-
reading of the *cogito* in 'Cogito et histoire de la folie' (for
Derrida, the *cogito itself* is the infinity exceeding any given
totality), the language of excess remains the same, in this case

represented in the notion of overflow, a figure already discussed in chapter 1: 'extériorité qui déborde infiniment la monade de l'*ego cogito*' (*ED*, p. 156) ('an exteriority infinitely overflowing the monad of the *ego cogito*' (*WD*, p. 106)), 'débordement non-spatial sur lequel se brise la métaphore' (*ED*, p. 157) ('a nonspatial overflowing, against which metaphor shatters' (*WD*, p. 106)).

It has already been remarked that the 'infinity' Derrida proposes, both directly and indirectly through his commentary of others, is not transcendental in the classical sense. It is not, for instance, the positive infinity of God. Its only defining characteristic is a negative one: it refuses any containment or delimitation. In a strange and difficult sense this infinity, while exceeding any given totality, is also 'finite' in that it 'inhabits' that totality. Or, put another way, the system, totality or structure is neither finite nor infinite, as Derrida argues in 'Violence et métaphysique': 'Un *système* n'est ni fini ni infini. Une totalité structurale échappe en son jeu à cette alternative. Elle échappe à l'archéologique et à l'eschatologique et les inscrit en elle-même' (*ED*, p. 180) ('A *system* is neither finite nor infinite. A structural totality escapes this alternative in its functioning. It escapes the archaeological and the eschatological and inscribes them in itself' (*WD*, p. 123)). The concept of 'jeu', to which Derrida refers frequently in texts of this period, is an interesting and important one, since it makes possible the paradox of a system being both finite and infinite, (de)limited and exceeded. Perhaps the most useful (but also the most notoriously misconstrued) definition of this concept is to be found in Derrida's discussion of Lévi-Strauss and structuralism in 'La structure, le signe et le jeu dans le discours des sciences humaines', where he opposes the classical concept of structure to the modern understanding of the term. The classical conception sees the structure as possessing a definite, fixed centre which, paradoxically, is both inside and outside of that structure. The paradox arises from the fact that, while the centre permits a combinatorial play of elements within the structure, it commands and limits that play and does not as such enter into the process of combination and substitution (*ED*, pp. 409, 410; *WD*, pp. 278, 279). This means that the system, or structure, is 'closed', as Derrida puts it. The traditional (and reassuring) conception of the closed structure is, however, disturbingly questioned when it is recognized that there is not necessarily any one privileged centre for a given structure, and that the play of substitution is therefore an infinite process. This would mean a certain 'opening' or 'openness' of the system, totality or structure, similar to the 'ouverture' spoken of in 'Force et signification'; an openness whose condition of possibility is, however, a certain enclosure. In a very instructive passage, Derrida contrasts the classical apprehension of the infinite (which is presumably placed outside of its finite, controllable structures) with the alternative manner of conceiving infinity afforded by the acentric structure. The context of the passage is a discussion of the problematic cohabitation in Lévi-Strauss' work of a certain, old-style empiricism and the ambition of establishing a rigorously scientific methodology in his own discipline, anthropology. On the one hand, Lévi-Strauss speaks of the impossibility of ever gathering all of the empirical data relevant to a specific discipline, the impossibility of totalization; on the other hand, for the scientist – for the linguist – such totalization is unnecessary, provided it is possible to elaborate a basic structure or syntax of the system described. The passage in question merits quotation in its entirety:

La totalisation est donc définie tantôt comme *inutile*, tantôt comme *impossible*. Cela tient, sans doute, à ce qu'il y a deux manières de penser la limite de la totalisation... La totalisation peut être jugée impossible dans le style classique: on évoque alors l'effort empirique d'un sujet ou d'un discours fini s'essoufflant en vain après une richesse infinie qu'il ne pourra jamais maîtriser. Il y a trop et plus qu'on ne peut dire. Mais on peut déterminer autrement la non-totalisation: non plus sous le concept de finitude comme assignation à l'empiricité mais sous le concept de *jeu*. Si la totalité alors n'a plus de sens, ce n'est pas parce que l'infinité d'un champ ne peut être couverte par un regard ou un discours finis, mais parce que la nature du champ – à savoir le langage et un langage fini, exclut la totalisation: ce champ est en effet celui d'un *jeu*, c'est-à-dire de substitutions infinies dans la clôture d'un ensemble fini. Ce champ ne permet ces substitutions infinies que parce qu'il est fini, c'est-à-dire parce qu'au lieu d'être un champ inépuisable, comme dans l'hypothèse classique, au lieu d'être trop grand, il lui manque quelque chose, à savoir un centre qui arrête et fonde le jeu des substitutions. (*ED*, p. 423)

(Totalization, therefore, is sometimes defined as *useless*, and sometimes as *impossible*. This is no doubt due to the fact that there are two ways of conceiving the limit of totalization... Totalization can be judged impossible in the classical style: one then refers to the empirical endeavour of either a subject or a finite richness which it can never master. There is too much, more than one can say. But nontotalization can also be determined in another way: no longer from the standpoint of a concept of finitude as relegation to the empirical, but from the standpoint of the concept of *play*. If totalization no longer has any meaning, it is not because the infiniteness of the field cannot be covered by a finite glance or a finite discourse, but because the nature of the field – that is, language and a finite language – excludes totalization. This field is in effect that of *play*, that is to say, a field of infinite substitutions only because it is finite, that is to say, because instead of being an inexhaustible field, as in the classical hypothesis, instead of being too large, there is something missing from it: a centre which arrests and grounds the play of substitutions.) (*WD*, p. 289)

What Derrida is describing here is a conception of the infinite that has become peculiarly his own, beyond the immediate context of his reading of Lévi-Strauss and structuralism, and which appears also to inform other texts in *L'écriture et la différence*. This is a *finite* infinity, what he elsewhere describes as the 'in-fini', something that is neither finite nor infinite, but literally, the infinite *within* the finite.[1] Continuing his commentary of Lévi-Strauss from the point of view of supplementarity, which he associates with the notion of play ('ce mouvement du jeu, permis par le manque, l'absence de centre ou d'origine, est le mouvement de la *supplémentarité*', *ED*, p. 423 ('this movement of play, permitted by the lack or absence of a centre or origin, is the movement of *supplementarity*', *WD*, p. 289)), Derrida argues that 'la *surabondance* du signifiant, son caractère supplémentaire, tient donc à une finitude, c'est-à-dire à un manque qui doit être *suppléé*' (*ED*, p. 425) ('the *overabundance* of the signifier, its supplementary character, is thus the result of a finitude, that is to say, the result of a lack which must be *supplemented*' (*WD*, p. 290)). With the term 'surabon-dance', borrowed from Lévi-Strauss but inflected and fore-grounded, there is again an infinity which is immeasurable excess, but here with the qualification that such an excess proceeds from a finite base, a base of deprivation ('manque') rather than of fullness or totality. This notion of the finite basis of infinite substitution or supplementarity already anticipates the next area of reflection, the moment of determination. As was learnt in the previous chapter, the infinite duration of force is nothing without the determination of inscription, it is not 'before' this determination in any logical or chronological sense. Expressed in Derrida's language, the system is *always already* determined.

INSCRIPTION

It was established above that Derrida's certain infinity is indeterminate (see, for example, *ED*, pp. 86, 87; *WD*, p. 57). However, the second moment of Derrida's model, the passage to determination or inscription, does not in any way eliminate this indeterminacy. The infinity of which Derrida speaks does not become determined *with* the moment of determination, but simply becomes apprehensible at that point, 'inhabiting' but exceeding the structure thus constituted. In chapter 1, it was observed that this passage to determination was also the occasion of anguish and pain; the passage is a passion and the inscription is violence. To begin with, I shall expand upon this peculiar attribution of violence to the moment of determination which, it transpires, is a persistent feature of Derrida's texts.

Foucault's *Histoire de la folie* is already a discourse on violence: the violence of a discourse that separates and excludes madness from the domain of reason. In 'Cogito et histoire de la folie', Derrida appears to accept and adopt this category of violence, though with certain qualifications. Derrida agrees, for example, with Foucault's contention that Descartes operates a 'coup de force' in the *Méditations*, but differs on the nature and location of that 'coup de force' in Descartes' text. For Foucault, the logical 'coup de force' effected by Descartes in the first of the

Méditations is but symptomatic of a wider, historically determinable moment at which the free circulation of the sane and insane in the medieval city gives way to their separation and segregation, with the 'grand renfermement' of the classical age. Derrida disagrees with Foucault as to the privileged historical localization of this separation: the division between reason and insanity is *already* accomplished, he claims, from the beginnings of logical discourse in Greece: 'La libre circulation des fous, outre qu'elle n'est pas si libre, si simplement libre que cela, ne serait qu'un épiphénomène socio-économique à la surface d'une raison déjà divisée contre elle-même depuis l'aube de son origine grecque' (*ED*, p. 64) ('The free circulation of the mad, besides the fact that it is not as simply free as all that, would only be a socioeconomic epiphenomenon on the surface of a reason divided against itself since the dawn of its Greek origin' (*WD*, p. 40)). Nevertheless, Derrida is in agreement with Foucault as concerns the structural necessity (and reality) of the division. In this connection, he speaks approvingly of Foucault's word 'décision':

Il s'agit donc d'accéder où le dialogue a été rompu, s'est partagé en deux soliloques: à ce que Foucault appelle d'un mot très fort la *Décision*. La Décision lie et sépare du même coup raison et folie; elle doit s'entendre ici à la fois comme l'acte originaire d'un ordre, d'un *fiat*, d'un décret, et comme une déchirure, une césure, une séparation, une discession. Je dirais plutôt *dissension* pour bien marquer qu'il s'agit d'une division de soi, d'un partage et d'un tourment intérieur du sens *en général*, du logos en général, d'un partage dans l'acte même du *sentir*. (*ED*, p. 62)

(The issue is therefore to reach the point at which the dialogue was broken off, dividing itself into two soliloquies – what Foucault calls, using a very strong word, the *Decision*. The Decision, through a single act, links and separates reason and madness, and it must be understood at once both as the [originary] act of an order, a fiat, a decree, and as a schism, a caesura, a separation, a dissection. I would prefer *dissension*, to underline that in question is a self-dividing action, a cleavage and torment interior to meaning *in general*, interior to logos in general, a division within the very act of *sentire*.) (*WD*, pp. 38–9)

The style of Derrida's argument, with its combination of close paraphrase and interpretation, is now becoming somewhat familiar. In this instance, as in his reading of Lévi-Strauss, Derrida follows Foucault's argument closely. At the same time, however, there is a certain inflection of Foucault's terms and the interpolation of Derrida's own figures, the effect of which is evidently not a neutral reading (though this does not necessarily mean a misreading) of Foucault. From the italicized word *Décision*, Derrida proceeds to a linguistic exploration of semantically and phonetically associated terms, 'déchirure-césure', 'discession-dissension'.[2] These terms are more Derrida's than Foucault's ('comme', 'je dirais plutôt'), and while Foucault obviously holds that the 'décision', like the 'coup de force', possesses an inherent violence, Derrida's conception of the 'torment' attendant upon the act of decision is at once more general and abstract than Foucault's violence, 'un partage et un tourment intérieur du sens *en général*' ('a cleavage and torment interior to meaning *in general*'). This is because, as Derrida points out, Foucault's 'décision' is historically determined, it occurs in the classical age. Derrida, on the other hand, views the 'décision' as a structure fundamental to the *logos*. As such, and despite his reference to the Greek origin of the *logos*, the 'décision' itself is ahistorical, it is not *in* history.[3] As a fundamental structure, it could be held to be analogous to the principle of inscription described in chapter 1, and what Derrida here names the 'torment' of decision is equivalent to the passion of inscription. In 'Force et signification', Derrida indeed says, apropos of the moment of inscription, that 'c'est le moment où il faut *décider* si nous graverons ce que nous entendons' (*ED*, p. 19, Derrida's emphasis) ('it is the moment at which we must *decide* whether we will engrave what we hear' (*WD*, p. 9)).

A further aspect of Derrida's treatment of the violence of decision in 'Cogito et histoire de la folie' is the *necessity* of such violence. He refers, for example, to 'le logos, dans la violence nécessaire de son irruption' (*ED*, p. 97) ('logos, in the necessary violence of its irruption' (*WD*, p. 62)). In 'Force et signification' it was also recognized that there is a certain necessity of the fall of force into form without which there is nothing, but the essential adherence of the two, the violence of necessity and the necessity of violence, is most systematically argued in *L'écriture et la différence* in the two chapters dealing with Artaud, 'La parole soufflée' and 'Le théâtre de la cruauté et la clôture de la représentation'. In these studies of Artaud, Derrida underlines the fact that while Artaud rejects the hegemony of the text and the spoken word in Western theatre, he does not intend to replace it with a mute theatre based entirely on improvised gesture. Far from being improvised, Artaud's projected new theatre would be rigorously *determined* and *codified*.[4] In both of Derrida's readings of Artaud (for example, *ED*, pp. 288 and 350 respectively; *WD*, pp. 192, 238–9), he points out that the Theatre of Cruelty, as Artaud named and conceived it, is cruel not in the conventional, moral sense, but rather in the special sense that it is rigorous, implacable, calculating (even 'mathematical') and finally, *necessary*. All of these terms occur in Artaud's texts, but Derrida's selection of them, what one might call his *inflected* reading of Artaud, inevitably indicates the extent to which Artaud's text comes to conform to, or rather, perhaps, confirm Derrida's model. What Derrida's commentary of Artaud teaches us is that the violence of decision, as he describes it, must not necessarily be understood to be violence in the specifically anthropological or moral sense. It is not, for example, 'mindless', 'uncontrolled' or 'gratuitous' violence, but first and foremost a lucid, applied and necessary violence, a violence that is closer to formal rigour than to human cruelty, an ontological rather than an anthropological violence.

One important feature of Derrida's model of inscription, as it emerged from the commentary of 'Force et signification' in the last chapter, is that the moment of inscription is, properly speaking, not a simple or single moment at all. It is, rather, both instance *and* insistence. Returning for an instant to 'Cogito et histoire de la folie', it is evident that the 'décision' that Derrida adopts and adapts from Foucault's *Histoire de la folie* is similarly not unitary in nature. In the course of 'Cogito et histoire de la folie', Derrida identifies Foucault's 'décision' with the notion of the 'crise' (crisis) as it repeatedly occurs in *L'histoire de la folie*: 'La crise, c'est aussi la décision, la césure dont parle Foucault' (*ED*, p. 96) ('the crisis is also decision, the caesura of which Foucault speaks' (*WD*, p. 62)). According to Derrida, 'cette crise a toujours déjà commencé et elle est interminable' (*ED*, p. 96) ('This crisis has always [already] begun and it is interminable' (*WD*, p. 62)). This then is the essential structure of what is variously called the crisis, the decision, or the inscription, a structure of non-originarity and repetition. It will be recalled that Derrida situated the decisional split in the *logos*, not *in* a historical period (as Foucault had done), but *since* its origin in Greek thought, 'depuis l'aube de l'origine grecque' (*ED*, p. 64). The split had always already taken place, and can therefore only be secondary. At the same time, Derrida reminds us that the crisis is congenital to the history (and the historicity) of our philosophy, that it occurs many times and continuously. It is also congenital in the most vital of senses, in that without the continuity of crisis, without such violent repetition, there would be nothing. In 'Force et signification', the fall of force into the singular inscription entails certain death. The epigraph to the second section of this text, a quotation of the painter Delacroix, provides an interesting, if unusual, illustration of the necessity of secondarity. For Delacroix, the singular line is a monstrosity, an impossibility: 'Il y a des lignes qui sont des monstres ... Une ligne toute seule n'a pas de signification; il en faut une seconde pour lui donner de l'expression. Grande loi' (*ED*, p. 27) ('There are lines which are monsters ... A line by itself has no meaning; a second one is necessary to give expression to meaning. Important law' (*WD*, p. 15)). Despite this, repetition, in Derrida's model, does not imply repetition of the same, a second apparition identically doubling the first; this too is death. The repetition of the sign is a *differential* repetition which refers to the same only through a system of other signs, as Derrida argues in 'Ellipse': 'Dès qu'un signe surgit, il commence par se répéter. Sans cela, il ne serait pas ce qu'il est, c'est-à-dire cette non-identité à soi qui renvoie régulièrement au même. C'est-à-dire à un autre signe qui lui-même naîtra de se diviser' (*ED*, p. 432) ('As soon as the sign emerges, it begins by repeating itself. Without this, it would not be a sign, would not be what it is, that is, the non-self-identity which regularly refers to the same. That is to say, to another sign, which itself will be born of having been divided' (*WD*, p. 297)). This continuous process of difference within identity means that the origin is essentially lost, dead: 'La mort est à l'aube parce que tout a commencé par la répétition. Dès lors que le centre ou l'origine ont commencé par se répéter, par se dédoubler, le double ne s'ajoutait pas seulement au simple. Il le divisait et le suppléait. Il y avait aussi une double origine plus sa répétition. Trois est le premier chiffre de la répétition' (*ED*, p. 435) ('Death is at the dawn because everything has begun with repetition. Once the center or the origin have begun by repeating themselves, by redoubling themselves, the double did not only add itself to the simple. It divided it and supplemented it. There was immediately a double origin plus its repetition. Three is the first number of repetition' (*WD*, p. 299)). Three is an odd number. The reassuring doubling of the same implied in dual (pure) repetition is disturbed and displaced by the asymmetry of three. In 'Ellipse', this differentiality is also expressed in the figure of an eccentric (excentric) circle, the ellipsis. Traditionally, the figure of the circle supposes a fixed, single and non-substitutable centre, assuring identical repetition, with each revolution returning to the same point. With the ellipsis this fixed centre is displaced (the ellipsis has two focuses, the centre, or origin, is doubled), so that repetition itself is difference, never the return of the same. But with this asymmetric (therefore dynamic) repetition and its eccentric circulation, we are once more already engaged in the following 'moment' of Derrida's model, in this case the third moment, that of the economy.

THE ECONOMY

In chapter 1 it was seen that the model of the economy allowed force and form to be thought together, thus avoiding the limitations of the metaphysical system of oppositions which presented them only as mutually exclusive alternatives. However, the passage in question (*ED*, p. 34; *WD*, pp. 19–20) has bearing mainly upon the conceptual necessity of the model of the economy (it is part of a 'strategy' – that of deconstruction – designed to undo the reductive oppositions of a whole tradition of metaphysics) and does not inform us greatly as to how the economy works. We are told that the economy takes into account both spatial differences and differences of force, but this requires some extension. I shall firstly return to the text of 'Cogito et histoire de la folie' for such extension.

It was seen above that the singular 'crisis' of which Foucault spoke in *L'histoire de la folie* was generalized by Derrida to apply to a repeated feature of the history of our philosophy, a feature which is in fact essential to its historicity, its very existence in and as a history. The passage in question requires closer attention, both for its phrasing and for its logical coherence with what can now be seen as an identifiable model of interpretation:

L'historicité propre de la philosophie a son lieu et se constitue dans ce passage, dans ce dialogue entre l'hyperbole et la structure finie, entre l'excès sur la totalité et la totalité close, dans la différence entre l'histoire et l'historicité; c'est-à-dire dans le lieu ou plutôt le moment où le Cogito et tout ce qu'il symbolise ici (folie, démesure, hyperbole, etc...) se disent, se rassurent et déchoient, s'oublient nécessairement jusqu'à leur réactivation, leur réveil dans un autre dire de l'excès qui sera aussi plus tard une autre déchéance et une autre crise. (*ED*, p. 94)

(The historicity proper to philosophy is located and constituted in the transition, the dialogue between hyperbole and the finite structure, between that which exceeds the totality and the closed totality, in the difference between history and historicity; that is, in the place where, or rather, at the moment when, the Cogito and all that it symbolizes here (madness, derangement, hyperbole, etc.) pronounce and reassure themselves then to fall, necessarily forgetting themselves until their reactivation, their reawakening in another statement of the excess which also later will become another decline and another crisis.) (*WD*, pp. 60–1)

Several terms call for comment. Firstly, 'folie', 'démesure', 'hyperbole', 'excès' are all varieties of the infinity characterizing the first moment, discussed above. Secondly, the 'passage', the 'lieu', 'différence' are varying descriptions of the second moment, the decision which situates and constrains the infinite in the finite structure. Significantly, this critical moment is described as 'déchéance', a fall – a moral fall – and this can be compared with the fall to inscription described in 'Force et signification' ('chute', 'déchéance'). Thirdly (and this is where the idea of economy is introduced), the second moment is *temporalized.* The fall from excess to finite totality is not unique: there is a continual reactivation of the fall, in time. Derrida continues:

Dès son premier souffle, la parole, soumise à ce rythme temporel de crise et de réveil, n'ouvre son espace de parole qu'en enfermant la folie … Mais cette libération violente de la parole n'est possible et ne peut se poursuivre, que dans la mesure où elle se garde, où elle est la trace de ce geste de violence originaire, et dans la mesure où elle se tient, résolument, en conscience, au plus proche de l'abus qu'est l'usage de la parole, juste assez près pour *dire* la violence, pour dialoguer avec soi comme violence irréductible, juste assez loin pour *vivre* et vivre comme parole. C'est en cela que la crise ou l'oubli n'est peut-être pas l'accident mais la destinée de la philosophie parlante qui ne peut vivre qu'en enfermant la folie mais qui mourrait comme pensée et sous une violence encore pire si une nouvelle parole à chaque instant ne libérait l'ancienne folie tout en enfermant en elle, dans son présent, le fou du jour. (*ED*, p. 94)

(From its very first breath, speech, confined to this temporal rhythm of crisis and reawakening, is able to open the space for discourse only by emprisoning madness … But this violent liberation of speech is possible and can be pursued only in the extent to which it keeps itself resolutely and consciously at the greatest possible proximity to the abuse that is the usage of speech – just close enough to *say* violence, to dialogue with itself as irreducible violence, and just far enough to *live* and live as speech. Due to this, crisis or oblivion is perhaps not an accident, but rather the destiny of speaking philosophy – the philosophy which lives only by emprisoning madness, but which would die as thought, and by a still worse violence, if a new speech did not at every instant liberate previous madness while enclosing within itself, in its present existence, the madman of the day.) (*WD*, p. 61)

It is a question here of life and death. It is a question also, once again, of inaugural violence, and a violence possessed of a certain necessity: the 'crise' is not accidental, but the very *destiny* of philosophical discourse. This original violence cannot, however, be integrally present, for this would surely mean death. The unitary, extreme fall expends the whole of its force: there is no survival. The single sign, like Delacroix's single line, is a monster, and monsters bear no progeny. The integral violence of the origin must therefore be distributed in lesser repetitions, as it were, so that the inaugural gesture may live on, carry on ('se poursuivre'). The 'trace' is a diminished effect of an originary, conditioning force in which that force is preserved ('se garde') and saved from singular annihilation. At the same time, the diminishment must not be such that contact is lost with the conditioning violence: this too would be certain death. Survival of the (reasoned) word ('parole') is only possible in the tension between the ongoing gesture of enclosure of madness (excess, immoderation) and its liberation. This tension between saving and expenditure, investment and consumption, is precisely an economy. On the following page Derrida argues: '*Au plus haut d'elle-même*, l'hyperbole, l'ouverture absolue, la dépense anéconomique est toujours reprise et surprise dans une *économie*. Le rapport entre la raison, la folie, la mort est une économie, une structure de différance dont il faut respecter l'irréductible originalité' (*ED*, p. 95) ('*At its height* hyperbole, the absolute opening, the uneconomic expenditure, is always reembraced by an economy and is overcome by economy. The relation between reason, madness, and death is an economy, a structure of deferral whose irreducible originality must be respected' (*WD*, pp. 61–2)). Derrida's employment of the word 'économie' at this juncture, though describing what is a dynamic relation between the dual polarities of saving and expenditure, containment and dissipation, is perhaps semantically more biased towards the former than the latter. 'Une économie' can in French, as in English, mean simply 'a saving', as in the phrase 'faire des économies'. Saving defers, it delays expenditure until a later date, and the idea of delay or deferment is rendered in this example by the neologism 'différance'. The word 'différance' is derived from the verb 'différer' (to defer, put off, adjourn) but in Derrida's overdetermined and re-motivated lexicon, it is also a homonym of 'différence'.[5] The coupling of 'différance-différence' thus provides an appropriately condensed description or definition of the economy, as Derrida conceives it: it is spatial difference, but also difference of force, implying a certain distribution in time, a temporal structure of adjournment ('*à la fois* différences de lieux et différences de force', *ED*, p. 34 ('*simultaneously* ... differences of site and differences of force', *WD*, pp. 19–20)). The economy is therefore the instance and the insistence of difference, or the deferment of absolute difference, which would be death.

This concept of a strategic adjournment of death in the economy, the economy of death, inevitably directs us to Bataille, in many senses *the* philosopher of the economy, whose dialogue with Hegel is the subject of 'De l'économie restreinte à l'économie générale'. In this chapter, Derrida concentrates on Bataille's reading or re-reading of Hegel's concept of mastery (*Herrschaft*) in the *Phenomenology*. For Derrida, Bataille's 'sovereignty' is an inflection and an extension of what was an already implicit, though in a sense repressed, dimension of Hegel's concept of mastery (*ED*, pp. 381–2; *WD*, p. 260). What Bataille does is operate a displacement, a minimal difference between the apparently identical ideas of 'sovereignty' and 'mastery'. Hegel's Master is master precisely and only because he has played with death, has put his life at stake, and has passed the test. The instance of death is therefore recuperated – negated and conserved – in the movement of the *Aufhebung* which is, in Hegel's terms, 'conscious negation'. Opposed to this is Hegel's 'abstract negativity', the properly inconceivable loss in the game with death, the loss of sense, a death that brings no returns: 'Cette mort pure et simple, cette mort muette et sans rendement' (*ED*, p. 375) ('This mute and nonproductive death, this death pure and simple' (*WD*, p. 255)). An extreme case such as this is literally out of play in what Derrida terms Hegel's 'economy of life' (ibid.). This economy is essentially conservative, it preserves from death, defers it; but it is not equivalent to the economy of 'différance' encountered above which is non-dialectical and non-recuperative. Hegel's economy of mastery is too *restricted* (*ED*, p. 376; *WD*, p. 256); it is bound to a *circular* reproduction of sense, typified in the encyclopedic sweep of Absolute Knowledge. In contrast, Bataille's inflection of 'sovereignty' proposes what is unthinkable in Hegel's closed economy, that is, precisely the precluded (negated, conserved) 'abstract negativity' that was its condition. However, to think the 'dépense sans réserve' which is the full exercise of Bataille's 'sovereignty' is impossible, for this is oblivion. In *La part maudite*, Bataille gives two definitions of the economy. The first is the restricted economy, the economy in the conventional sense of the word, confined to the study of the management of wealth. The second is the general economy, which is not (Bataille's) sovereignty itself, but a certain writing close to the non-sense that is sovereignty unbridled (*ED*, pp. 396–7; *WD*, p. 270). The 'general economy' therefore lies in the almost imperceptible transition (the minimal difference) between Hegel's closed economy of mastery and Bataille's senseless expenditure of sovereignty, closer to the conditions dialecticized by the former. Instead of a circulation of value, as in the closed economy, the general economy permits a continual destruction of it (*ED*, p. 398; *WD*, p. 271). Extrapolating from what was learnt above on the subject of repetition in 'Ellipse', it could be advanced that Hegel's circular economy of Absolute Knowledge is identically repetitive, while the general economy of Bataille–Derrida is *elliptically* so, offering as it does the insistent displacement rather than the identity of concept.

It can be gathered from the preceding analysis that the dimension of violence characteristic of the instance of decision does not cease with the elliptical circulation of the economy. The economy is itself, according to Derrida's expression in 'Violence et métaphysique', an '*économie de guerre*' (*ED*, p. 220) ('*economy of war*' (*WD*, p. 148)), a continual act of violence. In 'Violence et métaphysique', Derrida summarizes Levinas' objection to what he considers to be the violence of the reductive (philosophical) concept. Levinas' own philosophy of non-violence posits the integrity of the 'infiniment autre', which is irreducible to any delimiting definition or category of 'le même'. Derrida, for his part, believes such a position to be untenable in that it leads to a philosophy of pre-logical silence which is prey to a still greater violence than that of conceptual determination, of the decision to speak. The choice is therefore between the lesser of two evils:

Cette guerre seconde, comme aveu, est la moindre violence possible, la seule façon de réprimer la pire violence, celle du silence primitif et pré-logique, d'une nuit inimaginable qui ne serait même pas le contraire du jour, d'une violence absolue qui ne serait même pas le contraire de la non-violence: le rien ou le non-sens purs. (*ED*, p. 191)

(This secondary war, as the avowal of violence, is the least possible violence, the only way to repress the worst violence, the violence of primitive and prelogical silence, of an unimaginable night which would not even be the opposite of day, an absolute violence which would not even be the opposite of nonviolence: nothingness or pure non-sense.) (*WD*, p. 130)

Violence contre violence. *Economie* de violence ... Cette *vigilance* est une violence choisie comme la moindre violence. (*ED*, p. 172)

(Violence against violence. *Economy* of violence. ... This *vigilance* is a violence chosen as the least violence.) (*WD*, p. 117)

On n'échappe jamais à *l'économie de guerre*. (*ED*, p. 220)

(One never escapes the *economy of war*.) (*WD*, p. 148)

Once again, we are confronted with the *necessity* of violence, or more exactly, a *certain* violence. The circulation of violence within the economy in a sense defers the insistent menace of integral annihilation by a still greater violence. This 'moindre violence', as Derrida terms it, is of the same structure as the 'différance' or 'trace' mentioned above, in that it constantly distributes and thereby defuses a greater, pre-logical violence in a series of acts of lesser violence. This does not occur in a singular 'coup de force' (of which Foucault accused Descartes), but in a plurality of decisional acts which persist as the *traces* of an originary violence, the diminished perpetration of it (*ED*, p. 94; *WD*, p. 61). It is useful here to recall the argument of 'Cogito et histoire de la folie', where the violent advent of the word can only persist or be in a state of tension between its nearness to and distance from the conditional violence – 'juste assez près pour *dire* la violence ... juste assez loin pour *vivre* et vivre comme parole' (*ED*, p. 94) ('just close enough to *say* violence ... and just far enough to *live* and live as speech' (*WD*, p. 61)). The 'trace' is both continuous with and distinct from its occasion, it constitutes the economy (the saving) of that occasion. In conclusion, again to quote Derrida assessing the necessity of a certain violence: 'toute philosophie de la non-violence ne peut jamais, *dans l'histoire*, – mais aurait-elle un sens ailleurs? – que choisir la moindre violence en une *économie de la violence*' (*ED*,

p. 136) ('*within history* – but is it meaningful elsewhere? – every philosophy of nonviolence can only choose the lesser violence within an *economy of violence*' (*WD*, p. 91, note 21)).[6]

The analysis of the threefold articulation of the model of inscription (infinity, inscription, the economy) undertaken in this chapter has both extended and given greater definition to the theory of writing that emerges from Derrida's critique of structuralism, examined in chapter 1. It has added to our understanding of the theory the concepts of play, substitution, the finite, 'différance'. At the same time it has brought into closer focus the importance of the category of violence, or a certain violence, and the structural necessity of this violence. The Hegelian resonance of Derrida's presentation of violence has already been mentioned, and it appears to be a persistent feature of Derrida's texts during this period. But it is also clear that his reading of violence does not simply repeat or reproduce the configurations of the Hegelian philosophy which has been so influential for his own, and for previous intellectual generations in France. While the Kojèvian reading of Hegel, for example, situates violence pre-eminently at the level of the conflict of consciousnesses, the violence described by Derrida is most frequently a pre- or rather non-anthropological violence; it is beyond the strictly anthropological or existential (the anguish, the *angustia* of writing is not necessarily individual, 'n'est pas essentiellement une modification ou un affect empiriques de l'écrivain', *ED*, p. 18 ('this anguish is not an empirical modification or state of the writer', *WD*, p. 9)). Such violence would be the necessary condition of the institution of any system, beyond the specific register of the subjective or intersubjective. This places writing, as violent inscription, at a level of determination most properly termed 'transcendental'. There is one key chapter in *L'écriture et la différence*, not yet discussed, which gives perhaps the most explicit formulation of a writing that transcends conscious agency, a writing that functions at a level both lower and higher than consciousness. This crucial chapter is 'Freud et la scène de l'écriture' to which I shall now turn.

CHAPTER 3

Beyond the seen of writing
('Freud et la scène de l'écriture')

L'image graphique n'est pas vue; et l'image acoustique
n'est pas entendue. La différence entre les unités pleines de
la voix reste inouïe. Invisible aussi la différence dans le
corps de l'inscription.

(GR1, p. 95)

(The graphic image is not seen; and the acoustic image is
not heard. The difference between the full unities of the
voice remains unheard. And, the difference in the body of
the inscription is also invisible.)

(GR2, p. 65)

After all, the simplest cybernetic circuit can be said to have
a memory of a dynamic nature – not based on static
storage but upon the travel of information around the
circuit.[1]

The text of 'Freud et la scène de l'écriture' is the transcript of
part of a lecture given by Derrida at the Institut de psychanalyse
in Paris in March 1966. In consequence, the text is preceded
and concluded by two explanatory notes summarizing the first
and final parts of the lecture which do not figure in the chapter
itself. Derrida's stated intention in 'La scène de l'écriture' is to
follow the metaphor of writing as it is increasingly adopted by
Freud in his descriptions of the psychical apparatus from his
earliest works onwards, from the *Project for a Scientific Psychology*
(1895) to 'A Note upon the "Mystic Writing-Pad"' (1925). As
Derrida indicates in the prefatory note, this programmatic
reading of Freud should be situated in the context of the
deconstruction of logocentrism, undertaken in a number of
contemporary texts, most notably in the article 'De la gram-

matologie' (*ED*, p. 293; *WD*, p. 196). Before entering into a detailed analysis of Derrida's reading of Freud, it is first necessary to open a brief parenthesis on the subject of logocentrism.

Probably Derrida's most sustained and systematic critique of logocentrism is to be found in *De la grammatologie*, published in 1967. In this now seminal work, Derrida demonstrates how, throughout the history of Western thought, writing in the common sense of the word has been consistently involved in a series of oppositions assigning to it only secondary status in man's spiritual, intellectual and practical experience. The Greek word *logos* implicitly associates the faculty of speech with the ideal of reason and rationality. The spoken word, the *phonè* or voice, is considered to enjoy a closer proximity to the inner 'truth' of the subject's consciousness, intuition and presence to him or herself. In contrast to this, scriptural language is seen to represent an artificial and external appendage or supplement to the 'natural' co-implication of *phonè*-consciousness; it is an auxiliary technology employed by human reason but never essential to reason itself. In *De la grammatologie*, Derrida's critique of this reduction or repression of writing takes the form of a critical engagement with a series of examples or 'symptoms' of the logocentric paradigm, from Plato and Rousseau through to Saussure and Lévi-Strauss. However, his objective is not merely to effect a form of rehabilitation of a long-repressed party (writing); his gesture is to move beyond the everyday understanding of writing in order to postulate a 'writing' more fundamental to signifying practices in general, a 'writing' that is the condition of all forms of expression, whether scriptural, vocal, or otherwise. Such a 'writing' is precisely an 'écriture avant la lettre', or 'archi-écriture', as Derrida terms it.[2] Nonetheless, writing in its normal sense, or, more exactly, a certain form of writing, remains a model of the generalized 'writing' that is its condition.

This brief account of Derrida's critique of logocentrism repeats what is now the standard interpretation and understanding of Derrida's philosophical project in *De la grammatologie* and adjacent texts. It is possible, however, that this standard interpretation also contains a bias towards what could be termed the first moment of Derrida's critique, the critical reading of texts representative of logocentric thought and the exposure of the specific premises or presuppositions subtending those texts.[3] This is not to say that the second moment of Derrida's argument, the reference to the fundamental structure of 'archi-écriture' is not mentioned or explained, but rather that it is often not the principal point of interest. One explanation for this is perhaps the limited use-value of what could be termed the 'ontological' part of Derrida's argument. For the most part, attention has focused on the potential of deconstruction as a critique – a powerful and radical critique – of entrenched and unquestioned habits of thought; if reference is made more specifically to aspects or articulations of the general theory of writing, such as 'jeu' or 'différance', then these are often simply projected onto the level of the empirical (literary or philosophical) text, and are not properly understood as a fundamental structure of which literary production is only one manifestation. Such a restriction of emphasis is to an extent understandable, given the impressive working examples of deconstructive reading provided in texts such as *De la grammatologie*, which have exerted much influence in the shaping of the literary critical canon in recent years. The problem with the resultant view of deconstruction as basically an *instrument* of criticism is that there is a concomitant tendency to forget the specificity (and originality) of the general theory of writing itself. The importance of deconstruction as a way of reading, as a *style* of criticism cannot, of course, be underestimated, but it is also arguable that 'deconstruction', as it has come to be called, is inseparable from Derrida's general theory of writing. The question of writing as treated in the earlier, programmatic texts is not an accidental or arbitrary 'theme' of deconstructive criticism, which might be detached from a methodological nucleus of 'deconstruction', but is an integral part of deconstruction – indeed, as will become increasingly clear, it *is* deconstruction. At a later stage I shall be attempting precisely such a redefinition, or rather, relocation of deconstruction. For the moment, however, I shall continue what has been my own

emphasis on the second moment of Derrida's theory, what I
referred to above as his 'ontology' of writing.

Freud's use of the scriptural metaphor at different stages of
his intellectual itinerary is not necessarily immediately and
obviously assimilable to Derrida's general theory of writing. In
the note introducing 'Freud et la scène de l'écriture', Derrida
indeed marks the distance he wishes to take with respect to the
panoply of concepts used by Freud. Such concepts belong,
irrevocably and in their entirety, he claims, to the system of
logocentric metaphysics. At the same time, the adherence of
Freudian discourse to this logocentric tradition is not without its
ambiguities; Derrida points also to Freud's critical and careful
handling of concepts, the self-conscious 'nominalism' of his
hypothetical constructions (*ED*, p. 294; *WD*, p. 198). Once
again, there are *two* manifestations or aspects of the same
thinker, and it is a question of extending that aspect which to
differing degrees resists the constraints and conventions of a
given metaphysical tradition. This is what Derrida proposes
with regard to the Freudian concepts of 'writing' and 'trace'
(*ED*, p. 295; *WD*, p. 198). These concepts are still massively
determined in Freud's work by their entrenchment in a given
history of positivistic and metaphysical thought, but Derrida's
practice in the main text of 'La scène de l'écriture' is to explore
the ways in which they might point beyond such determination.
He argues that Freud's discourse is at the same time foreign to
the tradition which, since Plato and Aristotle, has consistently
used graphical metaphors to illustrate the relationship between
reason and experience, perception and memory. According to
Derrida, Freud's use of the graphical metaphor is not simple, its
purpose is not purely illustrative or didactic; rather, his
approach to writing destabilizes the familiarity and reassurance
of didactic or illustrative representations of it. Again, Derrida is
proposing a kind of defamiliarization of the everyday perception
of writing, parallel to the 'strange' or 'bizarre' movement of
inscription described in 'Force et signification': Freud's handling of the metaphor of writing makes *enigmatic* what we
conventionally believe to be 'writing', and stimulates reflection
on the meaning of metaphor and writing in general (*ED*,

pp. 296–7; *WD*, p. 199). The familiar, didactic, or illustrative use of the figure of writing is invariably associated in Derrida's argument with *phonetic* writing, and he is at pains to emphasize that Freud's graphical metaphors do not normally involve phonetic or alphabetical writing but, rather more frequently, non-phonetic writing. But before proceeding to writing itself, it is necessary to prepare the way by considering how Derrida accommodates what in Freud is at first not a scriptural metaphor with his own particular model of inscription or writing.

VIOLENCE

Freud's ambition in the *Project for a Scientific Psychology*, published in 1895, was to provide a psychology that would be a natural science, based entirely upon neuro-physiological data.[4] One particular problem of such a project was how to explain the processes of memory and perception (which Freud considered to be mutually exclusive), the difficulty residing in the fact that such processes require both a permanent alteration of nervous tissue and its continued capacity for further alterations. In order to circumvent this difficulty, Freud in effect breaks with the neurological description proper and sets forth a *metaphorical* model, including the hypothesis of 'contact-barriers' and 'facilitations' (*ED*, p. 298; *WD*, p. 200). That this model is no longer properly and purely neurological is evident in the both hesitant and boldly speculative hypotheses advanced by Freud in the *Project*, and this anticipates his later renunciation of any attempt to present a psychology based upon physiology (though, as Derrida notes, Freud never totally abandoned this ambition). It is the hypothesis of the contact-barriers and facilitations, as formulated in the *Project*, which is of particular interest to Derrida. Freud suggests two classes of neurones, permeable and non-permeable. The permeable neurones be-have as if they had no contact-barriers and therefore allow excitations to pass through them without any structural alteration taking place. The impermeable neurones, on the other hand, offer differing degrees of resistance to excitation in the form of contact-barriers, thereby allowing the opening of facilitations in the nervous tissue. If Derrida considers this hypothesis remarkable for its speculative boldness, then no less remarkable is his own reading of the phenomenon of facilitation (*Bahnung*), which in French is translated as 'frayage': 'Le frayage, le chemin tracé ouvre une voie conductrice. Ce qui suppose une certaine violence et une certaine résistance devant l'effraction. La voie est rompue, brisée, *fracta*, frayée' (*ED*, p. 298) ('Breaching, the tracing of a trail, opens up a conducting path. Which presupposes a certain violence and a certain resistance to effraction. The path is broken cracked, *fracta*, breached' (*WD*, p. 200)). This statement is remarkable because of its degree of consistency with the model of inscription described in chapters 1 and 2 above. It will be remembered that in Derrida's model there is always, and necessarily, a *passion* of inscription. The decisional passage is always the occasion of violence, the passage is a passion. Such is the case in this particular instance: the inauguration of the facilitation supposes a certain violence, and a certain resistance to its infraction, and this idea of aggressive incursion is enhanced by the etymological relation, underlined by Derrida, between the terms 'effraction', '*fracta*', 'frayée'. (As has already been seen, this verbal negotiation or exploration of the object is often an essential part of Derrida's argument.) Derrida's emphasis upon the violence of the facilitation thus inaugurated is not necessarily misplaced or foisted upon Freud's text. Indeed, shortly afterwards he notes the particular privilege Freud accords to pain: 'C'est parce que le frayage fracture que, dans l'*Esquisse*, Freud reconnaît un privilège à la douleur. D'une certaine manière, il n'y a pas de frayage sans un commencement de douleur et "la douleur laisse derrière elle des frayages particulièrement riches"' (*ED*, p. 301) ('It is because breaching breaks open that Freud, in the *Project*, accords a privilege to pain. In a sense, there is no breaching without a beginning of pain, and "pain leaves behind it particularly rich breaches"' (*WD*, p. 202)). The dimension of violence is therefore at least nominally present in Freud's text. Despite this, Derrida's foregrounding of the violence inherent in the opening of the facilitation, underlined in the linguistic overdetermination of the chain 'effraction-fracta-frayée', suggests an inflection of, or a reading beyond, Freud's text, a strategy which is doubtless now familiar to the reader. This is particularly clear in a later passage of 'La scène de l'écriture' where it is more precisely a question of the metaphor of writing, and where Derrida speculates upon the idea of writing as breaching, and the communication between the graphic breach and that of the pathway. Here again, a vocabulary of violence is discernible:

Il faudrait donc examiner de près – nous ne pouvons naturellement le faire ici – tout ce que Freud nous donne à penser de la force de l'écriture comme 'frayage' dans la répétition *psychique* de cette notion naguère neurologique: ouverture de son propre espace, effraction, percée d'un chemin contre des résistances, rupture et irruption *faisant route* (*rupta, via rupta*), inscription violente d'une forme, tracé d'une différence dans une nature ou une matière, qui ne sont pensables comme telles que dans leur *opposition* à l'écriture. La route s'ouvre dans une nature ou une matière, une forêt ou un bois (*hylè*), et il y procure une réversibilité de temps et d'espace. Il faudrait étudier ensemble, génétiquement et structurellement, l'histoire de la route et l'histoire de l'écriture. (*ED*, p. 317)

(We ought thus to examine closely – which we cannot do here – all that Freud invites us to think concerning writing as 'breaching', in the *psychical* repetition of this previously neurological notion: opening up its own space, effraction, breaking of a path against resistances, rupture and irruption *becoming a route* (*rupta, via rupta*), violent inscription of a form, tracing of a difference in a nature or a matter which are conceivable as such only in their *opposition* to writing. The route is opened in nature or matter, forest or wood (*hylè*), and in it acquires a reversibility of time and space. We should have to study together, genetically and structurally, the history of the road and the history of writing.) (*WD*, p. 214)

This passage should be compared with a passage of *De la grammatologie* which is striking for the similarity of its terms. The context of the passage is not, however, a study of Freud's neurological or scriptural models, but a critical commentary of Lévi-Strauss' autobiographical text, *Tristes tropiques*. The chapter in which this passage occurs is appropriately entitled 'La violence de la lettre: de Lévi-Strauss à Rousseau', and Derrida's critique of Lévi-Strauss bears upon the latter's depiction of what he considers to be the violent and destabilizing effect of the introduction of writing to the non-literate culture of the Nambikwara Indians, one of the 'sociétés sans écriture' he encounters in the Brazilian forests. Characteristically, Derrida passes beyond Lévi-Strauss' supposition that the introduction to, or presence of, writing in a culture represents a repressive violence, in order to posit an essential violence conditioning writing as it is commonly accepted ('l'écriture au sens courant') and linguistic expression in general. In the passage in question, Derrida explains and reflects upon the implications of the *picada* which crosses the large territory occupied by the Nambikwara. The entire passage is in parentheses:

Picada (piste grossière dont le 'tracé' est presque 'indiscernable de la brousse': il faudrait méditer d'ensemble la possibilité de la route et de la différence comme écriture, l'histoire de l'écriture et l'histoire de la route, de la rupture, de la *via rupta*, de la voie rompue, frayée, *fracta*, de l'espace de réversibilité et de répétition tracé par l'ouverture, l'écart et l'espacement violent de la nature, de la forêt naturelle, sauvage, salvage. La *silva* est sauvage, la *via rupta* s'écrit, se discerne, s'inscrit violemment comme différence, comme forme imposée dans la *hylè*, dans la forêt, dans le bois comme matière; il est difficile d'imaginer que l'accès à la possibilité des tracés routiers ne soit pas en même temps accès à l'écriture). (*GR*1, p. 158)[5]

(*Picada* (a crude trail whose 'track' is 'not easily distinguished from the bush'; one should meditate upon all of the following together: writing as the possibility of the road and of difference, the history of writing and the history of the road, of the rupture, of the *via rupta*, of the path that is broken, beaten, *fracta*, of the space of reversibility and of repetition traced by the opening, the divergence from, and the violent spacing, of nature, of the natural, savage, salvage, forest. The *silva* is savage, the *via rupta* is written, discerned, and inscribed violently as difference, as form imposed on the *hylè*, in the forest, in wood as matter; it is difficult to imagine that access to the possibility of a road-map is not at the same time access to writing).) (*GR*2, pp. 107–8)

The evident homology between this and the previous passage indicates a certain insistence of interpretation on Derrida's part, the persistence of a model, quite apart from the immediate context of Freud or Lévi-Strauss. In this model, the necessity of a certain violence in the inauguration of a system, in the informing of a 'matter', would appear to be fundamental. Again it must be stressed that such violence is not to be understood in a strictly anthropological sense, that this violence both precedes and transcends the instance of the human or the subjective. In the example of Freud's neurological model, violence is the result of resistance at a primary level, of the encounter of a force and a counter-force in the production of the facilitation. In the example of Lévi-Strauss' writing lesson, violence inhabits Nambikwara society before its chief 'learns' the fatal craft of writing, and indeed inhabits spoken language itself, which for Lévi-Strauss (and for logocentric philosophy in general) is the medium *par excellence* of proximate communication, and therefore regarded as natural and non-oppressive in its employment. As Derrida shows in his reading of the 'guerre des noms propres', where the ethnologist encourages the Nambikwara children to divulge their secret names, resulting in an escalation of denunciation and recrimination, violence is always already at work in the structuring of the social system (here in the system of naming), there is a necessary precession of violence in the constitution of any coded space: 'Antérieure à l'éventualité de la violence au sens courant et dérivé, celle dont parlera la "Leçon d'écriture", il y a, comme l'espace de sa possibilité, la violence de l'archi-écriture, la violence de la différence, de la classification et du système des appellations' (*GR*1, p. 163) ('Anterior to the possibility of violence in the current and derivative sense, the sense used in "A Writing Lesson", there is, as the space of its possibility, the violence of the arche-writing, the violence of difference, of classification, and of the system of appellations' (*GR*2, p. 110)).[6] Such violence *is* memory, whether psychical or social memory. In both of the present examples (Freud and Lévi-Strauss), the quality of reversibility, of traversability in both directions (as along a path or a road), upon which memory depends, is in its turn dependent upon this preliminary, coding violence.

SUBSTANCE

If facilitation is the violent inscription of a force or difference in a hypothetical medium ('*hylè*', 'nature ou matière', as Derrida puts it), Derrida nevertheless insists upon the only partly quantitative nature of the facilitation thus described. He wishes to dissociate Freud's postulate of facilitation from the idea of a present, empirical substance. Though Freud, he claims, intends to speak the language of full and present quantity, to remain safely within the simple opposition between a transparent quality of consciousness and an opaque quantity of memory, his concept of the facilitation is highly resistant to this (*ED*, p. 299; *WD*, p. 201). Freud reasons that if each of the contact-barriers offered equal resistance to excitation, thereby occasioning an equality of facilitations, then there would be no memory since no facilitatory path could be preferred over another: all would be equally traversable. In a sense, there would be only one facilitation, whereas memory resides in the differences between facilitations (*Project*, p. 361). Derrida interprets this in the following manner: 'La trace comme mémoire n'est pas un frayage pur qu'on pourrait toujours récupérer comme présence simple, c'est la différence insaisissable et invisible entre les frayages. On sait donc déjà que la vie psychique n'est ni la transparence du sens ni l'opacité de la force mais la différence dans le travail des forces. Nietzsche le disait bien' (*ED*, p. 299) ('Trace as memory is not a pure breaching that might be reappropriated at any time as simple presence; it is rather the ungraspable and invisible difference between breaches. We thus already know that psychic life is neither the transparency of meaning nor the opacity of force but the difference between the exertion of forces. As Nietzsche has already said' (*WD*, p. 201)). Psychical processes are neither force nor form, if one returns to the formulations of 'Force et signification': they arise, rather, from the differences between force and form.

The effect of Freud's formulation of difference in the *Project*, and Derrida's interpretation of it, is therefore to reduce the importance of the substantial support of the phenomenon of memory. Derrida is extremely interested in this reduction of substance, and sensitive to Freud's increasing recourse to metaphorical schemas in and after the *Project*, a tendency that corresponds with a movement away from the anatomical representation of psychical processes. Freud, for all his attempts to present his psychology as a branch of natural science, dealing with observable and quantifiable substances, increasingly finds it necessary to pass beyond the histological point of view in order to provide a satisfactory account of the complex functionings of the psyche, so much so that what was intended to be an empirically-based enquiry, ultimately cedes to the formal, the metaphorical and the speculative.[7] For example, the facilitations described in the *Project* come to be defined more in terms of the hypothesized relations between them than in terms of their substance, 'relations structurelles plus importantes que les termes de support' (*ED*, p. 303) ('structural relations more important than their supporting terms' (*WD*, p. 204)) – that is, the differences between facilitations, and not the substance of the facilitations themselves. The epigraph to the main text of 'Freud et la scène de l'écriture', quoted from the *Project*, expresses precisely this hesitant effacement, or parenthesis of substance which is clearly of such great interest to Derrida: '*Worin die Bahnung sonst besteht, bleibt dahingestellt,* En quoi consiste d'ailleurs le frayage, la question en reste ouverte' (*ED*, p. 296; *Project*, p. 362) ('In what pathbreaking consists remains undetermined' (*WD*, p. 198)). Similarly, the Derridean trace, which is evidently more general in its field of reference than the Freudian psychic trace, is not a substance; it is, Derrida constantly reiterates, *nothing*: 'La trace *n'est rien,* elle n'est pas un étant, elle excède la question *qu'est-ce que* et la rend éventuellement possible' (*GR*1, p. 110) ('The trace is *nothing,* it is not an entity, it exceeds the question *What is?* and contingently makes it possible' (*GR*2, p. 75)). The trace, like the movement of 'différance' from which it cannot be separated, is not a thing, but a structure, a principle, or, as it was described in an earlier instance, a structuring principle. Derrida's model of inscription is a structural model, that is, its purpose is not empirical description, but the setting forth of the conditions of possibility of systems of signification. Such conditions are unobservable, they are not perceptible as such. The trace is not a visible, intuitable entity, but 'la différence *insaisissable* et *invisible* entre les frayages' (*ED*, p. 299, my emphasis) ('the *ungraspable* and *invisible* difference between breaches' (*WD*, p. 201)).

The reduction of substance and the formulation of difference which Derrida foregrounds in his reading of Freud is both faithful to the letter of Freud's text and consistent with Derrida's own conception of inscription, as was the case with his reading of violence. What we have here is a form of cohabitation of two descriptions or models, and a circulation or exchange of concepts between them. At the same time, just as a certain Freud remains firmly determined by the positivistic science of his period, so Derrida's reading of difference and writing in a certain (other) Freud is in its own way part of a more general contemporary paradigm. Derrida's interpretation or inflection of Freud's model of the psychical system is not simply a theoretical idiolect or monad, constructed *ex nihilo* and in abstraction of a particular state of science. While it may owe something to previous philosophies of difference (Hegel, Nietzsche, Heidegger), there is also a sense in which Derrida's reading of Freud would be impossible without the modern development of cybernetic and information theory, even if he does not appear to make any direct use of the concepts and terminologies of these disciplines. More than in other chapters of *L'écriture et la différence*, and indeed more than in *De la grammatologie* (which draws attention to the important parallel between these sciences and the emergent philosophy of the gram), the influence of such a context is particularly evident in 'Freud et la scène de l'écriture', and there is a definite similarity between Derrida's interpretation of Freud in this text and certain aspects of cybernetic theory. This similarity has already been pointed out by Wilden in his discussion of 'Freud et la scène de l'écriture' in *System and Structure*, where he compares Derrida's reading of difference in Freud with Bateson's conception of information as difference.[8] According to Bateson, what is important is not so much the quantities of energy or substance supporting the transmission of information, as the differences that the information represents. In another discussion of Freud, which joins in many respects Derrida's analysis in 'La scène de l'écriture', Wilden quotes Buckley:

> Though 'information' is dependent upon some physical base or energy flow, the energy component is entirely subordinate to the particular form or structure of variations that the physical base or flow may manifest ... This structured variation – the marks of writing, the sounds of speech, the molecular arrangement of the genetic code of DNA, etc. – is still only raw material or energy unless it 'corresponds' to, or matches in some important way, the structure of variations of other components to which it may thereby become dynamically related.[9]

Wilden's reading of Freud in *System and Structure*, like Derrida's in 'La scène de l'écriture', therefore situates Freud between two paradigms: the thermodynamic paradigm of the late nineteenth and early twentieth centuries, which is concerned with forces, quantities, substances; and the informational paradigm of the present period, which deals with differences, relations, forms. While many critics of Freud point to the weakness of his bioenergetic, causal explanations of mental processes, Wilden and Derrida show how this traditional substantialist-materialist perspective is in Freud's text also coupled with a semiotic understanding of such processes. Though, as Wilden indicates, the terminology differs, his and Derrida's readings of Freud are in this respect essentially the same.[10]

Freud's open question concerning the substance of the facilitation (*Worin die Bahnung sonst besteht, bleibt dahingestellt*), and the tentative hypotheses he constructs in response, are thus a departure from a traditional, materialist conception of psychical processes. This traditional, empirical premise of substantial presence also presupposes in a sense a *present tense* of perception. However, the temporal structure of Freud's description of the institution of the facilitation would also appear, under Derrida's analysis, to escape the simple formulation of a here and now.

One special feature of Derrida's model of inscription discussed in chapters 1 and 2 above was that the violent opening of inscription is not unitary or integral in nature. The integral appearance of force in a singular instance is simultaneously its annihilation. But it is also apparent that such integral failure is avoided and deferred by a certain repetition of difference. With the model of the psyche elaborated in the *Project*, the differentiation between facilitations necessary to the functioning of memory is also fundamental to what Freud calls the 'primary function of neuronic systems' or 'primary process', that is, the efforts of the organism to maintain at the lowest possible level the quantity of external excitation to which it is subject (*ED*, p. 302; *WD*, p. 203; *Project*, pp. 361–2). In the *Project*, Freud describes the organism as inhabiting a physical world of powerful macro-forces, forces which pose a continual threat to the conservation and survival of the organism. The setting-up of facilitations in the spatial dimension permits otherwise fatal quantities of excitation from the external world to be meted out and stored, but equally important is the distribution of excitations in discrete repetitions, or periodic differences (*Project*, p. 371). With these concepts of adjournment (through distribution), of temporal as well as spatial difference (interval and repetition), it is hardly surprising that Derrida should interpret them as examples of the principle of 'différance':

Toutes ces différences dans la production de la trace peuvent être réinterprétées comme moments de la différance. Selon un motif qui ne cessera de gouverner la pensée de Freud, ce mouvement est décrit comme effort de la vie se protégeant elle-même en *différant* l'investissement dangereux, c'est-à-dire en constituant une *réserve* (*Vorrat*). La dépense ou la présence menaçantes sont différées à l'aide du frayage ou de la répétition ... N'est-ce pas déjà la mort au principe d'une vie qui ne peut se défendre contre la mort que par l'*économie* de la mort, la différance, la répétition, la réserve? (*ED*, pp. 300–1)

(All these differences in the production of the trace may be reinterpreted as moments of deferring. In accordance with a motif which will continue to dominate Freud's thinking, this movement is described as the effort of life to protect itself by deferring a dangerous cathexis, that is, by constituting a reserve (*Vorrat*). The threatening expenditure or presence are deferred with the help of breaching or repetition ... Is it not already death at the origin of life which can defend itself against death only through an *economy* of death, through deferment, repetition, reserve?) (*WD*, p. 202)

The potential death standing at the origin of life is adjourned by its distribution and repetition through and in life. Death inhabits the economy of life, it is congenital to it ('la vie *est* la mort', *ED*, p. 302 ('life *is* death', *WD*, p. 203)). This presence of death in life, a death that is, in a sense, introjected, mastered through its internalization, is a subject to which I shall return at a later stage. In the present example, it is evident that the 'death' described by Derrida is formally equivalent to the 'infinity' encountered in other contexts. This infinity, it will be recalled, is both the condition of a system and the force that continues to inhabit the system. What is more, the mode of such habitation is not a peaceful one: the threat of integral disruption inherent in the first instance of decision is diminished, but continued in a series of acts of lesser violence in what Derrida described as the 'economy' of violence. It could therefore be proposed that death *is* integral violence *is* (a certain) infinity. The repeated instance of decision, inscription or (in this case) breaching adjourns the absolute, infinite violence of death. It was noted in chapter 2 that the threefold articulation of infinity-inscription-economy was not reducible to a temporal sequentiality; each 'moment' was always already implicit in the others. This means that the differential repetition to which Derrida refers in 'Ellipse', for example, is not the iteration of a pure and definite first manifestation: what appears to be *the* inscription (the advent of the sign, the inauguration of a system, and so on) is always already double, and the uneven third is the first number of repetition (*ED*, p. 435; *WD*, p. 297). The very idea of a primary instance was problematized and in all cases was seen to be affected by the temporal quality of 'secondarity'. Returning now to Freud's model of the psyche, it is apparent that, with respect to the problem of originarity, repetition and sequentiality, it is absorbed into the Derridean model by virtue of Freud's concept of *Nachträglichkeit* or *Verspätung*.

If the breach of facilitation in Freud's model is in a sense repeated by further, periodic passages of excitation, then Derrida does not accept that such repetition is the iteration of a first time. Against Freud's assertion that the facilitation probably results from a single passage of a large quantity of excitation, Derrida argues that repetition has already occurred with the 'first' breach:

Car la répétition ne *survient* pas à l'impression première, sa possibilité est déjà là, dans la résistance offerte *la première fois* par les neurones psychiques. La résistance elle-même n'est possible que si l'opposition des forces dure ou se répète originairement. C'est l'idée même de *première fois* qui devient énigmatique. Ce que nous avançons ici ne nous paraît pas contradictoire avec ce que Freud dira plus loin : ' ... le frayage est probablement le résultat du passage unique (*einmaliger*) d'une grande quantité'. A supposer que cette affirmation ne renvoie pas de proche en proche au problème de la phylogénèse et des frayages héréditaires, on peut encore soutenir que dans la *première fois* du contact entre *deux* forces, la répétition a commencé. (*ED*, p. 301)

(For repetition does not *happen* to an original impression; its possibility is already there, in the resistance offered the *first time* by the psychical neurones. Resistance itself is possible only if the oppostion of forces lasts and is repeated [from] the beginning. It is the very idea of a *first time* which becomes enigmatic. What we are advancing here does not seem to contradict what Freud will say further on: 'Facilitation is probably the result of the single (*einmaliger*) passage of a large quantity.' Even assuming that his affirmation does not lead us little by little to the problem of phylogenesis and hereditary breaches, we may still maintain that in the *first time* of the contact between *two* forces, repetition has begun.) (*WD*, p. 202)

In the following pages of 'La scène de l'écriture', Derrida supports his reading of the non-originarity of the facilitation with reference to the twin Freudian concepts of *Verspätung* ('retardement', delay) and *Nachträglichkeit* ('l'après-coup', after-effect) which, he claims, are central to Freud's thought ('concepts directeurs de toute la pensée freudienne', *ED*, p. 303 ('concepts which govern the whole of Freud's thought', *WD*, p. 203)), his great discovery. In Freudian theory, the concept of *Verspätung-Nachträglichkeit* refers to a scene which is not understood, hence not properly conscious at the moment of its perception, and which, while retained in the unconscious, is only given its full significance in a later, conscious re-enactment of it. Freud's idea of 'delay' thus tends to fictionalize the supposed origin of a repetition, or at least, it parenthesizes the possibility of direct perception of the origin, thereby rendering to memory the function of deferred perception. As Derrida indicates, in *The Interpretation of Dreams* such an origin is taken to be a 'theoretical fiction', and the traumatic historical event in *Moses and Monotheism* assumes its full sense and effect for the collective psyche only after a period of delay or 'latency' (*Latenzperiode*) (*ED*, pp.   203; *WD*, p. 203).[11]

Of course the substa   , or rather the reduced substantiality, of the facilitat   d its indeterminate origin in time are not separable attrib   ough the order of exposition followed so far might suggest   is is so. The relationship between them is irreducible, a   ir essential cleavage is made especially evident when De   onsiders how Freud is obliged to account for the 'puzz   enomenon of consciousness. The difficulty Freud encou   t this stage is that while the permeable neurones serve th   se of mastering quantitative stimuli from the external w   rmitting of no facilitation, and the impermeable neuro   ponsible for memory admit no quality, the phenomenon   iousness is qualitative *and* requires a certain facilitation. F   therefore of necessity obliged to propose a third class of n   nes which are permeable and yet permit complete facilitation, afterwards returning to their former state. But, Freud asks, how can one have complete facilitation which does not arise from quantity? The problem is resolved by recourse to *periodic* differences, that is, differences taking place in time, at discrete intervals, without there being any spatial differentiation whatsoever. As Derrida indicates, the transient facilitations of consciousness arise 'du temps pur, de la temporalisation pure en ce qui l'unit à l'espacement: de la périodicité. Seul le recours à la temporalité et à une temporalité discontinue ou périodique permet de résoudre la difficulté et l'on devrait patiemment méditer ses implications' (*ED*, pp. 304–5) ('From pure time, from pure temporalization in its conjunction with spacing: from periodicity. Only recourse to temporality and to a discontinuous or periodic temporality will allow the difficulty to be resolved, and we must patiently consider its implications' (*WD*, p. 205)). If it is accepted that the facilitations of memory are made in a hypothetical medium or *hylè* (with, as has been seen, their own period, though this is, according to Freud, 'monotonous', *ED*, p. 305; *WD*, p. 205), then those of consciousness are pure interval or spacing. At the limit of the effacement of quantity, therefore, is differential time, the period, which, asserts Derrida, is pure difference, the condition of any opposition between quantity and quality: 'Différence pure, encore, et différence entre les diastèmes. Le concept de *période en général* précède et conditionne l'opposition de la quantité et la qualité, avec tout ce qu'elle commande' (*ED*, p. 305) ('Pure difference, again, and difference between diastems. The concept of a *period in general* precedes and conditions the opposition between quantity and quality, and everything governed by this opposition' (*WD*, p. 205)). Substance would therefore appear to be wholly absent from the psychic scene when it is a question of the transient and discontinuous processes of perception and consciousness. But if this is the case, *where* exactly do such discontinuous processes operate?

SPACE

If Derrida willingly pursues the points at which Freud departs from a purely anatomico-biological (empirical, substantialist) conception of the workings of memory and perception, it does not follow that the concomitant reduction of the substantiality of the facilitation or memory trace and problematization of its temporal determination implies a rejection of its spatiality. It is not a disincarnate, ideal entity or form, nor simply a delocalized energy. On the contrary, it is locatable in a structure, a structure which is not, however, describable in the empirical terms of anatomy. Freud's description of the structure of the psychical apparatus becomes a *topography* rather than an anatomy. Despite this, the topographical description of the psychical apparatus appears to be in some respects less important to Freud than the dynamical description. For example, in the final chapter of *The Interpretation of Dreams*, Freud attempts to correct and complete the conventional spatial representation of the psychical apparatus with an account of its energetics. To suppose that an unconscious thought, after 'translation', breaks through into the preconscious, and from there accedes to consciousness, is not to say that there has been a simple change of location, nor that the unconscious thought and its conscious 'translation' subsist in differing locations. This, in Derrida's eyes, would suggest the transposition or transportation of a formation present in the unconscious, that is, possessing a definite spatial (and, one assumes, temporal) delimitation. Such a simplistic metaphor of location would not take proper account of the components of force and energy in the functioning of the psychical apparatus. The reader is again reminded of the reasoning of 'Force et signification', when Derrida refers to 'le danger qu'il y aurait à immobiliser ou refroidir l'énergie dans une métaphorique naïve du lieu' (*ED*, p. 315) ('the danger involved in immobilizing or freezing energy within a naive metaphorics of place' (*WD*, p. 212)). He continues his quotation of *The Interpretation of Dreams* with Freud's remark that the accession of an unconscious thought to consciousness is attributable to the investment and withdrawal of energy, that is, to the dynamics of innervation, rather than to the topographical configuration of the psychical apparatus. At the same time, however, Derrida stresses the irreducibility of the spatial component, indicating 'la nécessité non pas d'abandonner mais de repenser l'espace ou la topologie de cette écriture' (*ED*, p. 315) ('the necessity not of abandoning but of rethinking the space or topology of this writing' (*WD*, p. 212)). He reminds us that Freud's emphasis upon the dynamic component in the passage mentioned above does not signify a renunciation of spatial localization:

Ne nous hâtons pas de conclure qu'en en appelant à l'énergétique contre la topique de la traduction, Freud renonçait à localiser. Si, nous allons le voir, il s'obstine à donner une représentation projective et spatiale, voire purement mécanique, des processus énergétiques, ce n'est pas seulement pour la valeur didactique de l'exposition: une certaine spatialité est irréductible, dont l'idée de système en général ne sourait se laisser séparer; sa nature est d'autant plus énigmatique qu'on ne peut plus la considérer comme le milieu homogène et impassible des processus dynamiques et économiques. (*ED*, p. 318)

(Let us not hasten to conclude that by invoking an energetics, as opposed to a topography, of translation Freud abandoned his efforts at localization. If, as we shall see, he persists in giving a projective and spatial – indeed, purely mechanical – representation of energetic processes, it is not simply for didactic reasons: a certain spatiality, inseparable from the very idea of system, is irreducible; its nature is all the more enigmatic in that we can no longer consider it as the homogeneous and serene milieu of dynamic and economic processes.) (*WD*, p. 215)

There is always, therefore, the necessity of the passage through the space of this world without which there is, properly speaking, nothing. Derrida persistently reminds us that if trace, inscription, writing are nothing or almost nothing, they are nonetheless not otherworldly, theological principles, Ideas or archetypes. The system, any system, can only operate given a certain space ('une certaine spatialité est irréductible, dont l'idée de système en général ne saurait se laisser séparer'). The word 'certain' is important, because at the same time that certain space is not simple; the milieu of psychical processes is not homogeneous, it is not what Derrida would call a familiar, empirical space. The question is, in which way is psychical space non-simple and non-homogeneous? It is probable that Derrida is referring to the fact that the psychical apparatus, as Freud describes it from the *Project* onwards, is a *stratified* system, a collection or consecution of systems, 'instances' or agencies. When, in the *Project*, Freud is obliged to introduce the intermediate neuronal system in order to account for the processes of Pcpt-Cs (see above), Derrida quotes his correspondence with Fliess (letter 39), noting that Freud 'slides' that system between those of the permeable and impermeable neurones. According to Derrida, this bold move ('cette dernière audace') anticipates the intercalatory sheet of the Mystic Writing-Pad (*ED*, p. 304; *WD*, p. 205). It also complicates the topographical representation of the psyche, suggesting the idea of the stratification of systems which Freud developed in subsequent studies and to which Derrida is particularly re-ceptive. This is because such stratification (or 'distribution' between instances) makes for the *virtualizing* of psychical space, its detachment from purely empirical observation or deter-mination. It could be said that with such a *complication* of space, there is no determinable first or last instance. Derrida suggests the example of Freud's model of the telescope in *The Interpretation of Dreams* as an illustration of how psychical operations are 'virtual' (Freud's term), localizable not in organic components, but between them (though Freud himself does not speak of 'stratification' in this instance).[12] As with the series of lenses of which the telescope (or microscope) is composed, the systems of the psychical apparatus, '*qui ne sont pas eux-mêmes du psychique*' ('*which are not in any way psychical entities themselves*') (Derrida's emphasis on Freud's text), are not in themselves open to direct perception (*ED*, pp. 318–19; *WD*, p. 215). Furthermore, just as the temporality of the facilitation was found to be inseparable from the parenthesizing of its substance, so too here the operation of the psychical apparatus *in time* interests Freud more than its anatomical or spatial description: 'Puis, c'est la marche de l'appareil qui intéresse Freud, son fonctionnement et l'ordre de ses opérations, le temps réglé de son mouvement tel qu'il est *pris* et repéré sur les pièces du mécanisme' (*ED*, pp. 319–20) ('Next, it is the operation of the apparatus which interests Freud, how it runs and in what order, the regulated timing of its movements as it is *caught* and localized in the parts of the mechanism' (*WD*, p. 216)). Freud dismisses the need to suppose a spatial ordering of the psychical systems, and contends that it is enough to envisage a fixed order by which excitation passes through the systems, that is, a *temporal* sequence of excitation.

It will be noticed that Derrida distinguishes between two series of representations in 'Freud et la scène de l'écriture', and he himself draws attention to this. On the one hand, there is the facilitation, the psychic trace, so far treated under the categories of violence, substance and time. On the other hand, there is the system, or structure, in which they are situated, consisting of an arrangement or consecution of systems. However, if the fa-cilitation, after the *Project*, is increasingly described metaphori-

cally as a form of writing within a stratified system – Freud
having abandoned the neurological and anatomical approach
– Derrida considers the two series of metaphors, system and
writing ('scène' and 'écriture') to be imperfectly matched, that
is, until their harmonization in the model of the Mystic Writing-
Pad: 'Désormais, à partir de la *Traumdeutung* (1900), la
métaphore de l'écriture va s'emparer *à la fois du problème de
l'appareil psychique dans sa structure et de celui du texte psychique dans
son étoffe*. La solidarité des deux problèmes nous y rendra
d'autant plus attentifs: les deux séries de métaphores – texte et
machine – n'entrent pas en scène en même temps' (*ED*, p. 307)
('From now on, starting with the *Traumdeutung* (1900), the
metaphor of writing will *appropriate simultaneously the problems of
the psychic apparatus in its structure and that of the psychic text in its
fabric*. The solidarity of the two problems should make us that
much more attentive: the two series of metaphors – text and
machine – do not come on stage at the same time' (*WD*,
p. 206)). And with the model of the Mystic Writing-Pad,
'Longtemps disjointes et décalées, les deux séries de métaphores
se rejoindront alors' (*ED*, p. 328) ('Long disjointed and out of
phase, the two series of metaphors will then be united' (*WD*,
p. 220)). If the graphical metaphor, according to Derrida's
analysis, informs and eventually determines both the structure
and the substance of Freud's representation of the psychical
apparatus, it is clear that such a metaphor of writing is far from
simple in its application.

WRITING

After the *Project*, therefore, Freud increasingly has recourse to
the scriptural metaphor when describing the elements, or rather
the operations, of memory: 'La trace deviendra le gramme; et
le milieu du frayage, un espacement chiffré' (*ED*, p. 305)
('Trace will become *gramme*; and the region of breaching a
ciphered spacing' (*WD*, p. 205)). Derrida quotes Freud's
correspondence with Fliess (letter 52) to illustrate this significant evolution in his thought. In this letter, Freud no longer
speaks of facilitations, but of signs, registrations and transcrip-

tions in his analysis of memory. In addition, Derrida underlines that in Freud's stratified model, the verbal stratum is far from occupying a privileged position; on the contrary, it is reduced to a mere instance within the general space of the psyche: 'le site du verbal y est assigné à l'intérieur d'un système d'écriture stratifiée qu'il est fort loin de dominer' (*ED*, p. 306) ('verbal phenomena are assigned a place within a system of stratified writing which these phenomena are far from dominating' (*WD*, p. 206)). This interest on Derrida's part in the reduction and relativization of the verbal within the divided and stratified topography of the psyche, can only be understood in the context of his general critique of logocentrism, discussed above. It is to be remembered that such reduction does not carry the intention of a hierarchical revolution by which the traditional auxiliary and subordinate of the spoken voice (writing) is rehabilitated and given absolute precedence. In 'La scène de l'écriture', Derrida's subsequent incursion into *The Interpretation of Dreams* emphasizes the fact that in dreams the logical, linear con-secution of conscious speech does not escape the distorting, alogical processes of the dream-work (see, for example, pp. 322, 323; *WD*, pp. 217, 218). But he also reminds us that alphabetical, phonetic writing (what he calls 'l'écriture au sens courant', writing in the conventional sense of the word), which is supposedly the direct transcription of the verbal, is equally subordinate to the same processes: 'Le verbal est investi et sa transcription phonétique est enchaînée, loin du centre, dans un filet d'écriture muette' (*ED*, p. 308) ('The verbal is cathected, and its phonetic transcription is bound, far from the center, in a web of silent script' (*WD*, p. 207)). But, it could be asked, what *is* this silent writing ('écriture muette') if it is not a familiar, transcriptural writing? How might it lay claim to the title of writing? Once again, of course, it is a question of a general writing that is the condition of any organized system, in this particular case, that of the dream. This general writing is itself non-manifest, in the same manner that the dream-work (with which it is here assimilated) is non-manifest. The question 'what is?' is not pertinent in this case, since such a non-manifest principle can only be deduced from its manifest effects and designated by analogy. The analogy adopted by Freud is in fact writing, but as Derrida indicated at the beginning of 'Freud et la scène de l'écriture', this is more frequently a non-alphabetical writing, that is, the Egyptian (or, to a lesser extent, Chinese) hieroglyphics. Derrida's evident attraction to Freud's analogy of the hieroglyph is easy to understand, since hieroglyphic script is not purely phonetic, but also pictographic and ideographic. The phonetic component is therefore simply a component and nothing more. One arrives at the phonetic expression of the hieroglyph only after a detour through the pictographic and ideographic components: it is not an immediately 'verbal' writing. More to the point, it does not give the illusion of being so, as is the case with phonetic writing. (Derrida would say that phonetic writing gives the illusion of transparency: it disappears before the voice that it transcribes in the same way that the voice is seen to be transparent in relation to the sense or intention it conveys.) This reduction of the importance of the phonetic element is obviously appropriate to Freud's view of the dream-work as an essentially *visual* process, selecting its material for its plastic rather than semantic properties. Derrida in turn considers the hieroglyph to be a particularly striking counter-example to certain assumptions of logocentric thought, the assumption, for example, of the immediacy and transparency of the vehicle or instrument of signification. Furthermore, Freud's predilection for the analogy of the hieroglyph is doubtless also partly coloured by his belief that the dream is a regression to the more 'primal' states of psychic life. In his archeology of the psyche, verbal residues occupy the uppermost, more recent (and therefore more conscious) strata of the psychical apparatus. Freud suggests that dreams generally follow old facilitations ('"Les rêves suivent en général des frayages anciens", disait l'*Esquisse*', *ED*, p. 307), and Derrida accordingly interprets the scene of the dream as a regressive path in 'un paysage d'écriture' ('a landscape of writing'), 'une forêt d'écriture' ('a forest of script') (*ED* p. 307; *WD*, p. 207).

It would be a mistake, however, to assume that what is being described here is a static topography of writing, somehow present in the unconscious and simply awaiting clear decipherment. It would be equally erroneous to assume that the value of the analogy of the hieroglyph lies entirely in its more immediately visual aspect, or in its highly coded nature. Not only does the dream-work operate idiomatically (idiolectically) – thereby rendering redundant a fixed code of interpretation – but the dream-work itself actually comes to assume an importance equal to that of the decoded content of the dream:

Mais il [Freud] fait de l'écriture psychique une production si originaire que l'écriture telle qu'on croit pouvoir l'entendre en son sens propre, écriture codée et visible 'dans le monde', n'en serait qu'une métaphore. L'écriture psychique, par exemple celle du rêve qui 'suit des frayages anciens', simple moment dans la régression vers l'écriture 'primaire', ne se laisse pas lire à partir d'aucun code... dans ses opérations, son lexique et sa syntaxe, un résidu purement idiomatique est irréductible... Autant qu'à la généralité et à la rigidité du code, cette limite tient à ce qu'on s'y préoccupe trop des *contenus*, insuffisamment des relations, des situations, du fonctionnement, et des différences. (*ED*, pp. 310–11)

(But [Freud] makes of psychical writing so originary a production that the writing we believe to be designated by the proper sense of the word – a script which is coded and 'visible in the world' – would be only the metaphor of psychical writing. This writing, for example the kind we find in dreams which 'follow old facilitations', a simple moment in a regression toward a 'primary' writing, cannot be read in terms of any code.... in its operations, lexicon and syntax a purely idiomatic residue is irreducible... As much as it is a function of the generality and the rigidity of the code this limitation is a function of an excessive preoccupation with *content*, and an insufficient concern for relations, locations, processes, and differences.) (*WD*, p. 209)

So the usefulness of the analogy of the hieroglyph in describing the dream processes resides not in the linear decoding of signifier into signified, but in its structure (stratification of pictographic, ideographic and phonetic elements) and hence its mode of operation. Derrida makes exactly this point in his preface to Abraham and Torok's book on Freud's Wolf Man. Quoting and commenting upon their use of the model of the hieroglyph, he writes:

'Le langage des organes et des fonctions serait donc à son tour un ensemble de symboles renvoyant à un langage encore plus archaïque et *ainsi de suite.* Ceci posé, il apparaît d'une logique sans faille de considérer l'organisme *comme un texte hiéroglyphique* sédimenté au cours de l'histoire d'une espèce, et qu'une investigation appropriée serait à même de déchiffrer' … Le modèle hiéroglyphique opérant *partout*, il est plus et autre chose qu'un modèle analogique. Il implique, d'une part, certes, que l'ultime objet reste encore, fût-ce comme nom ou corps 'propres', un texte à déchiffrer, mais aussi, d'autre part, que son écriture ne soit pas essentiellement verbale ou phonétique… On évitera néanmoins l'interprétation simpliste ou scripturaliste, on évitera d'omettre l'opération d'un 'sujet' ou le fonctionnement opératoire du symbole, on évitera de substantialiser l'objet-texte, le 'symbole-chose considéré comme hiéroglyphe, ou texte symbolique', comme 'symbole mort'. Dans ce dernier cas, nous n'aurions devant nous que ce 'catalogue de hiéroglyphes' auquel le *Verbier* ne se réduit en aucun cas: au moment même où il isole un unique 'mot-chose' tenu pour mort ou léthargique, il en explique la genèse opératoire, l'efficace vivante et vigilante. (*F*1, pp. 38–9)[13]

('The language of bodily organs and functions would thus in turn be a set of symbols referring back to an even more archaic language, *and so forth.* This being so, it would seem logically flawless to consider the organism as a *hieroglyphic text*, deposited in the course of the history of the species and which an appropriate investigation should be in a position to decipher' … The hieroglyphic model at work *everywhere* … is more, and other, than an analogical model. It implies on the one hand, of course, that the ultimate object still remains, even as a 'proper' name or body, a text *to be deciphered*, but it also implies that that writing is not essentially verbal or phonetic… We shall nevertheless avoid the simplistic, 'scripturalistic' interpretation; we shall avoid omitting the 'subject's *operation*' or the operative functioning of the symbol. We shall avoid turning the object-text into a substance, the 'symbol-thing considered as a hieroglyphic, or symbolic text' into a 'dead symbol'. If these things were not avoided, we would be faced with nothing but a 'catalogue of hieroglyphics', to which *The Magic Word* can in no way be reduced: at the very moment *The Magic Word* isolates a unique 'word-thing' hitherto considered dead or lethargic, it explains the symbol's operative genesis, its vibrant, vigilant effectiveness.) (*F*2, pp. xxviii–xxix)

Again, there is the metaphor of stratification ('*comme un texte hiéroglyphique* sédimenté'), and what Derrida says here of the hieroglyphic model (it is more and something else than a simple analogy) will also apply to the later model of the Mystic Writing-Pad.

In Abraham and Torok's words, therefore, the hieroglyph is not to be regarded as a dead symbol awaiting decipherment, but rather is to be seen from the point of view of its production. It is the figure of a *process* of writing rather than of a static script, and this process is, properly speaking, invisible. It is beyond what is *seen* of writing in the common sense of the word. The naive, empirical conception of a writing present and open to decipherment ('écriture codée et visible "dans le monde"' ('a script which is coded and "visible in the world"')) is subtended by a more radical form of writing that produces both signifier and signified, that is the process of 'signifiance' (*ED*, p. 311; *WD*, p. 209). What is essential in Derrida's reading of Freud is not the static scene of writing, but its dynamic *mise en scène*: 'Freud et la [mise en] scène de l'écriture.'[14]

The psychical scene of writing is therefore not simple. It is present and perceptible neither here, nor (potentially) elsewhere. One does not pass behind the manifest scene in order to discern its corresponding, latent scene, but rather in order to appreciate the differential operations of the unconscious, of the dream-work, of 'writing', those operations that serve to conceal and defer the presentation of the originary scene. Derrida makes a similar point in his text on 'La différance', which is approximately contemporary to 'Freud et la scène de l'écriture':

Une certaine altérité – Freud lui donne le nom métaphysique d'incon-scient – est définitivement soustraite à tout processus de présentation par lequel nous l'appellerions à se montrer en personne. Dans ce contexte et sous ce nom, l'inconscient n'est pas, comme on sait, une présence à soi cachée, virtuelle, potentielle. Il se diffère, cela veut dire sans doute qu'il se tisse de différences et aussi qu'il envoie, qu'il délègue des représentants, des mandataires; mais il n'y a aucune chance pour que le mandant 'existe', soit présent, soit 'lui-même' quelque part et encore moins devienne conscient. (*M*i, p. 21)

(A certain alterity – to which Freud gives the metaphysical name of the unconscious – is definitively exempt from every process of pres-entation by means of which we would call upon it to show itself in person. In this context, and beneath this guise, the unconscious is not, as we know, a hidden, virtual, or potential self-presence. It differs from, and defers, itself; which doubtless means that it is woven of differences, and also that it sends out delegates, representatives, proxies; but without any chance that the giver of proxies might 'exist', might be present, be 'itself' somewhere, and with even less chance that it might become conscious.) (*M*2, pp. 20–1)

The idea of the delegate, proxy or representative could be compared to the stratification of agencies (*Instanzen*) composing the psychical apparatus as Freud describes it, agencies which, it should also be noted, can perform the role of censuring authorities, to the effect that there is never a simple or unequivocal translation between them. But, as has already been discovered, Freud's hierarchy of agencies does not cohere simply in the spatial realm, it cannot be explained simply from the 'topographical point of view'. More significantly, the 'dynamic point of view' takes the consecution of agencies in time, the *order* in which an excitation passes through them, to be an essential characteristic of psychical processes. The term 'différance' expresses, in its appropriately ambivalent form, precisely this separation ('espacement') or differentiation of agencies in space and time, and correlatively, the impossibility of assigning to them a supreme agency or originary instance: there is no Court of First (or last) Instance.

If the scene of writing is non-manifest and ultimately undisclosable, this is because it is dynamic and differential in nature and is therefore not subject to the delimitation of definitive decipherment. In this context, Derrida refers to 'ce travail d'écriture qui circule comme une énergie psychique entre l'inconscient et le conscient' (*ED*, pp. 314–15) ('the labor of writing which circulates like psychic energy between the unconscious and the conscious' (*WD*, p. 212)), or 'le labeur souterrain d'une impression' ('the subterranean toil of an impression'), 'une trace travailleuse' ('a laborious trace') (*ED*, p. 317; *WD*, p. 214). Work and (a certain) circulation are of course the attributes of the economy, the model of a working, dynamic system already encountered in chapters 1 and 2 above. In 'Freud et la scène de l'écriture', the 'économie de la mort', the saving, sparing, reserving of death, is the economy that works, as a derivative of the primary process, to preserve life. The multiplication of pathways or facilitations within the system of the psyche, their spatial and temporal redistribution of potentially fatal levels of excitation, defers the definitive and integral failure that is the fate of all systems. But since it has become properly a question of life and death – of *survival*, it will be seen – it is now time to investigate the model of the Mystic Writing-Pad, which *almost* acquires the autonomy of the living psyche.

THE MYSTIC WRITING-PAD

As was discovered earlier, Derrida considers there to be two sets of metaphors emanating from the *Project* which develop in a specific direction in subsequent texts. The two metaphors concern the psychic and the system, the elements of the psyche and the topographical arrangement of the system in which they are located. According to Derrida, the orientation of these two metaphors in texts following the *Project* is towards a figure of writing, but this figure does not at first apply equally to both system and psyche. The psychical component is more im-mediately affected by the graphical metaphor, whereas the system continues to be described by analogy with mechanical instruments. It is only with the model of the Mystic Writing-Pad that both system and psyche are subsumed under the scriptural metaphor.

The Mystic Writing-Pad is the subject of a brief article, 'A Note upon the "Mystic Writing-Pad"', published by Freud in 1925.[15] Derrida considers that the Mystic Pad resolves the difficulties of all the models hitherto proposed to account for the mental functions of perception and memory, which Freud believed to be mutually exclusive. Previous models had failed to explain the dual capacity of the psychical apparatus for both retention and infinite reception of stimuli. The models of the telescope, or the microscope, for example, as described in *The Interpretation of Dreams*, could imitate only the receptive (or perceptive), but not the retentive, capacity of the psychical apparatus. The mechanics of the Mystic Pad itself are simple. It is composed of three layers: topmost is a sheet of transparent celluloid; beneath this is a fragile layer of waxed paper; under which there is finally a wax or dark resin slab. One writes with the pointed stylus upon the uppermost layer of celluloid:

> At the points at which the stilus touches, it presses the lower surface of the waxed paper onto the wax slab, and the grooves are visible as dark writing upon the otherwise smooth whitish-grey surface of the celluloid. If one wishes to destroy what has been written, all that is necessary is to raise the double covering-sheet from the wax slab by a light pull, starting from the free lower end. The close connection between the waxed paper and the waxed slab at the places that have been scratched is thus brought to an end and it does not recur when the two surfaces come together once more. The surface of the Mystic Pad is clear of writing and once more capable of receiving impressions. But it is easy to see that the permanent trace of what was written is retained upon the wax slab itself and is legible in suitable lights. ('Note', pp. 431–2)

The ingenious laminated structure of the Mystic Pad does not simply provide an appropriate model of the dual function of the psychical apparatus (retention and infinite reception). In addition to this, it imitates the related tendency of the apparatus to maintain at the lowest possible level the quantities of excitation coming from the external world (Freud's 'primary function of neuronic systems', mentioned earlier). This is because the uppermost celluloid sheet protects the fragile second layer of waxed paper from the sharp point of the writing stylus in the same way, Freud maintains, that the protective shield placed before the systems Pcpt-Cs., described in *Beyond the Pleasure Principle*, diminished the force of external stimuli (*ED*, p. 331; *WD*, p. 224; 'Note', pp. 432, 433). But beyond Freud's evident satisfaction with the Mystic Pad as a model for the processes of perception and memory expressed in the 'Note', are perceivable Derrida's own motivations and preferences which cause him to accord special privilege to the device and to the article describing it. The Mystic Pad possesses a number of qualities which would, no doubt, be of particular interest to Derrida, given the specific orientation of his reading of Freud and what has already been learnt regarding that orientation.

Firstly, the model of the Mystic Pad accounts directly for the action of inscription, the production of the trace, the institution of a writing. The graphical metaphor which Derrida follows through texts subsequent to the *Project*, while it posits a 'text' of the psyche and a certain translation between its stratified instances, does not properly address the problem of the production of the elements of the psychical system, as was the case in the *Project*. With the Mystic Writing-Pad, the *passional* dimension of inscription once more enters the scene of writing, for the Mystic Pad, Freud remarks in his short article, 'is a return to the ancient method of writing on tablets of clay or wax: a pointed stilus scratches the surface, the depressions upon which constitute the "writing"' ('Note', p. 431). The writing upon the Mystic Pad is therefore incisional; it 'does not depend on material being deposited on the receptive surface', but rather upon the material differentiation of that surface. Predictably, Derrida ascribes to this indented inscription, 'ses reliefs et ... ses dépressions' (*ED*, p. 332) ('its ... reliefs and depressions' (*WD*, p. 225)), the quality of violence previously attributed to the production of the facilitation. At the close of 'La scène de l'écriture', for example, he refers to Freud's 'métaphores du chemin, de la trace, du frayage, de la marche piétinant une voie ouverte par *effraction* à travers le neurone, la lumière[16] ou la cire, le bois ou la résine pour *s'inscrire violemment* dans une nature, une matière, une matrice ... référence infatigable à une pointe sèche et à une écriture *sans encre*' (*ED*, p. 338, my emphasis) ('metaphors of the path, trace, breach, of the march treading down a track which was opened by *effraction* through neurone, light or wax, wood or resin, in order *violently to inscribe itself* in nature, matter or matrix... the untiring reference to a dry stilus and a writing *without ink*' (*WD*, p. 229)). It should be noted that this violent inscription is made in a particular medium (here 'nature', 'matière', 'cire', 'bois', elsewhere, 'forêt', '*hylè*', etc.). Similarly, the wax, resin and celluloid of the Mystic Pad, its materiality, emphasize the necessity of the medium of inscription, without which there would be no possibility of signification or memory. Signification does not reside in an other-worldly, inner palace of faculties, but requires the passage through, that is, a passion *in*, the world. Without such a passage it is nothing. However, this is not to say that Derrida is advancing in 'La scène de l'écriture' a 'materialist' as against an 'idealist' conception of psychical or signifying processes. The preceding discussions of substance, time and space on the contrary lead to the conclusion that such an opposition in itself is devoid of sense. Psychical processes are dependent upon a material support, but they are at the same time neither substantial nor localizable, as has been seen. With the model of the Mystic Pad, this virtual nature of the inscription, its non-localizability, resides in the fact that neither the gesture nor the medium of inscription is simple. This introduces my second point.

The gesture and medium of inscription cannot be simple because, unlike the slate or the piece of paper whose space is that of a 'classical geometry' (*ED*, p. 329; *WD*, p. 229), the Mystic Pad is a *stratified* volume. The inscription is therefore distributed, and its violence thereby diminished, between the differing instances of the Mystic Pad. This differentiation of the medium of the Mystic Pad, its division (or delegation) of differing functions, should be directly related to the movement of inscription which defuses the integral violence of the 'origin' through spatial difference. Inevitably, such defusion is not singular or instantaneous, and must also occur in time. Consequently, again in accordance with Derrida's model of inscription, the stratiform Mystic Pad also – and perhaps more importantly – implies a consecution of instances. Derrida is especially receptive to this temporal dimension of the Mystic Pad, deeming it the most *interesting* analogy suggested by the device. He writes:

Jusqu'ici il n'était question que de l'espace de l'écriture, de son étendue et de son volume, de ses reliefs et de ses dépressions. Mais il y a aussi un *temps de l'écriture* et ce n'est pas autre chose que la structure même de ce que nous décrivons en ce moment. Il faut compter ici avec le temps de ce morceau de cire. Il ne lui est pas extérieur et le bloc magique comprend en sa structure ce que Kant décrit comme les trois modes du temps dans les *trois analogies de l'expérience*: la permanence, la succession, la simultanéité. Descartes, lorsqu'il se demande *quaenum vero est haec cera*, en peut réduire *l'essence* à la simplicité intemporelle d'un objet intelligible. Freud, reconstruisant une *opération*, ne peut réduire ni le temps ni la multiplicité de couches sensibles. Et il va relier un concept discontinuiste du temps, comme périodicité et espacement de l'écriture, avec toute une chaîne d'hypothèses qui vont des *Lettres à Fliess* à *Au delà*. (*ED*, pp. 332–3)

(Until now, it has been a question only of the space of writing, its extension, and volume, reliefs and depressions. But there is as well a *time of writing*, and this time of writing is nothing other than the very structure of that which we are now describing. We must come to terms with the temporality of the wax slab. For it is not outside the slab, and the Mystic Pad includes in its structure what Kant describes as the three modes of time in *the three analogies of experience*: permanence, succession, simultaneity. Descartes, when he wonders *quaenam vero est haec cera*, can reduce its *essence* to the timeless simplicity of an intelligible object. Freud, reconstructing an operation, can reduce neither time nor the multiplicity of sensitive layers. And he will link a discontinuist conception of time, as the periodicity and spacing of writing, to a whole chain of hypotheses which stretch from the *Letters to Fliess* to *Beyond the Pleasure Principle*.) (*WD*, p. 225)

The time of writing *is* the structure of the Mystic Pad. The consequence of this is that, as Derrida notes shortly beforehand, perception is never present to itself. The structure of the Mystic Pad excludes this, since inscription upon the surface of the celluloid will disappear once contact with the two lower layers is interrupted: it retains no permanent trace. The present of a perception can only be read afterwards (*nachträglich, après coup*, as Derrida would say) and under the superficial strata of the psyche, upon the wax slab which is equivalent to the unconscious: 'Le "perçu" ne se donne à lire qu'au passé, au-dessous de la perception et après elle' (*ED*, p. 332) ('The "perceived" may be read only in the past, beneath perception and after it' (*WD*, p. 224)). Perception proper is never primary, can only occur through the intermediary of another agency. There is an inherent non-originarity or delay in conscious (verbal) thought, which is the effect of this delegating structure. The inscription can never be present simply *once*, and requires a certain repetition that problematizes any assignation of a unitary origin. Such repetition is equivalent to the discontinuity or periodicity to which Derrida refers above, the interruption and re-establishment of contact between the different strata of the Mystic Pad. The following description of the trace summarizes the essential elements of Derrida's interpretation of Freud's model:

> Les traces ne produisent donc l'espace de leur inscription qu'en se donnant la période de leur effacement. Dès l'origine, dans le 'présent' de leur première impression, elles sont constituées par la double force de répétition et d'effacement, de lisibilité et d'illisibilité. Une machine à deux mains, une multiplicité d'instances ou d'origines, n'est-ce pas le rapport à l'autre et la temporalité originaires de l'écriture, sa complication 'primaire': espacement, différance et effacement originaires de l'origine simple, polémique dès le seuil de ce qu'on s'obstine à appeler la perception? (*ED*, p. 334)

> (Traces thus produce the space of their inscription only by acceding to the period of their erasure. From the beginning, in the 'present' of their first impression, they are constituted by the double force of repetition and erasure, legibility and illegibility. A two-handed machine, a multiplicity of agencies or origins – is this not the [originary] relation to the other and the [originary] temporality of writing, its 'primary' complication: spacing, deferring, and erasure of the simple origin, polemics [from] the very threshold of what we persist in calling perception?) (*WD*, p. 226)

It is here, however, that one encounters the limits of the compelling analogy that Derrida implicitly draws between Freud's model and his own. This is because the ephemerality of the trace, which is an essential postulate of Derrida's model (he asserts later that 'une trace ineffaçable n'est pas une trace', *ED*, p. 339 ('an unerasable trace is not a trace', *WD*, p. 230)), appears to concern only the perceptual extremity of Freud's representation of the psychical apparatus. As Derrida argues, the equivocal trace problematizes from the start 'ce qu'on s'obstine à appeler la perception', and this is of course consistent with his criticism in works contemporary to *L'écriture et la différence* (*La voix et le phénomène, De la grammatologie*) of the traditional association in Western metaphysics of the concepts of perception and consciousness with the present tense and verbal enunciation. Derrida had indeed pointed out earlier in 'La scène de l'écriture' that for Freud, the pre-conscious is the seat of the verbal faculties (*ED*, pp. 307, 316; *WD*, pp. 207,

215). In the model of the Mystic Pad, the systems of pre-conscious-consciousness are represented by the two uppermost layers of the celluloid sheet and the waxed paper. The wax or resin slab is therefore the unconscious. It is this stratum or extremity of the apparatus which, one might argue, poses a limit to Derrida's inflected reading of Freud. Derrida holds that Freud's stratified Mystic Pad, its non-simple structure, extricates it from the simplistic, traditional metaphor of the soul or psyche as an inscribed wax tablet. This metaphor assumes an objectifiable essence of the inscription upon the soul, its immutable substance and, above all, its eternal presence or timelessness. Such was Descartes' conception of the wax-like soul (*quaenam vero est haec cera*), and before him, Plato took the writing upon the surface of the soul to be the incorruptible index of eternal truths, '*inscription* de la vérité dans l'âme' ('inscription of truth in the soul') as Derrida says in 'La pharmacie de Platon' (*D*1, p. 172; *D*2, p. 149).

It is true, as Derrida convincingly demonstrates, that in Freud's model of the Mystic Pad, durational time and space are irreducibly implicated. At the same time, Freud appears to adopt a traditionally essentialist perspective when it is a question of the unconscious itself. The transient processes of the conscious periphery of the psychical apparatus do not appear to apply to the space of the unconscious. Freud consistently asserts, for example, that the traces of the unconscious are indestructible, and Derrida is obviously resistant to this. In the note which concludes 'La scène de l'écriture' (this note recapitulates the last part of the lecture which is not included in the transcribed text), he directly addresses the problem:

Il faut donc radicaliser le concept freudien de trace et l'extraire de la métaphysique de la présence qui le retient encore ... La trace est l'effacement de soi, de sa propre présence, elle est constituée par la menace ou l'angoisse de sa disparition irrémédiable, de la disparition de sa disparition. Une trace ineffaçable n'est pas une trace, c'est une présence pleine, une substance immobile et incorruptible ... Cet effacement est la mort elle-même et c'est dans son horizon qu'il faut penser non seulement le 'présent', mais aussi ce que Freud a sans doute cru être l'indélible de certaines traces dans l'inconscient où 'rien ne finit, rien ne passe, rien n'est oublié'. (*ED*, p. 339)

(Thus the Freudian concept of trace must be radicalized and extracted from the metaphysics of presence which still retains it ... The trace is the erasure of selfhood, of one's own presence, and is constituted by the threat or anguish of its irremediable disappearance, of the disappearance of its disappearance. An unerasable trace is not a trace, it is a full presence, an immobile and uncorruptible substance ... This erasure is death itself, and it is within its horizon that we must conceive not only the 'present', but what Freud doubtless believed to be the indelibility of certain traces in the unconcious, where 'nothing ends, nothing happens, nothing is forgotten'.) (*WD*, pp. 229–30)

Freud's belief in the indestructibility of the unconscious trace, as the above quotation indicates, also inevitably implies the *timelessness* of unconscious processes. The Freud of the *Project* said that the time of the unconscious was 'monotonous' and without quality (*Project*, pp. 371–2). In the main text of 'La scène de l'écriture', Derrida wrestles (as he had wrestled before with Freud's difficult assumption of a single institution of the facilitation) with the 'redoutable problème de la temporalisation de ladite "intemporalité" de l'inconscient' ('the formidable problem of the temporalization and the so-called "timelessness" of the unconscious'), asserting that: 'Ici plus qu'ailleurs l'écart est sensible entre l'intuition et le concept freudiens. L'intemporalité de l'inconscient n'est sans doute déterminée que par opposition à un concept courant du temps, concept traditionnel, concept de la métaphysique, temps de la mécanique ou temps de la conscience' (*ED*, p. 318) ('Here, more than elsewhere, the gap between Freud's intuition and his concepts is evident. The timelessness of the unconscious is no doubt determined only in opposition to a common concept of time, a traditional concept, the metaphysical concept: the time of mechanics or the time of consciousness' (*WD*, pp. 214–15)). It would appear that for Freud (or a certain Freud) there is in a sense a last instance, both temporally and spatially, and that this instance is the unconscious. This is one limit upon Derrida's interpretation of Freud.

The third, and final, point concerning the Mystic Pad (in my opinion, the most interesting point) has to do with the limit which Freud himself recognizes in the analogy between the Mystic Pad and the human psyche. This is most interesting because, as Freud articulates this limit, Derrida delineates the second limitation to his interpretation of Freud, concerning the question of life and death. Freud accepts that his model of the Mystic Pad fails to imitate the actual operation of human memory in two important respects:

> We need not be disturbed by the fact that in the Mystic Pad no use is made of the permanent traces of the notes that have been received; it is enough that they are present. There must come a point at which the analogy between an auxiliary apparatus of this kind and an organ which is its prototype will cease to apply. It is true, too, that once the writing has been erased, the Mystic Pad cannot 'reproduce' it from within; it would be a mystic pad indeed if, like our memory, it could accomplish that. ('Note', p. 433)

These two limitations are in effect one: they arise from the fact that the Mystic Pad does not possess the living autonomy of the human psychical apparatus, that is, in Freud's words, it does not dispose of and use the capacity of *cathexis*. Playing upon the etymological derivation of the word 'maintenance', Derrida interprets the limit Freud assigns to the analogy of the Mystic Pad as follows: 'Cette machine ne marche pas toute seule. C'est moins une machine qu'un outil. Et on ne la tient pas d'une seule main. Sa temporalité se marque là. Sa *maintenance* n'est pas simple ... Il faut au moins deux mains pour faire fonctionner l'appareil, et un système de gestes ... une multiplicité organisée d'origines' (*ED*, p. 334) ('The machine does not run by itself. It is less a machine than a tool. And it is not held with only one hand. This is the mark of its temporality. Its *maintenance* is not simple ... At least two hands are needed to make the apparatus function, as well as a system of gestures ... an organized multiplicity of origins' (*WD*, p. 226)). And shortly afterwards, he repeats:

> La machine ne marche pas toute seule, cela veut dire autre chose: mécanique sans énergie propre. La machine est morte. Elle est la mort ... La représentation est la mort ... Une représentation pure, une machine, ne fonctionne jamais d'elle-même. Telle est du moins la limite que Freud reconnaît à l'analogie du bloc magique. Comme le premier mot de la *Note*, son geste est alors très platonicien. Seule l'écriture de l'âme, disait le *Phèdre*, seule la trace psychique a pouvoir

de se produire et de se représenter elle-même, spontanément ... La vie comme profondeur n'appartient qu'à la cire de la mémoire psychique. Freud continue donc d'opposer, comme Platon, l'écriture hypomnési- que à l'écriture *en tè psuchè*, elle-même tissée de traces, souvenirs empiriques d'une vérité présente hors du temps. Dès lors, séparé de la responsabilité psychique, le bloc magique, en tant que représentation abandonnée à elle-même, relève encore de l'espace et du mécanique cartésiens: cire *naturelle*, extériorité de *l'aide-mémoire. (ED*, pp. 335–6)

(That the machine does not run by itself means something else: a mechanism without its own energy. The machine is dead. It is death ... Representation is death. ... A pure representation, a machine, never runs by itself. Such at least is the limitation which Freud recognizes in his analogy with the Mystic Pad. Like the first section of the 'Note', his gesture at this point is extremely Platonic. Only the writing of the soul, said the *Phaedrus*, only the psychical trace is able to reproduce and to represent itself spontaneously ... Life as depth belongs only to the wax of psychical memory. Freud, like Plato, thus continues to oppose hypomemnic writing and writing *en tei psychei*, itself woven of traces, empirical memories of a present truth outside of time. Henceforth, the Mystic Pad, separated from psychical re- sponsibility, a representation abandoned to itself, still participates in Cartesian space and mechanics: *natural* wax, exteriority of the *memory aid*.) (*WD*, p. 227)

This passage follows closely in certain respects Derrida's argument in 'La pharmacie de Platon': Plato uses the model or metaphor of writing in order to describe the inner life of the soul, but at the same time considers writing in the common sense of the word to be an external supplement, appendage or aide (cf. Freud's example of the *Hilfsapparat* in the 'Note') to the living and autonomous space of the psyche (*D*1, p. 172; *D*2, p. 149). Derrida therefore sees the limitation Freud places upon the autonomy of the Mystic Pad as an extension of the philosophical tradition which admits as self-evident (and establishes an implicit relationship between) the oppositions of natural- artificial, essential-supplementary, internal-external, eternally present-contingent, living-dead, autonomous-dependent. He resists the simple verdict that the Mystic Pad is itself helpless (it needs *maintenance*, must be manipulated with the hand), echoing his criticism in 'La pharmacie de Platon' of Plato's suggestion that graphical writing is like the dependent and irresponsible son in need of paternal assistance (*D*1, p. 87; *D*2, p. 77). Freud, he proposes, does not completely follow the implications of his own thought:

Tout ce que Freud a pensé de l'unité de la vie et de la mort aurait dû pourtant l'inciter à poser ici d'autres questions ... Loin que la machine soit pure absence de spontanéité, sa *ressemblance* avec l'appareil psychique, son existence et sa nécessité témoignent de la finitude ainsi suppléée de la spontanéité mnésique. La machine – et donc la représentation – c'est la mort et la finitude *dans* le psychique. Freud ne s'interroge pas davantage sur la possibilité de cette machine qui, dans le monde, a au moins commencé à *ressembler* à la mémoire, et lui ressemble toujours davantage et toujours mieux. (*ED*, p. 336)

(All that Freud had thought about the unity of life and death should have led him to ask other questions here ... Far from the machine being a pure absence of spontaneity, its *resemblance* to the psychical apparatus, its existence and its necessity bear witness to the finitude of the memnic spontaneity which is thus supplemented. The machine – and consequently, representation – is death and finitude *within* the psyche. Nor does Freud examine the possibility of this machine, which, in the world, has at least begun to *resemble* memory, and increasingly resembles it more closely.) (*WD*, pp. 227–8)

The very possibility of the metaphorical passage between psyche and model – their resemblance – would indicate a more fundamental relationship between the two, in this case that of writing in the very general sense that Derrida attributes to it. However, familiar as this particular proposition may seem at this stage, it is argued here in the difficult context of supplementarity, life and death. The Mystic Pad is not simply *any* analogy of the functions of human memory; it does not simply resemble or simulate human memory in a number of significant ways. It is also, as Derrida repeatedly calls it, a machine, an instrument, a piece of technology. Like the piece of paper used as a memorandum which Freud, at the start of the 'Note', takes to be a 'materialized portion' of the memnic apparatus, the Mystic Pad is an aid to, an extension of, memory, a *Hilfsapparat* (Freud) or a *supplement* (Derrida) to memory. Derrida's reading of the logic of supplementarity, undertaken at length in other, contemporary texts,[17] is again applicable in this case: what is normally perceived to be integral, endowed of life and in need of no assistance, is nevertheless dependent (or becomes dependent) upon an external agent that supplements its activities but which is itself without autonomy. But the very act of supplementation throws doubt upon the supposedly integral and self-sufficient nature of what is supplemented: how can that which is auto-mobile and self-sustaining also require the vehicle or support of the auxiliary? The co-operation of 'death' and 'life' in the mutual commerce (or economy) of supplement and supplemented inevitably exposes the essential lack – or death – at the heart of the supplemented party. The ultimately uneasy cohabitation of the Mystic Pad and of spontaneous human memory in the 'Note' – Freud cuts short the analogy when it becomes a question of life and death – is an index of the death that inhabits the living psyche ('la mort et la finitude *dans* le psychique' ('death and finitude *within* the psyche')). This essential complicity of life and death means that if one is to recognize a certain 'death' within the living soul, then one must correspondingly accept also a certain 'life' or autonomy of its purported external auxiliary, writing. The idea or practice of 'writing' cannot therefore be subsumed under the normally accepted category of an auxiliary technology:

Ici la question de la *technique* (il faudrait peut-être trouver un autre nom pour l'arracher à son problématique traditionnelle) ne se laisse pas dériver d'une opposition allant de soi entre le psychique et le non-psychique, la vie et la mort. L'écriture est ici la *technè* comme rapport entre la vie et la mort, entre le présent et la représentation, entre les deux appareils. Elle ouvre la question de la technique: de l'appareil en général et de l'analogie entre l'appareil psychique et l'appareil non-psychique. (*ED*, p. 337)

(Here the question of *technology* (a new name must perhaps be found in order to remove it from its traditional problematic) may not be derived from an assumed opposition between the psychical and nonpsychical, life and death. Writing here, is *technè* as the relation between life and death, between present and representation, between the two apparatuses. It opens up the question of technics: of the apparatus in general and of the analogy between the psychical apparatus and the nonpsychical apparatus.) (*WD*, p. 228)

With this fundamental interrogation of the meaning and function of technology in relation to the human, Derrida is touching on a central problem of cybernetic theory regarding the processes of control and communication in the animal and the machine and the possible analogies between the two. Already in 'La scène de l'écriture', there have been allusions to what might be taken as contemporary equivalents of Freud's model of the Mystic Pad: when, for example, Derrida refers to Freud's abrupt termination of his analogy between human memory and 'cette machine qui, dans le monde, a au moins commencé à *ressembler* à la mémoire, et lui ressemble toujours davantage et toujours mieux' (*ED*, p. 336) ('this machine, which, in the world, has at least begun to *resemble* memory, and increasingly resembles it more closely' (*WD*, p. 228)). This is a clear reference to the (then) current advances in computing and artificial intelligence, for Derrida continues: 'Beaucoup mieux que cet innocent bloc magique: celui-ci est sans doute infiniment plus complexe que l'ardoise ou la feuille, moins archaïque que le palimpseste, mais comparé à d'autres machines à archives, c'est un jouet d'enfant' (*ED*, pp. 336–7) ('Its resemblance to memory is closer than that of the innocent Mystic Pad: the latter is no doubt infinitely more complex than slate or paper, less archaic than the palimpsest; but, compared to other machines for storing archives, it is a child's toy' (*WD*, p. 228)). While Freud's model provides a limited approximation of mental functions, modern simulations of these 'vital' or 'human' processes challenge even more radically the line of demarcation drawn between the natural and the artificial.[18] The effect of cybernetic explanation, the modelling of human mental processes on mechanical control systems and vice versa, is to relativize the difference between living and mechanical systems, pointing towards a theory of complex systems in general. The philosophical implication of cybernetic theory would therefore tend to be a certain parenthesis of the anthropological or the anthropomorphic, as Derrida argues in *De la grammatologie* apropos of the trace, a central concept of cybernetic theory: 'A supposer que la cybernétique puisse déloger en elle tous les concepts métaphysiques – et jusqu'à ceux d'âme, de vie, de valeur, de choix, de mémoire – qui servaient naguère à opposer la machine à l'homme, elle devra conserver... la notion

d'écriture, de trace, de gramme, ou de graphème' (*GR*1, p. 19)
('If the theory of cybernetics is [to free itself of] all metaphysical
concepts – including the concepts of soul, of life, of value, of
choice, of memory – which until recently served to separate the
machine from man, it must conserve the notion of writing,
trace, grammè, or grapheme' (*GR*2, p. 9)). In 'Freud et la scène
de l'écriture', the trace is similarly presented as a basic process
of the system, before and beyond conscious agency. If the
subject is not an integrally 'living' consciousness, then this trace
is not, cannot be, an absolutely 'dead' substance, animated and
informed from without, like a passive instrument handled by its
user. Derrida's descriptions of the trace indeed frequently
emphasize the qualities of dynamism and autonomy; the
inauguration of the facilitation is described for example in terms
of a working, productive trace: 'travail *itinérant* de la trace,
produisant et non parcourant sa route, de la trace qui trace, de
la trace qui se fraye elle-même son chemin' (*ED*, p. 317) ('the
itinerant work of the trace, producing and following its route, the
trace which traces, the trace which breaks open its own path'
(*WD*, p. 214)). Such descriptions are contrasted with the
conventional conception of the psychic script as a lifeless,
petrified archive: 'présence impassible d'une statue, d'une
pierre écrite ou d'une archive' (*ED*, p. 313) ('the serene
presence of a statue, of a written stone or archive' (*WD*,
p. 211)), 'présence impassible de signes pétrifiés' (*ED*, p. 322)
('the impassive presence of petrified signs' (*WD*, p. 217)),
where the implication is that a living consciousness or intentionality is required to animate or (to borrow Freud's term)
cathect the dead signs passively inscribed on the inner tablet of
the psyche. Unlike the traditional understanding of writing as a
tangible relic of its institution, as a static archive, monument or
scripta manent, the trace is the perpetual *survival* of the mortal first
instance, it economizes life through the elliptical and discontinuous repetition of that instance: 'Il faut rendre compte de
l'écriture comme trace survivant au présent de la griffe, à la
ponctualité, à la *stigmè*' (*ED*, p. 331) ('We must account for
writing as a trace which survives the scratch's present, punc-
tuality, and *stigmè*' (*WD*, p. 224)).

The ultimate effect of Derrida's reading of Freud in 'La scène de l'écriture' is thus to displace the absolute distinction between internal and external, when such a distinction is applied to the 'human' or the 'living' as against the 'artificial' and the 'dead'. It could be said, borrowing the topological term used in *La dissémination*, that there is an *invagination* of psychical with worldly space, since this space is, as Derrida suggested earlier, 'ni dehors ni dedans' (*ED*, p. 304) ('neither outside nor inside' (*WD*, p. 204)). Inner 'life', and the 'death' outside of it, are totally and inseparably implicated. Paradoxically, or so it seems, life is never integrally living. Its condition is an inherent death, or composition with death, without which it would be nothing, that is, death. Integral presence is death, 'la pureté de la vie est la mort' ('the purity of life is death'), says Derrida in *Glas* (*GL*1, p. 137a; *GL*2, p. 118a). His critique of logocentrism, of the metaphysics of presence, is precisely that it represses the difference or death implicit in all technology, all extensions of the 'living' through which life (reproduction and survival) is made possible, and rests upon the illusion of a living continuum of presence, the conscious self or voice that exists without interruption, the so-called 'présent-vivant' of the phenomenologists. The logic of life is, on the contrary, to be both life and not-life. Its articulation in space has the structure of invagination; in time, the structure of discontinuity. This would be equivalent to the 'flickering up and passing-away' (*Aufleuchten und Vergehen*) of consciousness in Freud's explanation of the process of perception, which the Mystic Pad achieves by the interruption and re-establishment of contact between its different layers, but which Freud compares also to 'feelers' which the unconscious would direct towards the external world and then retract (*ED*, p. 333; *WD*, p. 225; 'Note', p. 433).

Twice in this chapter, I have proposed a parallel between Derrida's theory of the trace, as it is elaborated in his dialogue with Freud's neurological and scriptural models, and aspects of cybernetic theory. The first comparison concerned Derrida's formulation of difference and its similarities with the cybernetic conception of information as difference. The second discussed the similar philosophical conclusions resulting from an in-

CHAPTER 4

The element of play
(écart, entame, [en]taille, articulation/double bande, tomber)

Mais la langue n'est que l'un de ces systèmes de *marques* qui ont tous pour propriété cette étrange tendance: accroître *simultanément* les réserves d'indétermination aléatoire *et* les pouvoirs de codage ou de surcodage, autrement dit de contrôle et d'auto-régulation.

(MC, p. 5)

(Language, however, is only one among those systems of *marks* that claim this curious tendency as their property: they *simultaneously* incline towards increasing the reserves of random indetermination *as well as* the capacity for coding and overcoding or, in other words, for control and self-regulation.)

(*TC*, p. 2)

Que se passe-t-il quand des actes ou des performances (discours ou écriture, analyse ou description, etc.) font partie des objets qu'ils désignent? Quand ils peuvent se donner en exemple de cela même dont ils parlent ou écrivent?

(CP, p. 417)

(What happens when acts or performances (discourse or writing, analysis or description, etc.) are part of the object they designate? When they can be given as examples of precisely that of which they speak or write?)

(*PC*, p. 391)

It has sometimes been the case in the preceding analyses that Derrida's argument is characterized by, and in certain instances may even turn upon, an element of verbal play. Such play is not simply confined to isolated puns or homonyms, but can assume the proportions of a highly organized system of associations, so that the reader is confronted with what appears to be an extremely *stylized* manner of argumentation, in which the effect of words is constantly felt. This happens, for example, in the closing pages of 'Force et signification', as was evident in the analysis in chapter 1. The word 'graver' was associated both with the motion of a weighty fall ('chute', 'déchéance', 'pesanteur') and the gesture of inscription. In chapter 3, the violence of the Freudian facilitation ('frayage') was seen to be given supplementary motivation in Derrida's text through the associative declension of 'effraction-fracta-frayée'. The status of verbal play of this type is often difficult to determine. On the one hand, certain etymological considerations may validate the logical grounding of such play; on the other hand, the play may be, for instance, purely homophonic, or anagrammatic, and would therefore appear to belong to what is normally taken to be poetic expression. Of course, this blurring of lines of generic demarcation is wholly intentional on Derrida's part. His later work, especially, often combines the most scrupulous and impeccable scholarship with a seemingly frivolous, and apparently arbitrary, distortion of terms and discourses. Furthermore, with a torsional movement that becomes a common feature of his texts, this undecidable or arbitrary element of his writing comes to imitate the inherent instabilities and uncertainties of its object. In other words, not only is Derrida articulating a particular description or interpretation of a specific object, but his own description or interpretation also becomes an example of that object.

It is certainly the case that these two characteristics – highly stylized word-play and a self-referential discourse – though present to some extent in works such as *L'écriture et la différence* or *De la grammatologie*, only become persistent and systematic in texts such as *La dissémination* and later *Glas* and *La vérité en peinture*. In an interview given in 1975, a similar point was put to Derrida: after *Glas*, especially, one part of his work is relatively 'classical' in its approach, whereas another part (texts such as *Glas* itself) remains 'unclassable'. Derrida's response was that such a distinction was already apparent within his earlier works, and that later, it is simply a question of the extension of this tendency (EC, pp. 97ff). Derrida would therefore disagree with verbal system that Derrida constructs in 'La dissémination', but intend instead to explore a text that is, from this point of view at least, somewhat simpler: Derrida's commentary of Rousseau's *Essai sur l'origine des langues* in *De la grammatologie*.

There is an interesting persistence of the word 'écart' in the chapters of *De la grammatologie* devoted to Rousseau. In these chapters there is no direct play upon the two words 'trace' and 'écart', but the structural relationship between them is apparent. This is particularly clear in the third chapter of *De la grammatologie*, which concentrates on the *Essai sur l'origine des langues*, and where Derrida follows Rousseau's attempts to account for the emergence of social formations and their development. A *sine qua non* of such formations is language, and it becomes apparent that Rousseau regards the different transitions he is obliged to hypothesize, in his descriptions of the genesis of a linguistic community, as somewhat unnatural departures from a natural state, what Derrida refers to as 'des écarts de nature'. Rousseau is in a sense caught in a double bind: on the one hand, he wishes to describe how the progress represented by the constitution of a linguistic community was achieved; on the other hand, such a description requires the intervention of a catastrophe that violates the (for him) ideal state of natural equilibrium in which the pre-linguistic community lived. If Rousseau must account for the creation and transformation of social groups in his *Essai* (languages require an established community and vice versa), then Derrida's reading of this necessity in Rousseau's text is typically expressed in terms of structures, systems and sets. In the final part of the chapter on the *Essai* (*GR*1, pp. 361–78; *GR*2, pp. 255–68) speaking of the passage from what Rousseau describes as the second (barbarous, pastoral and pre-social) state to the third (social) state, Derrida writes: 'Le passage d'une structure à l'autre – par exemple de l'état de nature à l'état de société – ne peut être expliqué par aucune analyse structurelle: un factum extérieur, irrationnel, catastrophique doit faire irruption. Le hasard ne fait pas partie du système' (*GR*1, p. 365) ('The passage from one structure to the other – from the state of nature to that of society for example – cannot be explained by any structural analysis: an external, irrational, catastrophic factum must burst in. Chance is not part of the system' (*GR*2, p. 258)). Again, as with the moment of inscription, the conditions of transformation are of a somewhat violent character: the perturbing intrusion from without is sudden and catastrophic. In Rousseau's narrative this external perturbation is explained in the following manner. The second, pre-social state (or system), as evidenced in the savage's natural indolence, is initially in equilibrium, as is the larger system that contains and determines it, the terrestrial system ('le système de la terre', *GR*1, p. 363; *GR*2, p. 256). This (for Rousseau) ideal and self-sufficient state of inertia can only, according to Rousseau's logic, be transformed from without ('Le hasard ne fait pas partie du système'). He proposes that some external agent (God) touched with His finger the axis of the earth so as to incline it very slightly in relation to the celestial axis (Derrida quoting Rousseau, *GR*1, p. 362; *GR*2, p. 256). From this minimal, digital intervention that literally revolutionizes the earth (turns it on its axis) come the catastrophic climatic changes that make necessary human co-operation, and hence language. Derrida's interpretation of Rousseau's solution merits quotation in its entirety, for it raises a number of extremely interesting points:

Comme la catastrophe de l'inquiétude et de la différenciation des saisons n'a pu être logiquement produite depuis le dedans du système inerte, il faut imaginer l'inimaginable: une chiquenaude parfaitement extérieure à la nature. Cette explication d'apparence 'arbitraire' répond à une nécessité profonde et elle concilie ainsi bien des exigences. La négativité, l'origine du mal, la société, l'articulation viennent *du dehors* … Il est d'autre part indispensable que cette extériorité du mal ne soit rien ou presque rien. Or la chiquenaude, le 'léger mouvement' produit une révolution à partir de rien … Une force presque nulle est une force presque infinie dès lors qu'elle est rigoureusement étrangère au système qu'elle met en mouvement … La chiquenaude est toute-puissante parce qu'elle déplace le globe dans le vide … Puissance infinie: le doigt qui incline un monde. Eloquence infinie parce que silencieuse: un mouvement du doigt suffit à Dieu pour émouvoir le monde. (*GR*1, pp. 363–4)

(As the catastrophe of disturbance and seasonal differentiation could not be logically produced from within an inert system, one must imagine the unimaginable: a little push entirely exterior to Nature. This apparently 'arbitrary' explanation responds to a profound necessity and thus reconciles many exigencies. Negativity, the origin of evil, of society, of articulation, comes *from without* ... On the other hand it is imperative that this exteriority of evil be nothing or nearly nothing. The little push, the 'slight movement' produces a revolution out of nothing ... A nearly nonexistent force is a nearly infinite force when it is strictly alien to the system it sets going ... The slight push is almighty because it shifts the globe in the void ... Infinite power: the finger that tips the world. Eloquence infinite because silent: a movement of the finger is enough for God to move the world.) (*GR2*, pp. 256–7)

The inauguration of an entirely new order is due to a minimal difference: the 'chiquenaude', the flick or flip, is 'rien ou presque rien' ('nothing or nearly nothing'). This is structurally equivalent to Derrida's descriptions elsewhere of the inscription or trace: it is itself nothing or next to nothing, a minimal cause that occasions a maximal effect. The 'trace' of the 'écart' or the 'écart' of the 'trace' is of a micrological dimension, but it will inaugurate or transform entire systems ('une force presque nulle est une force presque infinie' ('a nearly nonexistent force is a nearly infinite force')).[1]

To speak simply of minimal cause and maximal effect, however, is perhaps too reductive. This chain of cause and effect, in Derrida's interpretation of Rousseau, does not have the completely deterministic character one might expect of it. There is an element of indeterminacy in Derrida's argument that requires closer attention. Following another commentator of Rousseau, Derrida notes the 'arbitrary' nature of Rousseau's explanation, an arbitrariness which, however, satisfies a deep necessity ('répond à une nécessité profonde'). This necessity is Rousseau's desire and conviction that the idyllic and stable system preceding socialization cannot by and of itself have produced the causes of its transformation; some external intervention is required. Again, one is close to a formulation of Derrida's logic of supplementarity, discussed above from the point of view of writing and human memory. Rousseau projects outside of the world system the evil he considers to be the cause of its destabilization. As Derrida indicates, this creates problems, for the efficient cause of such destabilization is *probably* God. On the one hand, Derrida argues, the cause is probably God because only God wields infinite power in a gesture that is near to nothing. On the other hand, the cause is perhaps not God because God cannot have willed catastrophe and because He would not have required the elements of chance and empty space in order to act efficiently (*GR*1, p. 363; *GR*2, p. 257). But Rousseau retains God. Derrida's undecidable causality (perhaps God, perhaps not) is shortly afterwards collapsed into the certainty that it *was* God who initiated the global revolution, since in Rousseau's 'theodicy' (Derrida's term, *GR*1, p. 364; *GR*2, p. 257), the relative evil of disequilibrium is dialectically compensated by the greater good of the awakening of man's perfectibility. However, according to Derrida's logic of supplementarity, the necessity for man's perfectibility to be activated by an external, supplementary cause, exposes the deficiency or empty space within the supposedly perfect system preceding socialization, the undecidable play (interval or vacuum) that inhabits the system of nature. There is a ghost (or god, or demon) in the machine that it is difficult to exorcize. Following Freud's logic of the uncanny, it could be argued that Rousseau's representation of the arbitrary author of the world revolution (Derrida: 'un Dieu joueur', *GR*1, p. 367 ('a player God', *GR*2, p. 260)) is a projection of what is already inherent in the system and which ought not to have come to light, in other words and in this case the essential instability of the system, its 'play'. Derrida writes: 'L'imagination est dans la nature et pourtant rien dans la nature ne peut expliquer son éveil. Le supplément à la nature est dans la nature comme son jeu. Qui dira jamais si le manque dans la nature est *dans* la nature, si la catastrophe par laquelle la nature *s'écarte d'elle-même* est encore naturelle?' (*GR*1, p. 364) ('Imagination is within Nature and yet nothing in Nature can explain its awakening. The supplement to Nature is in Nature as its play. Who will ever say if the lack within nature is *within* nature, if the catastrophe by which Nature [*deviates*] *from itself* is still natural?' (*GR*2, p. 258)). The reflexive voice of the italicized '*s'écarte d'elle-même*' is significant, for Derrida is suggesting, contrary to Rousseau's external projection of chance ('Le hasard ne fait pas partie du système' ('Chance is not part of the system')), that the natural state or system in fact possesses an *autonomous* tendency to destabilization, a play ('jeu') inherent in its constitution.[2]

Such chance irregularities ('écarts') are consistently viewed as scandalous or inconceivable by Rousseau, but at the same time, he must compensate for them. Society must compensate for them. Thus the evil of the catastrophe that inaugurates society is recuperated by way of the theodicy of perfectibility; the evil that is society (a product of man's perfectibility) is vindicated by appeal to its reparatory effect upon the vagaries of nature:

Entre les accidents de la nature et le mal social, il y a une complicité qui manifeste d'ailleurs la Providence divine. La société ne se crée que pour réparer les accidents de la nature ... La formation des sociétés a joué un rôle compensateur dans l'économie générale du monde. Née de la catastrophe, la société apaise la nature déchaînée. Il faut qu'elle ait à son tour ce rôle régulateur sans quoi la catastrophe eût été mortelle. La catastrophe elle-même obéit à une économie. Elle est *contenue*. (*GR*1, p. 367)

(Between the accidents of nature and social evil, there is a complicity that, moreover, manifests Divine Providence. Society is created only to repair the accidents of nature ... The formation of societies played a compensatory role in the general economy of the world. Born of catastrophe, society appeases unfettered Nature. It must in its turn have that regulatory role without which the catastrophe would have been mortal. The catastrophe itself follows an economy. It is *contained*.) (*GR*2, p. 260)

There is evidently a strong structural coherence between this interpretation and Derrida's understanding of inscription, as it has been described above. To begin with, the inaugural catastrophe is of a violent nature, as is the instance of inscription. In addition, not only is the initial instance violent, it is also potentially mortal. What was metaphorically the *fall* to inscription was subject to the binary undecidability of 1 or 0, the risk of life or death: 'si graver sauve ou perd la parole' (*ED*, p. 19) ('whether writing preserves or betrays speech' (*WD*, p. 9)). Rousseau's natural catastrophe is similarly a 'fall' or 'accident', there is the risk of integral annihilation in the initial deviation, 'sa chance ou sa malchance' (*GR*1, p. 367) ('its good or ill fortune' (*GR*2, p. 259)). Survival is possible only through the countering force of a further deviation (a further evil, but a lesser evil) that cancels the harmful effects of the first. The supplement of society is a move to restore a certain equilibrium or, in Derrida's words, to 'effacer l'écart'.

It is symptomatic that Derrida uses the word 'economy' to describe this state of affairs. The economy, it has been seen, is the dynamic redistribution or diminished repetition of the instance of inscription or determination, its contained perpetuation. A similar structure is perceptible in this particular context where Derrida argues that 'la catastrophe elle-même obéit à une économie. Elle est *contenue*' ('the catastrophe itself follows an economy. It is *contained*')). But it is easy to see that while this is a regulated economy, it is not a closed or restricted one; the advent of society is not, cannot be, the last word, so to speak. It does not restore the equilibrium that existed prior to socialization. Indeed, it could be argued that the concept of equilibrium is a theoretical fiction, required as a foundation or fixed point from which all further development – progress and/or degeneration – might be measured.[3] The theory of original equilibrium is a fiction because the pre-social world system was in any case itself unstable in a virtual sense. In its turn, the social system that regulates and contains the excesses of nature, again according to the logic of supplementarity, is not inviolably self-sufficient or self-sustaining, and would itself contain the vacant space or indeterminacy necessarily present in the pre-social system. Such 'play' in the system would, at a later stage, precipitate further catastrophe and further transformation. An example of this would be 'la chance et le mal de l'écriture' ('the "luck" and the evil of writing') – the ambivalent supplement of writing – which for Rousseau is an external, but again paradoxically necessary, infraction upon the integrity of the voice, and an agent of social dislocation and alienation (*GR*1, p. 367; *GR*2, p. 259). The undecidable 'écart' is therefore congenital to any system, whether it be the terrestrial system, the social system contained within it, or the linguistic system that is a subset of the social system. Every economy, or more exactly every *general* economy (what Derrida referred to above as 'l'économie générale du monde'), is open to destabilization from an indeterminate source, is always already in crisis. As Derrida asserted in 'Cogito et histoire de la folie', 'cette crise a toujours déjà commencé et elle est interminable' (*ED*, p. 96) ('this crisis has always [already] begun and it is interminable' (*WD*, p. 62)). This *series* of crises is precisely the rhythm of history and the rhythm of life.

ALTERATION AND DEGRADATION ('ENTAME')

The rhythm, however, is not a regular one. In 'Ellipse', Derrida proposed that the first number of repetition is the uneven three, and in 'Spéculer – sur "Freud"', he argues that the rhythm of walking is affected by a necessary disequilibrium.[4] The rhythm of repetition can only be differential or differentiating, elliptical rather than identically circular. In 'Signature, événement, contexte', Derrida points out that the Sanskrit root of the word 'iteration' (*itara*, 'other') associates the idea of repetition with alteration or modification (*M*1, p. 375; *M*2, p. 315). The use of the terms 'altération' or 'altérer' is frequent in *Marges* and other texts of the same period and, apart from the sense of alteration or modification, in French these words also refer to the process of distortion or debasement. A constant theme of *De la grammatologie* is what a number of authors regard as the scandalous decline – 'chute' or 'dégénérescence' – arising from the introduction into a system of an element they would consider to be foreign to the system. In Rousseau it is the series of 'écarts de nature' which distance human existence from its ideal, homeostatic origins. With Lévi-Strauss, the Nambikwara Indians lapse (momentarily) into the political reality of mystification and exploitation when the intruder (the ethnologist) transmits the technology of writing to the chief. In each case, the unexpected (and unwelcome) intrusion is discovered to be always already quite at home within the system (the *unheimlich* is in reality quite *heimisch*), being in fact both the cause of its destabilization and the compensatory containment or regulation of it. Again, there is a word which appears to encapsulate, in its condensed semantic space, a number of these ideas (inauguration, decline, violation from without, a certain moral affect). The word is 'entamer'. Like the chance encounter of the words 'trace' and 'écart', a chance in a sense made necessity by its absorption into the system of Derrida's argument, the word 'entamer' exercises a similar attraction upon the various elements of Derrida's system.

The relationship between inscription and the verb 'entamer' was referred to briefly in chapter 1 above ('C'est, *in historiam*, la chute de la pensée dans la philosophie, par laquelle l'histoire est *entamée*', *ED*, p. 45) ('*In historiam*, it is the fall of thought into philosophy which gets history under way' (*WD*, p. 27)). In *De la grammatologie*, the logic of the 'entame' is operative in Derrida's description of Rousseau's concept of 'articulation' in language. For Rousseau, articulation introduces difference into the continuum of pure voice that he considers to be characteristic of the 'pre-linguistic' state of affairs. Derrida's interpretation of this articulation reads as follows: 'Celle-ci entame le langage: elle ouvre la parole comme institution née de la passion mais elle menace le chant comme parole originelle' (*GR*1, p. 344) ('It broaches language: it opens speech as institution born of passion but it threatens song as original speech' (*GR*2, p. 243)). The use of the verb 'entamer' in this context is open to at least four interpretations, all of which are necessarily related. Firstly, 'entamer' can mean to cut into, to incise. Articulation therefore divides the continuum of the inarticulated cry by the violence of an incision. Secondly, and by association, 'entamer' means to begin, to open: articulation is the inauguration of language proper ('elle *ouvre* la parole'); before it, the natural voice expressed nothing. It is therefore a necessary violence. But, thirdly, the gesture of incision will equally diminish or degrade the medium in which it is practised: another meaning of 'entamer' is to wear or break down, shake or weaken, and indeed shortly afterwards Derrida concludes that '*la langue naît donc du processus de sa dégénérescence*' (*GR*1, p. 345, Derrida's emphasis) ('*thus language is born out of the process of its own degeneration*' (*GR*2, p. 242)). Finally, associated with this material sense of degradation is a moral sense: 'entamer' can mean to harm, damage or cast a slur upon a person (its Low Latin root *intaminare* is translated as 'to dirty or sully'). The *scandal* of articulation (and its structural equivalents, writing, the supplement in general, etc.) is a persistent feature of Derrida's reading of Rousseau. The invariant element in these differing nuances is the basic duality of the word: it expresses both inauguration and decline, birth and dissolution, and suggests not the paradox or opposition, but the irreducibility of these pairs.

In *La vérité en peinture*, where Derrida draws attention to the continuity of his reference to the 'entame' ('Je suis ici la conséquence de ce que j'avais appelé il y a longtemps, avant d'en venir au tour de la peinture, l'*entame* de l'origine', *VP*, p. 16 ('I follow here the logical succession of what I long ago called, before getting around to the turn of painting, the *broaching* of the origin', *TP*, p. 11)), there is an interesting filiation established between 'entame', 'entaille', and 'taille'. The latter two words are of particular significance in the chapter 'Parergon', and with them one returns to the figures of infinity and inscription.

INFINITY IN THIS WORLD. THE STANDING SUBJECT ('[EN]TAILLE')

In the fourth, and last section of 'Parergon', 'Le colossal' (*VP*, pp. 136–68; *TP*, pp. 119–47), Derrida broaches the question of Kant's notion of the sublime as expounded in his third *Critique*. He begins by considering the relationship between the words 'column' and 'colossus'. Though at first sight these words have nothing in common, Derrida points out that the word 'colossus' originally conveyed the sense of something upright, erect, before acquiring the sense of size ('taille'). He indicates the communication of this with the image of the erect phallus and Freud's Medusa complex, as set forth in *Glas*. However, extrapolating from Kant's text, Derrida opposes the column and the colossal in that for Kant the former is an example of the finite products of human artistry, those products that do not exceed the human scale ('taille', 'mesure'):

La maîtrise de l'artiste humain y opère en vue d'une fin, elle détermine, définit, informe. En décidant des contours, à border la forme et la taille, elle mesure et domine. Or le sublime, il n'y en a, s'il y en a, qu'à déborder : il excède la taille et la bonne mesure, il n'est plus proportionné à l'homme et à ses déterminations. (*VP*, p. 139)

(The mastery of the human artist here operates with a view to an end, determining, defining, giving form. In deciding on contours, giving boundaries to the form and the cise,[5] this mastery measures and dominates. But the sublime, if there is any sublime, exists only by overspilling : it exceeds cise and good measure, it is no longer proportioned according to man and his determinations.) (*TP*, p. 122)

The colossal, on the other hand, partakes of the sublime, and the sublime can only be found in a certain nature (not the nature of, for instance, the horse, which is destined for a definite purpose or end). The nature of the sublime is to be colossal, immeasurable, higher than the high: 'Très haut, absolument haut, plus haut que toute hauteur comparable' (*VP*, p. 141) ('Very high, absolutely high, higher than any comparable height' (*TP*, p. 122)).

The measure of the column and the excess of the colossal do not exist in themselves; they are qualities of the perceiving subject. For example: '*Colossal* (*kolossalisch*) qualifie donc la présentation, la mise en scène ou en présence, la prise en vue plutôt de quelque chose, mais de quelque chose qui n'est pas une chose, puisque c'est un concept. Et la présentation de ce concept en tant qu'il n'est pas présentable. Ni simplement imprésent-able : *presque imprésentable*' (*VP*, p. 143) ('*Colossal* (*kolossalisch*) thus qualifies the presentation, the putting on stage or into presence, the catching sight, rather, of some thing, but of something which is not a thing, since it is a concept. And the presentation of this concept inasmuch as it is not presentable. Nor simply unpresentable: *almost unpresentable*' (*TP*, p. 125)). Derrida notes Kant's distinction between the operations of the *apprehensio* and the *comprehensio aesthetica* (*Auffassung* and *Zusam-menfassung*). The first can continue *ad infinitum*, whilst the second soon reaches the limits of its capacities (*VP*, p. 145; *TP*, p. 126). However, even for the faculty of *apprehensio*, the presentation of the colossal is *almost* too much. The question arises as to how the excess of the colossal is presented as a concept ('Comment s'y prendre avec le *colossal?*', *VP*, p. 144 ('How to deal with the *colossal?*', *TP*, p. 126); 'Comment … l'infinité s'*annoncerait*-il dans le fini?', *VP*, p. 150 ('How could … [infinity] be *announced* in the finite?', *TP*, p. 131)). The solution to this lies in the question of size ('taille'), though Derrida imparts a peculiar, if characteristic, dual inflection to the word 'taille'. At the beginning of 'Parergon', he remarked that the word did not itself at first relate directly to the idea of size or measure: 'Avant la grandeur, et d'abord celle du corps humain … "taille" aura marqué le trait d'une coupe, le tranchant d'une épée, toutes les incisions qui viennent à entamer une surface ou une épaisseur pour y frayer une voie, y délimiter un contour, une forme ou une quantité (coupe de bois ou de tissu)' (*VP*, p. 137) ('Before referring to size, and above all that of the human body … *taille* marked the line of a cut, the cutting edge of a sword, all the incisions which come to broach a surface or a thickness and open up a track, delimit a contour, a form or quantity (a cut(ting) of wood or cloth)' (*TP*, p. 120)). 'Coupe', 'tranchant', 'incisions', 'entamer', 'frayer une voie', all of these words express the passional or violent aspect Derrida wishes to lend to the word 'taille', in addition to its sense of size or measure. This prepares the way for the later explanation of how the colossal or sublime can be perceived as such. If the excess of the colossal is not susceptible to measure, if the sublime is not subject to the comprehension or economy of reason (*VP*, p. 150; *TP*, p. 131), then it is nevertheless true that they come to be represented, as such, here and now. This presentation of the sublime is violent:

Il présente inadéquatement l'infini dans le fini et l'y délimite violemment. L'inadéquation (*Unangemessenheit*), la démesure, l'incommensurable se présente, se laisse présenter, dresser là, mettre debout devant (*darstellen*) comme cela même … Une présentation inadéquate de l'infini présente sa propre inadéquation, une inadéquation se présente comme telle en sa propre béance, elle se détermine en son contour, se taille et s'entaille comme incommensurable au sans-taille. (*VP*, p. 151)

(It inadequately presents the infinite in the finite and delimits it violently therein. Inadequation (*Unangemessenheit*), excessiveness, incommensurability are presented, let themselves be presented, be stood up, set upright in front of (*darstellen*) as that inadequation itself. ... An inadequate presentation of the infinite presents its own inadequation, an inadequation is presented as such in its own yawning gap, it is determined in its contour, it cises and incises itself as incommensurable with the without-cise.) (*TP*, p. 132)

The condition of the sublime is therefore the reflexive – and violent – cutting down to size ('se taille et s'entaille') of that which is immeasurable ('sans-taille'). The infinite column of the colossus is truncated: 'Tout cela se passe donc autour d'une colonne infinie mais tronquée, à la limite du tronc, à la place de la troncature ou du tranchant, sur le trait de bordure, fin comme une lame, qui définit la taille' (*VP*, p. 153) ('Thus all this goes on around an infinite but truncated column, at the limit of the trunk, at the place of the truncation or the cutting edge, on the borderline, fine as a blade, which defines the cise' (*TP*, p. 134)). Like the difference of inscription, which in 'Force et signification' was defined as the point of intersection or articulation of force and form, the presentation of the sublime subsists in the extremely fine, blade-like edge ('bordure', 'tranchant') of its severed infinity. This fine line between finite and infinite *is* the sublime.

But the sublime itself is nothing in nature. It was remarked above that the colossal is not a thing but a concept, and it is therefore to be sought on the side of the subject. The ascription of the sublime to nature itself is simply a *projection* of the subject's apprehension of it (*VP*, p. 151; *TP*, p. 132). However, not only is the sublime constituted on the side of the human subject, but more precisely it proceeds from the size or stature (again, 'taille') of the human subject. The absolute standard by which large can be compared (or preferred) to small is the human body: 'Or cette première mesure (subjective, sensible, immédiate, vivante) procède du corps... *C'est le corps qui s'érige en mesure*. Il fournit l'unité de mesure mesurante et mesurée: du plus petit et du plus grand possible, du minimum et du maximum, comme du passage de l'un à l'autre... Tout se mesure ici à la taille du corps' (*VP*, p. 160) ('This primary (subjective, sensory, immediate, living) measure proceeds from the body ... *It is the body which erects itself as a measure.* It provides the measuring and measured unit of measure: of the smallest and the largest possible, of the minimum and the maximum, and likewise of the passage from the one to the other.... Everything is measured here on the scale of the body' (*TP*, p. 140)). But this confrontation – and measurement – of larger and smaller is neither serene nor simple. There is a forceful erection of the human stature against the vertical excess of the sublime, two columns of force. On the following page Derrida speaks of the 'corps à corps' (clinch, hand to hand) of the sublime and the imagination. The imagination is the intermediary between reason and the senses and has two sides, edges or measures ('tailles'): 'L'imagination est la taille parce qu'elle a deux tailles. La taille a toujours deux tailles: elle dé-limite. Elle a la taille de ce qu'elle délimite et la taille de ce qu'elle dé-limite, de ce qu'elle limite et de ce qui s'y libère de sa limite' (*VP*, p. 162) ('Imagination is the cise because it has two cises. The cise always has two cises: it de-limits. It has the cise of what it delimits and the cise of what it de-limits, of what it limits and what is liberated in it of its limits' (*TP*, p. 140)). As has been seen, the delimitating powers of the imagination are derived from the operations of *comprehensio*, whilst its capacity to proceed to infinity is due to the faculty of *apprehensio*. Paradoxically, the ideal experience of the sublime resides at a point between the two: the 'corps à corps' is not immediately proximate, but requires a certain distance. It could be argued that there is not simply the infinite opening of the apprehension of the sublime, but equally (and necessarily) the finite closure of the imagination's comprehension of it. The mediating double edge ('Ce double trait d'une taille qui limite et illimite à la fois', *VP*, p. 165 ('This double trait of a cise which limits and unlimits at one and the same time', *TP*, p. 144)) is in a sense the suspension of the infinite ascension of *apprehensio* at the same time that it is the exceeding of the finite limit of *comprehensio*. Just as the colossus was violently cut down to size, so too the forcefully erect human subject who measures him- or herself against the sublime presentation (aspires to its infinity in his or her apprehension of it) must bow to the delimitating constraints of the finite. This double suspension of the imagination (of *comprehensio* and *apprehensio*) is described as a fall, a fall that is not without a certain pleasure: 'Et quand l'imagination atteint son maximum et éprouve le sentiment de son impuissance, de son inadéquation à présenter l'idée d'un tout, elle retombe, elle s'abîme, elle sombre en elle-même (*in sich selbst zurück sinkt*). Et cette retombée abyssale ne la laisse pas sans une certaine émotion positive' (*VP*, p. 163) ('And when the imagination attains its maximum and experiences the feeling of its impotence, its inadequacy to present the idea of a whole, it falls back, it sinks, it founders into itself (*in sich selbst zurück sinkt*). And this abyssal fall-back does not leave it without a certain positive emotion' (*TP*, p. 142)). Adopting Derrida's own system of puns, and following the sexual imagery that runs throughout 'Parergon', it could be argued that the 'bande' of the colossally sublime is resisted by the 'contre-bande' of the standing subject and that they fall in a 'double bande' (a punning allusion to the double bind, to which Derrida in fact refers on page 148 (*TP*, p. 129)).

The word 'taille', in its many incarnations in 'Parergon' – cut, incision, the edge of a blade, size or stature – thus functions as a mediator, both in the movement of Derrida's argument and in the logic of the object it describes (the sublime). Like the difference of inscription, the 'taille' itself *does not exist*, either as a concept in Derrida's text, or as a quality of its object: 'cette double taille ne se compare qu'à elle-même. Car la limite n'existe pas. Même s'*il y* en *a*, la taille de cette entame n'existe pas, elle ne commence jamais, nulle part. Ni originaire ni dérivée, comme la trace de chaque trait. C'est cela, ce qui se présente sans taille' (*VP*, p. 166) ('this double cise is compared only with itself. For the limit does not exist. Even if *there is* some, the cise of the broaching does not exist, it never begins, anywhere. Neither originary nor derived, like the trace of each trait. That is what is presented without cise' (*TP*, p. 145)). Just as one was able in 'Force et signification' to speak of the economy or system of Apollo and Dionysus, so here, one might refer to a system or economy of the sublime and the subject that is both open and closed. The condition of such a system is the 'taille', the indeterminate point of *articulation* of the sublime object and the standing subject, and (in the subject's imagination) of *apprehensio* and *comprehensio*. It is now time to consider more closely this peculiar word, 'articulation'.

ARTICULATION AND DOUBLE BIND

Articulation – the act or state of being joined together, or the form or manner in which a thing is jointed – is the condition of articulation, the act or process of speaking or expressing in words. This is what Derrida appears to be saying with, but at the same time beyond, Rousseau in *De la grammatologie* ('L'articulation', *GR*1, pp. 327–78; *GR*2, pp. 229–68). According to a now familiar schema, Rousseau's articulation is the cause both of the inauguration of language and its degradation. Before the advent of articulated language there is the theoretical fiction of a continuity and presence of pure voice; for Rousseau, pure voice (accent, song, or cry) is more vowel than consonant, and the harsh, Nordic consonant, the agent of articulation, is an infraction to the plenitude of the vowel: 'Le devenir-langage du cri est le mouvement par lequel la plénitude parlée commence à devenir ce qu'elle est en se perdant, en se creusant, en se brisant, en s'articulant. Le cri se vocalise en commençant à effacer la parole voyelle … Le chapitre *De l'écriture* doit d'abord … évoquer l'*oblitération* de l'accent par l'articulation consonantique' (*GR*1, p. 381) ('The becoming-language of the cry is the movement by which spoken plenitude begins to become what it is through losing itself, hollowing itself out, breaking itself, articulating itself. The cry vocalizes itself by beginning to efface vocalic speech … "On Script" must first … evoke the *obliteration* of the accent by consonantal articulation' (*GR*2, p. 270)). Despite this, the calamity of this fall from paradise is also a godsend: 'Cet accident malheureux est aussi un "progrès naturel"' (*GR*1, p. 344) ('This unhappy accident is also a "natural progress"' (*GR*2, p. 248)). Without it, neither spoken language, nor subsequently, writing, would have come into being. Following the same logic that applied in Rousseau's description of the origins of society, the unnatural, supplementary deviation is retrospectively seen to be a necessary development. Later, for example, writing will function as a remedy and a foil to the alienating expansion of the state.

There is, however, a second logic at work in Derrida's text with respect to the word 'articulation'. Beyond the reference to the linguistic phenomenon described in Rousseau's text, the consonantal differentiation of pure vowel or voice, responsible for the appearance of language, there is the more general aspect of articulation as a fundamental structure of phenomena. Central to this generalized conception of articulation is Derrida's emphasis on the anatomical image, implicit in the etymology of the word. This is evident in 'Le cercle linguistique de Genève' in *Marges*, where, discussing the importance of the word and concept of 'articulation' in Rousseau's *Essai*, Derrida quotes Saussure:

'Une certaine définition de ce qu'on appelle *langage articulé* pourrait confirmer cette idée. En latin, *articulus* signifie "membre, partie, subdivision dans une suite de choses"; en matière de langage, l'articulation peut désigner ou bien la subdivision de la chaîne parlée en syllabes, ou bien la subdivision de la chaîne des significations en unités significatives; c'est en ce sens qu'on dit en allemand *gegliederte Sprache* … ' (*M*1, p. 182)

('One definition of *articulated speech* might confirm that conclusion. In Latin, *articulus* means a member, part, or subdivision of a sequence; applied to speech, articulation designates either the subdivision of a spoken chain into syllables or the subdivision of the chain of meanings into significant units; *gegliederte Sprache* is used in the second sense in German.') (*M*2, p. 151)

This figure of the articulated limb is also a feature of Derrida's reading of Kant's third *Critique* in *La vérité en peinture*, when he focuses on the problem of the gulf (*Kluft*) between the domains of understanding and reason, a gulf which is apparently impassable. Kant proposes the analogy of a bridge which might join the two sides of the gulf. This intermediary between the differing orders of reason and understanding consequently becomes a middle joint (*Mittelglied*), the agent of their articulation:

L'entendement et la raison ne sont pas deux facultés disjointes, elles s'articulent dans un certain travail et dans un certain nombre d'opérations qui engagent précisément l'articulation, c'est-à-dire le discours. Entre les deux facultés, en effet, un membre articulé, une troisième faculté entre en jeu. Ce membre intermédiaire que Kant nomme justement *Mittelglied*, articulation moyenne, c'est le jugement (*Urteil*) ...

Le *Mittelglied* formant ainsi l'articulation du théorique et du pratique (au sens kantien), nous nous enfonçons dans un lieu qui n'est *ni* pratique *ni* théorique ou bien *à la fois* pratique et théorique. (*VP*, p. 45)

(The understanding and reason are not two disconnected faculties; they are articulated in a certain task and a certain number of operations which involve, precisely, articulation, i.e., discourse. For between the two faculties, an articulated member, a third faculty comes into play. This intermediary member which Kant names precisely *Mittelglied*, middle articulation, is judgment (*Urteil*) ...

Since the *Mittelglied* also forms the articulation of the theoretical and the practical (in the Kantian sense), we are plunging into a space that is *neither* theoretical *nor* practical or else *both* theoretical *and* practical.) (*TP*, p. 38)

Like the articulating edges of force and form (the difference of inscription) or the subject and the sublime object (the double-edged 'taille'), judgement is itself not properly determinate ('*ni* ... *ni*, *à la fois*' ('*neither* ... *nor*, *both* ... *and*')),[6] and like these articulating edges, it appears to be the condition of intersection of two differing orders (here reason and understanding). Derrida indicates on this and the following page how Kant wishes for the *Mittelglied* that is judgement to be both detachable accessory (one might translate: supplement) and a necessary hinge in the system of understanding and reason. In fact, the instance of judgement is both the condition of the difference – or gulf – between the faculties of understanding and reason, and of their connection. This idea of connection and separation is expressed in the word 'articulation', when it is understood in its anatomical sense, for the articulation of limbs is both a differentiation, or separation, of parts, and a joining of them. The difference of articulation is not an absolute severing of relations, it is simultaneously the opening and closure of a cleft, the infliction and healing of an injury (the pathological metaphor is, both here and elsewhere, Derrida's). This double movement, this double bind of coherence and separation, is the movement of all the systems that Derrida describes. The articulating instance opens ('s'écarte') like a wound to a possible death ('dépense absolue') that is reappropriated, or rather deferred, by the simultaneous closure (or healing) of the rift. Precisely such a movement is suggested in the passional tear of Heidegger's *Riss*, to which Derrida refers in the introduction to *La vérité en peinture*: 'Heidegger, dans *L'Origine de l'œuvre de l'art*, nomme le "trait" (*Riss*) qui n'ouvre pas seulement au-dessus du gouffre mais tient ensemble les rives adverses' (*VP*, p. 10) ('Heidegger in the *Origin of the Work of Art* names the "stroke" (*Riss*) which not only opens above the gulf but also holds together the opposite edges of it' (*TP*, p. 6)). Similarly in *Glas*, the use of the word 'penser', 'to think', is clearly intended to connote 'panser', 'to dress' or 'bandage', in Derrida's discussion of Hegel's remarks on the necessity of philosophy. The reappropriation of the passional, traumatic beginning of philosophy is compared to the dressing of a wound:

Le besoin de philosophie (*Bedürfnis der Philosophie*) ... surgit dans l'*entre*, l'écart étroit d'une scission, d'un clivage, d'une séparation, d'une division en deux. Un se divise en deux, telle est la source douloureuse de la philosophie : '*Entzweiung ist die Quelle der Bedürfnisses der Philosophie.*' La raison procède alors, s'affaire à penser la blessure, réduire la division, revenir en-deçà de la source, auprès de l'unité infinie.[7] (*GL*1, p. 109a)

('The Need of Philosophy' ('Bedürfnis der Philosophie') ... upsurges in the *between*, the narrow gap of a split, a cleavage, a separation, a division in two. One divides itself in two, such is the distressing source of philosophy : '*Entzweiung ist die Quelle der Bedürfnisses der Philosophie.*' Therefore reason proceeds to busy itself thinking the wound, to reduce the division, to return this side of the source, close by the infinite unity.) (*GL*2, p. 95a)

In each of these examples, there is what I have referred to as a 'double bind' of opposing forces or tendencies. The term 'double bind' is normally attributed to Gregory Bateson, who first formulated the concept in his studies on schizophrenia and alcoholism. In Bateson's work, the double bind refers to the power relationship involving two or more persons in which one person, the 'victim', is subject to contradictory or paradoxical injunctions on the part of one or more individuals occupying a position of authority with respect to the victim. The individual's 'solution' to this no-win situation is one form or another of psychological disorder.[8] In Derrida's text, the psychological and situational content of the concept of double bind, as formulated in Bateson, appears to be all but lost: the term is appropriated and systematized through its verbal form as much as through its conceptual content, and is subjected to a series of punning deformations. Derrida's transliteration into French of the double bind, 'double bande', yields a number of meanings or associations. There is the sexual dimension apparent in *Glas* and *La vérité en peinture*, which is related in *Glas* in particular to the circular 'bande', the satisfaction of Hegel's reappropriating return. This pun extends even to the designation of the two parallel, interacting bands or columns of text that are the format of *Glas*.[9] More appropriate to the present context of the pathological metaphor, however, is the connection of the 'double bande' with the verb 'bander' ('to bind' or 'bandage'), again a connection that is made in both *Glas* and *La vérité en peinture*. This in turn relates metonymically with the figure of *chiasmus* (an anatomical and rhetorical figure), the crossing-over or interweaving of two bands or ribbons, a configuration also encountered in certain of the paintings of Titus-Carmel included in *La vérité en peinture*, depicting two sticks bandaged together at each of their ends, or the binding of the separate extremities of two pieces of wood or pipe (*VP*, pp. 285, 289; *TP*, pp. 248, 252). It could be said that these paintings represent, or are approximate to, 'experiments' in articulation.[10]

The figure of the double bind proliferates, both as concept and metaphor, across a series of texts from *Glas* onwards. However, what might be called the 'weak' links established between the different manifestations of the 'bande', often based on purely arbitrary (phonetic, figural) association, at the same time produce in Derrida's text what is logically a 'strong' conceptual field. The logic of the double bind is the paradoxical conjunction of both structure (binding, restriction) and the transgression of structure (expenditure, dissipation) in a given system. Apart from the extremely elliptical treatment of the double bind in *Glas* and *La vérité en peinture*, this logic is also apparent in Derrida's reading of Freud's *Beyond the Pleasure Principle* in 'Spéculer – sur "Freud"'(*La carte postale*). Thematically, 'Spéculer – sur "Freud"' is in some respects a continuation of Derrida's previous study of Freud, 'La scène de l'écriture', discussed in the preceding chapter. One important element of this study is the role of the facilitation in the primary processes of the psychical system: the function of memory is also related to the organism's primal reflex of self-preservation from what might be harmful levels of excitation. In 'Spéculer – sur "Freud"', describing what is basically the same process (the so-called 'primary process'), Derrida shifts his attention from the memory trace to the Freudian concept of binding (*Bindung*): the psychical system restricts and binds, but at the same time permits the continued circulation of forces impinging upon it from both without and within. Derrida calls this double bind of containment and excess, of restriction and free circulation the 'économie bindinale':

Economie du lien ou de la liaison (*bind*, bande, double bande, double bind, et contre-bande). Le *Binden* allemand, concept ou métaphore, joue un rôle formidable, on le sait, dans ce texte et dans cette problématique. Tout semble s'y jouer ou plutôt nouer dans la stricture plus ou moins lâche de l'énergie, dans des liens ou des liaisons plus ou moins dissoutes, détachées, résolues, absoutes (*aufgelöst*).[11] (*CP*, pp. 415–16)

(Economy of the tie or the bond (*bind*, band, double band, double bind, and contra-band). The German *Binden*, concept or metaphor, plays, as we know, a formidable role in this text and this problematic. Everything seems to be played out, or rather knotted, in the more or less loose stricture of energy, in the more or less dissolved, detached, resolved, absolved (*aufgelöst*) ties or bonds.) (*PC*, p. 389)

Derrida's analysis of Freud's pleasure principle in 'Spéculer – sur "Freud"' demonstrates how the very condition of pleasure resides in a certain restriction of it, that is, a certain unpleasure

('Le principe même du plaisir se manifesterait comme une sorte de contre-plaisir, bande contre bande qui vient limiter le plaisir pour le rendre possible', *CP*, p. 426 ('The very principle of pleasure would manifest itself as a kind of counter-pleasure, band contra band which comes to limit pleasure in order to make it possible', *PC*, p. 399)). The economy of pleasure operates between the two infinities (the term is Derrida's) of absolute constraint and absolute expenditure. Derrida's homophonic play on the terms 'jouer' ('to play') and 'nouer' ('to knot') neatly expresses this conjunction or articulation of restricted and free energy (or rather the *differential* distribution of energy, the *degrees* of freedom or restriction in the circulation of energy, 'plus ou moins lâche', etc.) within the psychical economy. There are simultaneously weak links which allow a certain latitude of play in the circulation of forces, and strong links without which the system would simply disintegrate; it is the tension or disparity between these different linkages which is the condition of possibility of the pleasure principle and, indeed, of life.

The problem of life, the logic of life, inevitably forms a central strand of Derrida's commentary in 'Spéculer – sur "Freud"'. Beyond the pleasure principle is death, or rather the relation to or mediation of death, Freud's *Umwege zum Tode*, already touched upon in the closing stages of 'La scène de l'écriture'. The ultimate destination of life is death. The ascendent force of Eros is worked from within by the descendent counter-force of Thanatos. The organism's drive to higher states of self-preservation and organization is inseparable from its tendency to entropic decline, the tendency to return to a state of quiescence or organic equilibrium, that is, death, the final dissipation of energies. The figures of articulation or double bind (simultaneously separation and adherence, binding and unbinding), as set forth in *La carte postale* and adjacent texts, are therefore also expressible in the vertical dimension of a combined movement of ascent and fall. It is to this particular figure that I shall now turn.

UNDECIDABILITY AND ABYSSAL DESCENT ('TOMBER')

The complementary polarities of ascent and fall were already apparent in the analysis of chapter 1. Nietzsche's standing, ascensional affirmation was profitless without composition with an earthbound writing. In this chapter it was seen that the vertical column of Kant's sublime apparition is, as it were, cut down to size in the measuring cipher of the standing subject. In each of these cases, the motion of descent, in particular, is inseparable from a sense of indeterminacy. The moment of inscription is subject to the binary undecidability of life or death, sense or insignificance ('si graver sauve ou perd la parole', *ED*, p. 19 ('whether writing preserves or betrays speech', *WD*, p. 9)), as is the fall from natural grace in Rousseau's description of the genesis of society ('sa chance ou sa malchance', *GR*1, p. 367 ('its good or ill fortune', *GR*2, p. 259))). In a more recent article, 'Mes chances', during a discussion of the Greek and Latin atomist theories, Derrida questions the convention that associates falling, the motion from top to bottom, with the idea of chance:

Pourquoi ce mouvement de haut en bas? Quand on parle de chance, pourquoi les mots et les concepts imposent-ils d'abord cette signification, cette direction, ce sens? Ce mouvement vers le bas, qu'il s'agisse de jet ou de chute? Pourquoi ce sens et cette direction ont-ils un rapport privilégié avec le non-sens ou l'insignifiance qu'on associe fréquemment au hasard? (MC, p. 8)

([Why] the downward movement? When chance or luck are under consideration, why do the words and concepts in the first place impose the particular signification, sense, and direction of a downward movement regardless of whether we are dealing with a throw or a fall? Why does this sense enjoy a privileged relation to the non-sense or insignificance which we find frequently associated with chance?) (*TC*, pp. 4-5)

Such accidental descent (Derrida associates 'chute', 'chance' and 'accident' through their Latin root, *cadere*) can also affect the standing subject: 'Dans ce cas, quand c'est l'homme ou le sujet qui tombe, la chute vient affecter la station debout. A sa position verticale elle imprime la déviation d'un clinamen dont les effets sont parfois irrésistibles' (MC, p. 9) ('In such a case, when man or the subject falls, the fall affects his upright stance and vertical position by engraving in him the detour of a *clinamen*, whose effects are sometimes inescapable' (*TC*, p. 5)). Derrida's introduction of the Lucretian *clinamen* at this juncture is extremely interesting, for a number of reasons. In the cosmology of Lucretius, the pre-phenomenal, primordial state of undifferentiated matter is represented as an infinitely descending cataract of atoms. Because these atoms move in parallel trajectories, from top to bottom, in a continuous stream, there is no contact between them, and therefore no possibility of existence as such. The *clinamen* is the oblique deviation or departure (in French, one would say 'écart') from this parallel and non-interacting descent of particles. The collision and combination (or 'agglutination') of atoms resulting from this swerve leads to the creation of the world and its phenomena.[12] It is important to note that the occurrence of the *clinamen* is purely arbitrary: quoting Lucretius, Derrida points out that it happens at an indeterminate time and place, '*incerto tempore … incertis locis*' (MC, p. 11; *TC*, p. 7).

Already, there is a clear structural similarity between Lucretius' theory of the *clinamen* and Derrida's conception of the trace and the 'écart'. In addition to the preconditions of descent and chance, there is the micrological character of the *clinamen*: Lucretius himself indicates that it is *nec plus quam minimum*.[13] What is more, though of minimal dimension, the *clinamen* is of maximal consequence, since it is the cause and condition of the world we inhabit and perceive, its origin and its inauguration (compare this with God's minimal inclination of the world's axis in Rousseau's theory of the origin of society, treated above).[14] Finally, like the trace, the *clinamen* is not a thing or an object, it is, properly speaking, nothing. More precisely, it is a movement, or an atom of movement (but not an atom), and is itself imperceptible. In Derridean terms, it might be described as pure spacing ('espacement').[15]

If the *clinamen* itself is an arbitrary deviation, with no a priori structure of determination and without cause, then the results of the fall that it occasions, or the fall that it affects, are similarly indeterminate. Playing upon the French expression 'bien' or 'mal tomber', Derrida indicates that the chance event, the accidental fall, may have unhappy or fortunate consequences, may be 'chance' or 'malchance'. However, once past this uncertain inauguration, it is in a sense legitimized and rendered necessary after the event, 'après coup', to borrow Derrida's term. As he remarks, there is an intertwining, an 'entrelacement' (one could equally say a chiasmus or double bind) of chance and necessity (MC, p. 10; TC, p. 6).

Significantly, what is at stake here is not simply the accidental descent of atoms or events, but also that of the linguistic unit or atom. Following Lucretius' proposition that the formation of objects from atoms is no different to the various combinations of letters in a phrase, that the letter is like an atom and vice versa, Derrida writes: 'L'élément indivisible, l'*atomos* de cette dissémination littérale produite par le supplément de déviation, c'est le *stoikheion*, mot qui désigne aussi la chose graphique, la marque, la lettre, le trait ou le point' (MC, p. 12) ('The indivisible element, the *atomos* of the literal dissemination produced by the supplement of deviation, is the *stoikheion*, a word at once designating the graphic element as well as the mark, the letter, the trait, or the point' (TC, p. 8)). And at a later point in 'Mes chances', remarking that Freud's discussions of chance are invariably concerned with proper names and numbers, Derrida argues:

On peut d'abord se demander ce qu'il y a de commun entre ces éléments, ces *stoikheia* que sont la lettre ou le trait, le nombre et le nom propre pour qu'ils se trouvent ainsi associés dans une même série et pour que leur rapport à la chance soit analogue. Ce qu'ils ont en commun, je dirai que c'est leur *insignifiance marquante*. Elle marque, elle est celle de la marque; elle est marquée mais surtout remarquable. Cette remarquable insignifiance les destine, elle les fait entrer dans le jeu de la destination et y imprime la déviation possible d'un *clinamen*. (MC, p. 20)

(One could initially ask oneself what these elements have in common – these *stoikheia* that include the letter or the trait, the number, and the proper name – such that they are to be found thus associated in the same series and such that their relation to chance would be analogous.

That which they have in common, I will claim, is their insignificance in marking. This insignificance marks. It belongs to the mark. It is marked but it is above all re-markable. This re-markable insignificance destines them, makes them enter into the play of the destination, and therein stamps the possible detour of a *clinamen*.) (*TC*, p. 15)

The oxymorons of '*insignifiance marquante*' and 'remarquable insignifiance', their phonetic and semantic cross-over, describe the combination or chiasmus of chance and necessity characteristic of the elements of a linguistic system. On the one hand, like the Lucretian atom, which in itself is characterless, the linguistic trait or mark, the name or number, has no intrinsic meaning, it is nothing; its insignificance permits it to 'emigrate' (Derrida's term) to other locations of the linguistic structure, to enter into other combinations. As Derrida remarks, such elements are related precisely in that their relation is arbitrary. This constitutes their indeterminate dimension, their tendency or potential to deviate from a determined meaning or function. On the other hand, and at the same time, a mark should be identifiable and therefore repeatable from one context to another, so that there is a subsistence of meaning. At the same time that it is differential, the mark should be indivisible (the defining characteristic of the *atomos*) and should possess a direction, a destination, in other words, a certain necessity of reference (MC, pp. 20–1; *TC*, p. 15).

At first sight, this argument appears extremely close to Saussure's theory of the arbitrariness of the sign and of its differential function in relation to other signs. However, its application is at once more general and far-reaching than Saussure's theory. Derrida insists that: 'Si je dis marque ou trace plutôt que signifiant, lettre ou mot, si je réfère cela au *stoikheion* démocritéen ou épicurien dans sa plus grande généralité, c'est pour deux raisons. Tout d'abord, cette généralité étend la marque au-delà du signe verbal et même du langage humain. C'est pourquoi j'hésite à parler d'"arbitraire du signe" comme Hegel et Saussure' (MC, p. 22) ('If I speak of the mark or the trace rather than the signifier, letter, or word, if I refer these to the Democritian or Epicurian *stoikheion* in its greatest generality, it is for two reasons. First of all, this generality extends the mark beyond the verbal sign and even beyond human language. Thus I hesitate to speak of the "arbitrariness of the sign" in the manner of Hegel and Saussure' (*TC*, p. 16)). Derrida's generalizing, via the atomists' *stoikheion* (letter, primary body, element), of the sign or linguistic trait is very much in keeping with what until now has been observed with regard to writing and system. The atomists' idea of the *stoikheion* (atom or letter) in a sense eliminates the distinction between the phenomenal and the linguistic, and implies a combinatorial principle at the base of all complex systems. Similarly, what in previous chapters I have named Derrida's 'model of inscription', though departing in many cases from the specific problem of the repression of writing in the history of Western, logocentric philosophy, was from the start most general in its application. The linguistic system, as described here with its double bind of divisibility and identity of elements, of the chance and the necessity of their combination, would appear to share an isomorphism of structure with a number of other, non-linguistic systems; whatever the system, the formal description appears to be constant. A possible comparison would be the scriptural metaphors of modern biological and cybernetic theory which describe the production and regulation of complex systems (living or otherwise) in terms of information, coding and communication. The influence of such theory on Derrida's thinking, the interference and intersection of its lexicon with his own, is clearly in evidence in the opening pages of 'Mes chances', where his vocabulary ('code', 'aléatoire', 'contrôle', 'auto-régulation', 'système') is visibly derived from the terminology of cybernetics and information theory. One is at once both near and far from the 'classical' formulation of 'archi-écriture'. Near in that the principle (a metamorphic notion of difference) remains more or less the same. Far in that the Hegelian and Heideggerian tenor of the earlier theory of writing (violence, non-originarity, etc.) is here given a sup-plementary dimension, a new rhetorical stratum, so to speak, with the association or appropriation of the discourse of systems theory:

Mais la langue n'est que l'un de ces systèmes de *marques* qui ont tous pour propriété cette étrange tendance : accroître *simultanément* les réserves d'indétermination aléatoire *et* les pouvoirs de codage ou de surcodage, autrement dit de contrôle et d'auto-régulation. Cette concurrence entre l'aléa et le code perturbe la systématicité même du système dont elle règle pourtant le jeu dans son instabilité. Quelle que soit à cet égard sa singularité, le système linguistique de ces traces ou de ces marques ne serait, me semble-t-il, qu'un exemple de cette loi de déstabilisation. (MC, p. 5)

(Language, however, is only one among those systems of *marks* that claim this curious tendency as their property: they *simultaneously* incline towards increasing the reserves of random indetermination *as well as* the capacity for coding and overcoding or, in other words, for control and self-regulation. Such competition between randomness and code disrupts the very systematicity of the system while it also, however, regulates the restless, unstable interplay of the system. Whatever its singularity in this respect, the linguistic system of these traces or marks would merely be, it seems to me, just a particular example of the law of destabilization.) (*TC*, pp. 2–3)

This *strange* tendency of all dynamic systems to combine chance and necessity, coding and indetermination, means that they are necessarily conservative (the condition of their existence and persistence) but equally inherently unstable (the condition of their dynamism). The inscription of the code, be it linguistic, genetic or otherwise, is never simply present as static script, but is perpetually affected by an element of indeterminacy, so that the code is in a state of continual transformation. Like the Lucretian *clinamen*, this element of play, this perpetual departure ('écart') from the norm, is percurrent, that is to say, it is not simply the 'origin' of the system, but the perturbing and contesting force that assures the unstable continuation of the system, its survival. I shall return to these questions in greater detail in the following chapter.

In addition to this gesture towards a general theory of systems, there is also in 'Mes chances' what might be called a 'performative' register of discourse. In common with a number of Derrida's later texts, the argument of 'Mes chances' adopts a 'torsional' posture, that is, it imitates rhetorically the structure and movement of the objects it describes. This could in fact be seen to be a logical extension, an enactment, as it were, of the theory of the isomorphism of systems advanced above. Derrida argues that the linguistic system is formally and functionally no different from other systems, is merely one of a number (though at the same time perhaps a special case) of systems that combine (bind or articulate) regulation and indetermination, chance and necessity. In turn, his own discursive system (a subset of the linguistic system) proceeds in an aleatory, but somehow necessary, fashion, practising the isomorphism it describes. There are a number of examples of this.

Like the arbitrary and accidental *clinamen*, Derrida's preliminary questions are thrown at random, and constellate in a necessary determination or meaning only after the event, 'Après coup' (MC, p. 7; *TC*, p. 4).[16] In the following argument, amidst his descriptions of falling atoms, events and letters, Derrida himself *falls* upon texts, theories and authors. He falls – somewhat necessarily, however – upon the atomist philosophers, the descent of atoms and the *parenklisis* or *clinamen*: 'Nous retombons ici nécessairement sur Démocrite, Epicure et Lucrèce' (MC, p. 11) ('At this point we necessarily fall upon Democritus, Epicurus and Lucretius again' (*TC*, p. 7)). The appearance of the atomists in his text imparts a whirlwind-like condensation to its diverse elements, like Epicurus' *systrophè* or vortical agglutination of atoms (MC, p. 12; *TC*, p. 8). His final piece of luck ('ma dernière chance') is to fall upon a text by Freud (*Leonardo da Vinci*), the subject of which is precisely the problem of prediction and destiny, chance and necessity (MC, p. 36; *TC*, p. 28).

This process of random collision, combination and intersection of texts is not a one-way process: Derrida is not only affected or diverted by, but also affects and diverts, the course or destination of the texts he encounters. For example, the second point, following Derrida's remarks on the generality of the 'trace' and 'marque' quoted above, is that he wishes to distance himself ('m'écarter') from the strictly atomist interpretation of the *stoikheion*. He continues: 'Ensuite je tenais à m'écarter à mon tour, dans cette référence même, de l'atomisme strict, de l'interprétation atomistique du *stoikheion*. Mon *clinamen*,

ma chance ou mes chances, voilà ce qui m'incline à penser
le *clinamen* depuis la divisibilité de la marque' (MC, p. 22)
('Then, within this very frame of reference, I prefer to diverge
in turn from strict atomism and the atomistic interpretation of
the *stoikheion*. My *clinamen*, my luck or my chances are what lead
me to think of the *clinamen* beginning with the divisibility of the
mark' (*TC*, p. 16)). Derrida would therefore contest the
indivisibility of the minimal element, the *atomos*, which is the
corner-stone, or last instance, of atomist materialism. This
departure or deviation from atomist doctrine, his inclination
towards the divisibility of the mark, constitutes his *clinamen*, his
chance or luck: 'Mon *clinamen*, ma chance ou mes chances.'

Parallel to the descent, the deviations and the collisions of
atoms and letters described in 'Mes chances', there are therefore
the chance encounters, inflections and conjugations of texts and
discourses in Derrida's argument itself. This co-implication or
'invagination' of internal and external space, of the subject and
the object of discourse, undermines the traditional, positivistic
assumption of the separation of (neutral) discourse and (passive)
object, and poses some difficult questions as to the status of such
discourse, as Derrida indicates in *La carte postale*: 'Que se passe-
t-il quand des actes ou des performances (discours ou écriture,
analyse ou description, etc.) font partie des objets qu'ils
désignent? Quand ils peuvent se donner en exemple de cela
même dont ils parlent ou écrivent?' (*CP*, p. 417) ('What
happens when acts or performances (discourse or writing,
analysis or description, etc.) are part of the object they
designate? When they can be given as examples of precisely that
of which they speak or write?' (*PC*, p. 391)).

Having concentrated on the subject of play in Derrida's texts,
both in the systems he describes and in his own descriptive
systems, this chapter might have taken any of a number of
possible trajectories through his work. As it happened, the path
chosen departed from the anagram of 'trace-écart', and
consequently attempted a reconstruction of part of the system of
associations, conceptual and metaphorical, to which it belongs.
Alternative paths are possible. Within the conceptual field of
the inscription ('écriture', 'marque', 'trace', etc.), one might,

for example, have begun with the punning association of 'marque-marche-marge', initiated in *Marges*. The word 'marche', for instance (walk, step, pace, working or running), refers in *La carte postale* both to Freud's limping gait (midway between standing and falling) in *Beyond the Pleasure Principle* – his hesitant speculative steps (the 'pas au-delà', the step beyond) and positivistic reservations (the 'pas au-delà', in the sense of not stepping beyond) – and also to the asymmetrical rhythm ('marche') of life or the psychical system, their oscillation between excess and containment.

Whatever the path taken through these complex verbal systems, as they are constructed in Derrida's texts, it appears therefore that the double-bound morphology of the system described remains the same. In the following chapter I shall attempt to relate this conception of system more explicitly to the biological and cybernetic models mentioned above.

CHAPTER 5

Evolution and the 'life' sciences

> Every system involving life or mind, or simulating life or mind, is an open system.[1]

> In *biology* there is an awakening tendency to inquire beyond the definitions which mechanism and vitalism have given for 'life' and 'organism', and to define anew the kind of Being which belongs to the living as such.[2]

> My own view is that deconstruction and everything else are ultimately contained by Darwin's tale – but that is another story and will wait for another day.[3]

In their general approach, the preceding chapters have been for the most part 'internal' commentaries of specific texts and passages, 'internal' in the sense that they have studied Derrida's treatment of system and writing in its own terms, giving due attention to the specificities and peculiarities of Derrida's philosophical idiom. Reference to the wider context of contemporary thought, as outlined in the Introduction, has been at most brief and episodic. In this chapter, I shall begin by inverting this perspective, dealing in more detail with the aspects of contemporary thought which contain important parallels with Derrida's work. This will serve as a means of introduction to a reading of *Glas*, *La dissémination*, and some of the more recent publications.

In the Introduction, I argued that the general conversion to the linguistic paradigm in French philosophy during the 1950s and 1960s could not be properly explained with reference to the dual influences of Heidegger and structuralism alone. While for many the examples of Heidegger and structuralism were the most immediate points of introduction to this new paradigm, it is clear that the paradigm itself extended across the spectrum of the sciences, reflecting what Serres called the new 'Leibnizianism'. In its turn, the minor epistemic shift occurring within the linguistic or structural paradigm, the shift during the 1960s from 'language' to 'writing', would be equally unintelligible if it were abstracted from the context of the post-war advances in the related fields of biology and cybernetic theory, a determining context to which Derrida himself refers. During the same period, contemporary to the rise of structuralism, some of the new insights provided by these disciplines were being given more general expression in the field of systems theory. Systems theory addresses the following problems:

1 the self-organization of complex systems and
2 their self-regulation through operations such as feedback;
3 the passage between the differing levels of integration of a system;
4 the modalities of openness and closure of a given system;
5 the question of teleology or finality;
6 the concept of code.

A full explanation of the above points would obviously require more time and space than is available within the parameters of the present discussion. In the following exposition of the elements of systems theory I shall therefore be tendentiously selective, concentrating in the main on the notions most directly relevant to the aspects of Derrida's work discussed so far: the open system; teleology and code. This will not exclude some discussion of the other points.

THE OPEN SYSTEM

According to Ludwig von Bertalanffy, generally acknowledged as the originator of systems theory, 'the system problem is essentially the problem of the limitations of analytical procedures in science'.[4] The basis and success of classical science since the seventeenth century has consisted in its strict adherence to the methodology of analysis and summation, the resolution of phenomena into isolable causal trains or 'atomic' units separated from their environment or context. A similar methodological closure has applied at the level of the observer or the subject: the observer is taken to be distinct and detached from the phenomenon observed, mind is severed from object and world. In the present century, however, this traditional methodology of closure and analysis has been increasingly called into question, partly as a result of the growing influence of the life sciences. For a more adequate understanding of the processes of change and exchange, for example, it is no longer considered appropriate to view the complex system in isolation from its ecology or environment. Gregory Bateson's work in psychology, cybernetics and communications theory, for example, leads him to a thoroughgoing revision of the concepts of 'self' and 'mind'. As he argues in *Steps to an Ecology of Mind*, 'the mental world – the mind – the world of information processing – is not limited by the skin'.[5] The subject–object dichotomy, which has dominated our modes of thinking since Descartes and before, is basically an error of 'punctuation', part and parcel of the 'epistemological fallacies of Occidental civilization'.[6]

As Walter Ong points out in his book *Interfaces of the Word*, this 'ecological concern', 'a significant biological and social issue' during the past thirty years or so, is anticipated in Heidegger's *Sein und Zeit*, where he 'treats "openness" frequently and at length'. In their turn, Heidegger's questions 'echoed earlier obscure questions generated in and around the evolutionary thinking culminating in Darwin's work, which had shown how species themselves, earlier thought of as the closed-system bases of life and taken to be major elements in philosophical thinking, are not fixed but develop through natural selection brought about by interaction between individuals and environment'.[7] The living organism, the open system *par excellence* (though all systems are more or less open), survives only through a relation of export and import of energy and information with its environment.

TELEOLOGY AND CODE

The concept of teleology, of the necessary orientation of a system towards a predetermined final state, is unacceptable to traditional science. The idea, inherited from Aristotle, is considered to imply a mysterious reversal of causality, ultimately a *theological* supposition of a future plenitude uncannily governing a present state. The success of Western technological science since the seventeenth century is commonly seen to be based on its adherence to the safely determinable, observable linearity of cause and effect, and the rejection of the teleological premise. In contrast, systems theory accepts the idea of a certain kind of teleology, of *finality*, but there is no mystical, theological or even vitalist colouring to this. As Bertalanffy explains:

> Finality can be spoken of also in the sense of *dependence on the future* ... happenings can be considered and described as being determined not by actual conditions, but also by the final state to be reached. The final state to be reached in future is not a *vis a fronte* mysteriously attracting the system, but only another expression for causal *vires a tergo* ... Biologists often regarded such formulas as somewhat uncanny, either fearing a hidden vitalism, or else considering such teleology or goal-directedness as 'proof' for vitalism. For with respect to animate rather than inanimate nature, we tend to compare finalistic processes with human foresight of the goal.[8]

A few pages later, Bertalanffy adds that 'true purposiveness is characteristic of human behaviour, and it is connected with the evolution of the symbolism of language and concepts'.[9] If Bertalanffy substitutes causality (the *vires a tergo*) for the apparent teleology or preformism operative in open systems, this does not mean that the systems concept of finality is simply a restatement of classical causality. On the one hand it is, since quite conventionally, the idea of the effect preceding the cause, of a reversal of the flow of time, is taken to be logically and materially impossible. Such a conception of inverted causality is constructed entirely from the anthropomorphic projection of the human faculty of 'foresight', which is dependent on the existence of linguistic and symbolic expression. On the other hand, with the systems concept of finality, the traditional notion of a *singular* and *linear* causality is no longer an essential postulate. This is because the causal agent identified in cybernetic explanation is the code or programme (a symbolic construct) responsible for the structuring or regulation of a given system, and the manner in which this code or programme is realized is not strictly determinate. In other words, there is a certain degree of predetermining constraint, but also the possibility of a given system occupying a number of different states. The system is regulated, restrained, contained by control mechanisms such as negative feedback, both internal and environmental, but at the same time is able to depart in different degrees and on different levels from the regulatory norm. This potentiality for alternative pathways, this element of play, is called *equifinality*. The definition of equifinality given by Bertalanffy is helpful in explaining the difference between open- and closed-system causality:

> In any closed system, the final state is unequivocally determined by the initial conditions... If either the initial conditions or the process is altered, the final state will also be changed. This is not so in open systems. Here, the same final state may be reached from different initial conditions and in different ways. This is what is called equifinality, and it has a significant meaning for the phenomena of biological regulation.[10]

In *System and Structure*, a text very much influenced by the work of Bateson and systems theory, Wilden cites Freud's concept of overdetermination as it is applied to the dream, the lapsus and the neurotic symptom as an example of equifinality:

> Overdetermination may be read to mean 'determined' in some classically causal fashion, but in fact the notion is quite different from causal explanation. All it says is that, because of the semiotic freedom of the system of communication in which the symptom occurs, 'there is more than one way of getting there'. In other words, although the system is indeed determined in some sense by the repertoire or the code from which the possible elements of the message are drawn, and by the syntactic laws of combination in the message itself, this determination is similar to that in language itself. In language, there is a very large number of ways of saying the same thing, and an infinite number of possible messages. Determined as it is by its code and by its syntax,

language is perhaps the most semiotically free of all representational and communicational systems – and is not ruled by causality, but by possibility, constraints, and by its pragmatic-semantic function, that of the transmission and reproduction of variety in the system.[11]

Wilden's description of language as possibly 'the most semiotically free of all representational and communicational systems' brings qualification to the above description of the living system as the open system *par excellence*. In fact, as Wilden suggests, it is the linguistic system, a subsystem of the (human) biological and social system, that is most open as a system. While it is governed, in the last instance, both by its socio-biological substratum and by the prescriptive constraints of its own internal rules, human language has the capacity to transgress these constraints without necessarily bringing about its own demise or deselection, something that is less possible, often impossible, at lower levels of organization.[12] The closure of language is finite, its openness appears infinite. Such unlimited (semiotic) freedom is ultimately held in check by the reality principle. In this sense, the relationship between the linguistic system and its somatic-social support (a cybernetic relationship – the symbolic or digital construct to an extent governs the activities of the system) is comparable to a contract passed between the two parties: the governing (linguistic) instance is allowed to play only if, in the last instance, this redounds to the advantage of the whole system (the biological unit, ultimately the species).[13] This is undoubtedly what Wilden means when he speaks of the 'pragmatic-semantic function' of language, that of 'the transmission and reproduction of variety in the system': the immediate functional value of certain forms of language may appear superfluous, meaningless, redundant, but the 'fictional' alternatives (the variety) they offer may be of long-term adaptive benefit to the total system.

If systems theory, like all modern science, rejects traditional teleological explanation (the system does not *know* where it is going), the open system does have a 'direction': it is goal-seeking (or teleonomic) in that it seeks primarily to persevere, to reproduce itself, that is, to perpetuate and reproduce an invariant structure (the code or programme). The code is, in a very special sense, the memory of the system, and its function is essentially a conservative one: to transmit an invariant structure. But what the code promises is always liable to interference or, to use the terminology of information theory, *noise*. There is no such thing as a channel of information devoid of noise, a pure message. In fact, a pure message is unthinkable, and the very condition of possibility of (new) information is noise. The process of morphogenesis, the production of new forms or structures, is dependent upon noise, both internal and environmental, which via natural selection is integrated into the code as new information.[14] This integration of noise is possible precisely because of the 'looseness' of connections in the system, the property of equifinality or redundancy defined above. Because the code changes while attempting to remain the same, reproduction will tend in each instance to be the replication of the same but different. Hence similar initial conditions may lead to dissimilar end-states. This process of divergence, or *multifinality*, is not amenable to deterministic or statistical calculation, its direction is not predictable in the same way that the development of a less complex (closed) system is predictable. Evolution is an example of a multifinal process.[15]

It is clear from the preceding account that systems theory translates what appears to be the increasing convergence of a number of different disciplines. As Bertalanffy remarks: 'There is a general tendency towards integration in the various sciences, natural and social [and] such integration appears to be centred in a general theory of systems.'[16] Bertalanffy's evaluation of the synthetic potential of systems theory could be questioned. For one thing, it might be seen to be too regional – that is, its models are too localized – to pretend to such a status: as has been seen, biological science in particular played a determining role in the development of systems theory. If the closed-system epistemology that systems theory is supposed to replace is considered to be mechanistic and reductionist (its models coming mainly from physical science), one of the charges made against systems theory is that it has an unacceptable bias towards organicism and is too dependent upon biological models. While recognizing this tendency in Bertalanffy's work, Wilden refuses to accept that systems theory as such is organicist.[17] It is difficult to disagree with Wilden here, especially if one reflects that the adoption by systems theory of biological models has taken place during a period in which the distinction between biology and adjacent sciences has become increasingly indeterminate – a symptom of the convergence or integration of disciplines mentioned by Bertalanffy above; where developments in molecular biology or cybernetics, for example, have placed a large question mark over what we mean when we speak of the 'life' sciences. Nevertheless, the important catalytic role played by biological science in particular in the formulation of systems theory should not be underestimated, especially as concerns the necessary strategic opposition to a hitherto dominant reductionism in physical science.

The step from these very general points back to the philosophy of Derrida is, inevitably, a tentative one. It is first necessary to re-emphasize that the objective here is not to *explain* Derrida's work from the point of view of systems science, for it quite obviously is not reducible to such a simple schema. At the same time, the resonances between Derrida's philosophy of inscription and systems theory are often quite remarkable, and this resemblance is clearly not entirely gratuitous. As has already been noted, Derrida himself draws attention to the generality of his own concept of the gram when he refers to the importance of the concepts of code and programme in modern biology and cybernetics (*GR*1, pp. 19, 103; *GR*2, pp. 9, 70, quoted in the Introduction above). In their turn, commentators of Derrida have variously pointed to the parallels between his conception of 'différence-différance' and the concepts of difference and feedback in cybernetics. Anthony Wilden's reading of Freud and Derrida in *System and Structure* compares Derrida's presentation of difference with Bateson's idea of information as difference, and he goes on to note the similarity of Derrida's and his own readings of Freud, over and above the obvious differences of idiom (see chapter 3 above). For her part, Irene Harvey asks: 'Is it not this reflexivity or "circular causality", characteristic of cybernetics, which Derrida himself is aiming towards with his notion of *différance* as economy?'[18] At various stages of the present study, there have been examples of the conceptual proximities indicated by Wilden, Harvey and others. Derrida's discussion of Freud's model of the Mystic Pad introduced the fundamental questions of simulation and the relationship between the human and the technological, 'life' and 'death', questions central to cybernetic theory. In a later text such as 'Mes chances', when discussing the role of the random and the undecidable in the functioning of language, Derrida's own vocabulary shows a marked inflection towards the terminology of systems theory, as observed in the previous chapter.

Despite the visible similarities and parallels outlined above, Derrida's approach to these theories remains far from systematic. As remarked in the Introduction, this is not particularly surprising, considering Derrida's own disciplinary specialization, but perhaps even more importantly, considering what would doubtless be a reticence on his part to submit to a critically limiting scientific discourse retaining strong and enduring links with a certain positivistic and logocentric tradition. So while it is clear that Derrida is aware of and conversant with the contemporary system-cybernetic paradigm, his dialogue with this paradigm is at most an oblique and allusive one.

In the absence of any determinable framework for these theories within Derrida's work, and given the importance of modern biology in systems theory, I shall begin my comparison of the two discourses by examining Derrida's use of *biological* metaphors. It is evident that Derrida's vocabulary, especially following *Glas* (though such a tendency is already visible in *La dissémination*), becomes increasingly concerned with the genealogical, the genetic and, both literally and metaphorically, the question of families and descendance. The frequency of these metaphors and their systematic organization lead to the conclusion that they are more than simply metaphors, that they constitute a kind of theory of reproduction in general. I shall also be arguing that this generalization of biological figures is symptomatic of the essentially *evolutionary* nature of system and writing, as Derrida describes them. But this is anticipation.

OPENNESS AND CLOSURE: THE CONTINUOUS AND THE DISCRETE

In the analyses presented in previous chapters, a central issue in the articulation of system and writing has been the problem of closure. For example, Derrida's critique of structuralism, examined in chapter 1, opposed the totalizing theories of structuralism with what was essentially an *open-system* model. Expressed in the language of 'Force et signification' (where there is frequent use of the words 's'ouvrir' and 'ouverture'), there is an 'excess' in the text that the structural analysis can never totally enclose or contain. This 'excess' was frequently expressed in terms of metaphors of flow and overflow, which in Derrida's punning French ('débordement', 'déborder') gives also the sense of 'un-framing' ('dé-border'), of the undoing of punctuation or closure, an image that becomes an important leitmotif of *La vérité en peinture*. The gesture of closure, we are constantly reminded in Derrida's texts, is the scientific gesture *par excellence*. Saussure's methodological isolation of the linguistic system as a formal and arbitrary construct, for example, rests upon the critico-theoretical instance of the decidable, upon the ideal of a pure interiority uncontaminated by external contingency, 'au-dedans impénétrable, invulnérable, non contaminable, immaculé, du système linguistique' (J, p. 103) ('the impenetrable, invulnerable, uncontaminable and immaculate interiority of the linguistic system'). Such isolation is practised not only in our approach to 'natural' systems, such as language, but also in our relationship with technology in the widest sense of the word. In Derrida's analysis of Freud's model of the Mystic Writing-Pad, it becomes apparent that, as well as functioning as a useful analogy for the psychical system as Freud perceives it, the Mystic Pad – or indeed any archival technology – is not simply external to the pysche, but is a kind of prosthetic device continuous with the system it supplements. From this point of view, the script would not simply reflect the psyche, and more specifically, its capacity for memorization; it would also, by virtue of a type of circular causality or feedback, actually influence its structure (which is not simply 'internal') and transform its *modus operandi*.[19] The technology of writing cannot therefore be counted as subsidiary and external to thought and speech, as an entire tradition from Plato to Rousseau and beyond has desired and described it to be. This tradition would see in writing a scandalous form of contamination of the purity of the closed inner circuit of thought-speech, an unnatural and unnecessary adjunct to the autonomous consciousness. The actual inevitability of such contamination, if one accepts that mind, language, writing, technology, society, are *open* systems, is one of the most insistent themes in Derrida's work.

On many levels, therefore, Derrida challenges the closed-system epistemology which has shaped Western thought since its Greek beginnings. At the same time, the structure or system, as Derrida describes it, is not purely and simply open, as has been seen in a number of instances. In equal measure, law, coding, closure, restriction are the conditions of possibility of the system. Infinity is possible only from a finite base, the sublime is only apprehended through composition with the finite *comprehensio*, through an economy of openness and closure. As Derrida argues in 'Spéculer – sur "Freud"': 'Tout se passe alors dans des différences de bandage. L'économie n'est pas générale. On entend souvent sous ce mot une économie simplement ouverte à une dépense absolue. Ici, jusque dans son effondrement ultime, l'économie serait stricturale' (*CP*, p. 426) ('Everything then occurs in the differences of binding. The economy is not general. The general economy is often understood as one simply open to absolute expenditure. Here, to the point of its ultimate collapse, economy would be strictural' (*PC*, p. 399)); or, in *Glas*: 'Pas d'économie absolument générale, d'exposition ou de dépense pure: une stricture plus ou moins forte' (*GL1*, p. 227b) ('No absolutely general economy, no exposition or pure expenditure: a strict-ure more or less strong' (*GL2*, p. 202b)). Similarly, on the level of technology, or 'supplementarity', it is clear that (for example) writing cannot be entirely implicated in the circuit of speech-thought. The 'relief' of thought and speech by writing depends upon the structure of delegation and detachment (death, absence, remote control, the play of *fort-da*) permitted by writing, the dialectical (con)striction of the passage from speech to writing. So writing is simultaneously continuous with thought-speech and separable from it: its relative closure to the levels it subsumes allows for a greater degree of play or semiotic freedom.

This double bind or *articulation* of open and closed, adherent and detached, described above, is often expressed in terms of topological figures in Derrida's texts, and such figures tend to be of a biological or anatomical kind. The word 'articulation' is itself etymologically associated with the anatomy of joints and limbs, as was noted in chapter 4. The articulating joint permits both linkage and separation; it is both a breakage in a continuum and a bridging of the breakage, like Foucault's 'Décision' ('La Décision lie et sépare') or Heidegger's *Riss*. Topologically, it exhibits the quality of *betweenness*. In his book *The Dimensionality of Signs, Tools and Models*, James Bunn draws attention to the various anatomical examples of betweenness: 'In our bodies…joints of various kinds, ligatures such as ligaments and synapses, are evolutionary results of "experiments" with betweenness. As with any other semiotic object of mediation, they separate and connect two boundaries of different media'.[20] These figures of ligature and ligament are particularly common in *Glas*, *La carte postale*, *La vérité en peinture* and later texts, whenever it is a question of the binding of disparate media or forces, whenever Derrida wishes to describe the undecidable coalition of opposites, and/or the indeterminate transition from the one to the other. In *Schibboleth*, for example, the combination of chance and necessity in the number thirteen depends on the binding stricture of a ligament: 'C'est l'un de ces nombres dans lesquelles se croisent, pour s'y consigner en une seule fois, l'aléa et la nécessité. Un ligament y tient ensemble la fatalité et son contraire, strictement' (*SCH*, p. 43) ('It is one of those numbers in which chance and necessity cross one another, so as to consign themselves in a single event. In this number, a ligament strictly holds together fatality and its opposite').

In Derrida's texts, the topological or anatomical figure representing the articulation of internal with external is most frequently the figure of *invagination*. This term is used in both pathology and embryology to describe the infolding of an organ or part, or of the outer layer of cells of an organism, to form a pocket in the surface. In Derrida's work, what is especially stressed is the anatomico-sexual dimension. This is apparent in 'La double séance' (*La dissémination*), where the topology of invagination seems to act as a foil to and displacement of the figure of the phallus, associated with logocentric thought and its methodological distinctions between the 'inside' and the 'outside' of systems. In the introductory section of *Marges – de la philosophie*, 'Tympan', which serves as a kind of figural frontispiece to the book, it becomes the structure of the inner ear, the convoluted pathways and passages which complicate the distinction between inside and outside, and which problematize the question of the limit, the boundary, the margin.

This brief survey of the categories of openness and closure in Derrida's work has been concerned with the spatial or topological aspect of the biological models he uses, but it has not addressed the problem of how such models might depict change. If Derrida is always describing an anatomy of articulation (reflected in his rhetoric of the *ni ... ni* or the *d'une part, d'autre part*) rather than an anatomy of punctuation (decision, dissection, closure), if no man or woman is an island, if every system can be touched (if only at a tangent and at a distance, as Rousseau's God touches the earth's axis), contaminated, then it would be legitimate to ask what this means, what the consequences might be. One would have to reply, with suitable caution as to the sense of 'meaning' or 'consequence', that the touched system enters time, the rhythm of history and of life, the irreversibility of a certain *telos*.

THE BIOLOGICAL REPRESENTATION OF THE TELEOLOGICAL

Openness to what and towards what? Opening, *ouverture*, also bears the temporal sense of inauguration, as was found in 'Force et signification'. It is the determining instance of a system, its passage into becoming and time: 'Cette ouverture est certes ce qui libère le temps et la genèse (se confond même avec eux)'

('This opening is certainly that which liberates time and genesis (even coincides with them)'). At the same time, inauguration holds the danger of integral determination, and therefore of delimitating closure: 'mais c'est aussi ce qui risque, en l'informant, d'enfermer le devenir. De faire taire la force sous la forme' (*ED*, p. 44) ('but it is also that which risks enclosing becoming by giving it a form. That which risks stifling force under form' (*WD*, p. 26)). This closure is the closure of *pre*determination: it will be remembered that Derrida is criticizing here the teleological bias of structuralist analysis in general. While most structuralisms in theory reject any form of teleological explanation, in practice their assumption of the organized (closed) totality relies upon an implicit acceptance of finality, of sense (*sens*), of directedness. It will also be remembered that Derrida proposes as an alternative to this predeterminist philosophy the idea of an indeterminate *telos*: 'S'il y a des structures, elles sont possibles à partir de cette structure fondamentale par laquelle la totalité s'ouvre et se déborde pour *prendre sens* dans l'anticipation d'un telos qu'il faut entendre ici sous sa forme la plus indéterminée' (*ED*, p. 44) ('If there are structures, they are possible only on the basis of the fundamental structure which permits totality to open and overflow itself such that it *takes on meaning* by anticipating a *telos* which here must be understood in its most indeterminate form' (*WD*, p. 26)). Very typically, Derrida does not reject out of hand the concept of the *telos*, but retains it in a modified form (it is indeterminate). I shall endeavour to explain, in the remainder of this chapter, what Derrida means when he says that the finality of the system can only be indeterminate. In terms of Derrida's biological figures, this will involve a transition from the topological to the combinatorial, from anatomy to *genetics*.

In the history of Western philosophy, teleological behaviour has habitually been a quality attributed first and foremost to living systems, to nature, plants, animals, man. Since Aristotle and before, the idea of purposeful development has been derived from the observation of natural, especially vital, phenomena: the acorn, for example, appears to be trying to realize the form proper to it (the oak) and each of its successive developments are directed towards that goal. All objects, says Aristotle, have their own, proper form, progressively realized during their respective histories: the end is contained in the beginning, the alpha is the omega. Any interference in this natural history Aristotle considers to be the violent or unnatural infraction of some external agency.[21] This vitalist basis of the teleological argument has a particularly strong legacy in Western metaphysics. Hegel, for example, uses the metaphor of the seed to explain the unfolding of the concept:

> The concept constitutes the beginning in philosophical treatment too. But here it is the substance of the thing, like the seed [*der Keim*] from which the whole tree unfolds. The seed contains all of its characteristics, the entire nature of the tree: the type of its sap, the pattern of its branches, etc. However, these are not preformed, so that if one took a microscope one would see the twigs and leaves in miniature, but they are instead enveloped in a spiritual manner [*eingehüllt auf geistige Weise*]. Similarly the concept contains the entire nature of the object and cognition is nothing but the development of the concept, the development of what is contained in the concept but has not yet emerged into existence, is not yet explicated, not yet displayed ...
>
> The enveloped being [*Das Eingehülltsein*] of the tree's nature, this simple seed [*Samenkorn*], is the product or result of the entire developed life of this tree.[22]

Hegel's metaphor of the seed, in accordance with the scientific culture of his time, avoids the pitfall of preformationism (the future configuration of the tree is not contained in miniature in the seed, but is 'enveloped in a spiritual manner'). Despite this, the basic premise of purposeful, predetermined development, by analogy with vital processes, remains. Indeed, in the Hegelian system the accidents or *peripeteia* envisaged by Aristotle as unnatural perturbations can be absorbed (recuperated, reappropriated) through the play of the dialectic, the more general evolution towards the Absolute remaining untouched.

This particular example from Hegel, illustrating the strong continuity of the teleological premise and its vitalist model in Western metaphysics, is also relevant to the present discussion because of the important role Hegel plays in Derrida's work in general, and in *Glas* in particular. The dialogue between the two thinkers, Derrida and Hegel, in the left- (and right-)hand columns of *Glas*, turns upon questions of biology, genealogy, the family, and prepares the way for the genetic metaphors of *La carte postale* and a number of other texts. To begin with, I shall concentrate on the differences between Derrida and Hegel in their understanding of the seed, the *Keim* or *germe*.

Derrida's reading of Hegel in *Glas* is a close, detailed and continuous one. By way of paraphrase and lengthy quotation, he follows, often word for word, Hegel's encyclopaedic discourse on the individual, the family, the state, and the passages between them. At the same time, Derrida's faithfulness to the letter of Hegel's text is shadowed by a second voice, a kind of interpretative bending of concepts fundamental to the Hegelian system. This second (questioning, interpellating) voice emanates partly from the commentary itself which occupies the left-hand column of the text, but also, more remarkably, from the right-hand column, the 'contre bande' of the commentary of Genet's fiction. A most interesting, and possibly the most important, aspect of this dialogue is Derrida's treatment of the concept of the seed or germ. This concept, according to Derrida, is a key component in Hegel's speculative dialectic, figuratively linking the different orders he describes:

Ce concept (de) germe (*Same*, semen, semence, sperme, graine) entre régulièrement en scène dans la dialectique spéculative ... qu'il s'agisse de l'ordre végétal, biologique, anthropologique, onto-logique en général. Entre tous ces ordres, elle assure un système de correspondances figuratives.

D'où ces figures s'exporteraient-elles? Quel serait leur lieu propre?

La figure de la semence ... est immédiatement déterminée: 1. comme la meilleure représentation du rapport à soi de l'esprit; 2. comme le trajet circulaire d'un retour à soi. (*GL*1, p. 35a)

(The concept (of) germ (*Same*, semen, seed, sperm, grain) regularly enters on the scene in speculative dialectics ... whether [it is a question] of the vegetal, biological, anthropological, or the onto-logical order in general. Among all these orders, speculative dialectics assures a system of figurative correspondences.

From where would these figures export themselves? What would be their own proper place?

The figure of the seed ... is immediately determined: 1. as the best representation of the spirit's relation to self; 2. as the circular path of a return to self.) (*GL2*, p. 27a)

The seed which anticipates (for example) the tree, and which is also its end, is an ideal figuration of the reappropriating return of mind to itself after its passage through nature or Experience. During this circular journey, nothing is lost, all contradictions along the way are resumed in the ascendent work of the *Aufhebung*. Expressed in Derrida's vocabulary of strictness or constraint (*striction, stricture, structure*):

Chaque totalité, chaque puissance procède à la striction de la précédente, l'étrangle et l'élève à la puissance suivante, selon un processus circulaire qui va comme de la graine à la plante puis de la plante à la graine. (*GL1*, p. 121a; see also p. 115a)

(Each totality, each power proceeds to the striction of the preceding one, strangles it, and raises it to the following power, according to a circular process which goes, as it were, from the seed to the plant, then from the plant to the seed.) (*GL2*, p. 105a; see also pp. 99–100a)

Le mouvement annulaire re-streint l'économie générale (compte tenu, c'est-à-dire non tenu de la perte) en économie circulante. Le resserrement, la restriction économique forme l'anneau du même, du retour à soi, de la réappropriation. (*GL1*, p. 271a)

(The annular movement re-stricts the general economy (account taken and kept, that is, not taken or kept, of the loss) into a circulating economy. The contraction, the economic restriction forms the annulus of the selfsame, of the self-return, of reappropriation.) (*GL2*, p. 244a)

Thus articulated upon the circular (annular, ring-like[23]) sweep of Absolute Knowledge is the triangle (or trinity) of the dialectic, which restrains the evolution of the system to the finality prefigured in its beginnings: 'Or la trinité a partie liée avec la structure circulaire qui ne peut ni s'assimiler ni laisser tomber le reste ... Le *Sa* fait le plein de sens dans l'unité sans reste d'une structure triangulo-circulaire' (*GL1*, p. 254a) ('Now the trinity is intimately bound up with the circular structure that can neither assimilate itself nor let the remain(s) fall ... *Sa* fills up (with) sense in the unity without remain(s) of a triangulo-circular structure' (*GL2*, p. 227a)).[24] Derrida's corrective to this closed, teleological loop, as it emerges from his commentary of the Hegelian system, is the concept of the general economy. In contrast to the perfect circulation of Hegel's restricted economy, which accounts for loss only by sublating it, in other words, by not taking account of it, the general economy takes note of the remainder (*reste*), the loss which cannot be recuperated (saved), which deviates (*s'écarte*) from the path of pure predetermination. The general economy circulates elliptically, asymmetrically. If this inflection of Hegel turns the circle into an ellipse, then the triangle becomes a square, whose four-sidedness opens the restricted dialectic of one-two-three ('écart', 'carte', 'quart', 'carré', *GL*1, p. 254a (*GL*2, p. 227a), 'le quatre des saisons', *GL*1, p. 260a (*GL*2, p. 233a)).

There are therefore three metaphors in circulation here: the seed, the circle, the triangle. I have just explained Derrida's metaphorical inflection of the figures of the circle and the triangle, but how can the figure of the seed account for the exorbitance, the (controlled) *démesure*, of the general economy? In its traditional form, that expressed in the quotation of Hegel above, and described by Derrida in his commentary of Hegel, it obviously cannot. In this incarnation, the seed is a closed monad, containing and mirroring in their virtuality all subsequent contingencies in the development of the system. The displacement of this particular representation of the seed takes place firstly by a process of pluralization: what Derrida proposes is not the serene unfolding of a singular germ or seed, but the plural scattering of *dissemination*, such as that described in his discourse on flowers in the right-hand column of *Glas*. As Derrida remarks in *La dissémination*, where this concept is first introduced: 'Il n'y a pas de première insémination. La semence est d'abord essaimée. L'insémination "première" est dissémination' (*D*1, p. 338) ('There is no first insemination. The semen is already swarming. The "primal" insemination is dissemination' (*D*2, p. 304)). In Derrida's text, therefore, the *germe*, far from being the *arche* and the *eschaton* of a given system, becomes the principle of dispersal and of random combination. This movement of dissemination, or germination, as Derrida sometimes calls it, has no predetermined pathway, its *telos* is indeterminate; in contrast with the ascent of the Hegelian system towards the Absolute, dissemination descends, and descends catastrophically.

Derrida's elaborate juxtaposition in *Glas* of alternative readings of the *germe* is visibly a *mise en scène* of two different traditions in Western metaphysics, materialism and idealism. These two traditions, sometimes convergent but most frequently divergent, have not normally coexisted on equal terms, since the materialist, or at least a *certain* materialist, strand has been more or less hidden or repressed by its idealist opponent. Derrida's reactivation of the materialist tradition in *Glas* is visible in his bending of the word *germe* towards an 'atomistic' interpretation, where the germ is not the self-contained, self-reproducing entity of idealist philosophy, but a fissiparous and proliferating particle which exists only in combination with other particles. As was learnt in the previous chapter, the pre-phenomenal universe described in atomist cosmology is one of undifferentiated matter, represented by a parallel, infinite descent or stream of atoms. As long as the atoms continue their linear, isolated trajectories, they are nothing and there is nothing. With the random inflection of the *clinamen*, however, these atoms converge, collide and agglutinate, thus inaugurating the world of things and phenomena. It is the third term here, the figure of agglutination, which occurs most obsessively in *Glas* in connection with the dissemination of seeds or atoms, primarily in the right-hand column of the text. This is a heavily determined word, since through the atomic unit of *gl*, it is articulated and associated with a host of other terms, both formally and semantically: 'angle', 'glu', 'glas', 'gala', 'loi galactique'. As Derrida indicates, 'l'agglutination ne prend pas seulement dans la pâte signifiante ... elle colle au sens' (*GL1*, p. 169b) ('agglutination not only takes hold in the signifying paste ... it also sticks to the sense' (*GL2*, p. 149b)). Again, one can observe here the reflexive or torsional register of Derrida's language. The text of the right-hand column of *Glas* appears to be isomorphic with its 'object', it disseminates and agglutinates like the seeds or atoms Derrida describes. This implied isomorphism is not simply metaphorical in nature, it is also something more than metaphor.

The inflection of idealist teleology towards atomist dissemination that takes place in *Glas* is not just a turning of the tables. This inflection is adjustment, not opposition; the effect of Derrida's deconstructions is not the reversal of hierarchies, but their displacement. As was mentioned above, Derrida does not reject the *telos* out of hand, but says that it is indeterminate, which is to say that it is really something else. Indeed, the atomist position itself cannot be reduced to the random collision (collusion, agglutination) of atoms, despite its abolition of gods and final causes. On the one hand, the infinite descent of atoms and the inflection of the *clinamen* are blind, random. The atom does not know where it is going, it has no intelligence, according to Lucretius: 'Certainly the atoms did not post themselves purposefully in due order by an act of intelligence, nor did they stipulate what movements each should perform.'[25] The motion of the fall itself is associated (etymologically, conceptually) with accident, chance, catastrophe, as Derrida noted in 'Mes chances'. The diverse phenomena of this world are thus the result of the chance encounters of atoms since time immemorial; since their indeterminate origin and in their infinite descent, they have conglomerated into every conceivable pattern.[26] On the other hand, not every imaginable pattern has subsisted; some configurations are more equal than others. If all were equal, this would lead to the formation of monsters:

It must not be supposed that atoms of every sort can be linked in every variety of combination. If that were so, you would see monsters coming into being everywhere ... But it is evident that nothing of this sort happens. We see that everything is created from specific seeds and born of a specific mother and grows up true to type. We may infer that this is determined by some specific necessity.[27]

Later in his text, Lucretius explains the non-viability of monsters from the point of view of environmental or anatomico-reproductive constraints, a type of natural selection.[28] So the atomist system is not devoid of natural laws, but describes the union or articulation of chance and necessity. The element of necessity, expressed by Lucretius in the figure of the seed – but

generalizable to all phenomena, he says – is not however the
same as the necessity that restricts the Hegelian seed to the
eternal return of the same, the necessity of the teleological. It is
certainly deterministic, but within, or before, that determinism
there is the play of random combination, the inflection of the
clinamen. In the following passage Lucretius describes the
recapitulation of the genetic traits of past generations:

> It may also happen at times that children take after their grand-
> parents, or recall the features of great-grandparents. This is because
> the parents' bodies often preserve a quantity of latent seeds, grouped
> in many combinations, which derive from an ancestral stock handed
> down from generation to generation. From these Venus evokes a
> random assortment of characters, reproducing ancestral traits of
> expression, voice or hair.[29]

What is being described here is *bisexual* reproduction, which, by
the mixing of seeds, introduces variety into the chain of being,
a variety complicated by the temporal lapse that can occur in
the transmission of characters (compare Freud's idea of the
latency period or *Verspätung*). Semination or insemination is
therefore neither pure, linear nor immediate: it is dissemination,
différance. The reappropriating return of seed to seed, the
satisfaction of the Hegelian accomplishment of Absolute Mind
is by contrast patri-linear. Continuing Derrida's remarks on
Hegel's use of the metaphor of the seed or sperm, quoted above:

> La figure de la semence ... est immédiatement déterminée: 1. comme
> la meilleure représentation du rapport à soi de l'esprit; 2. comme le
> trajet circulaire d'un retour à soi. Et dans la description de l'esprit qui
> revient à lui-même à travers son propre produit, après s'y être perdu,
> il y a plus qu'une simple commodité rhétorique à donner à l'esprit le
> nom de père. (*GL*1, p. 35a)

> (The figure of the seed ... is immediately determined: 1. as the best
> representation of the spirit's relation to self; 2. as the circular path of
> a return to self. And in the description of the spirit that returns to itself
> through its own proper product, after it lost itself there, there is more
> than a simple rhetorical convenience in giving to the spirit the name
> father.) (*GL*2, pp. 27–8a)

And later: 'Un germe infini, l'esprit ou Dieu s'engendrant ou
s'inséminant naturellement lui-même, ne tolère pas la différence

sexuelle' (*GL*1, p. 134a) ('An infinite germ, spirit or God engendering or inseminating itself, naturally, does not tolerate sexual difference' (*GL*2, p. 116a)) (see also, *GL*1, pp. 38–40a (*GL*2, pp. 30–1a) for God as self-inseminating, self-conceiving father).[30] The variety introduced into the system by sexual difference (bisexual reproduction), by Venus' deferred and random rearrangement of characters (equivalent to 'noise' injected into a chain of transmission) is on the other hand productive of *new* structures. Unlike the stately return to the same implied in idealist teleology (a single line of descent, a male economy), there is a continuous drift of differences which has no origin and knows of no determinate future. The system is not pulled into the future by a mysterious first (and last) principle, but is pushed *a tergo* by what is handed down, selected and recombined, from its ancestral past. This philosophy is, in essence, a philosophy of *evolution*.[31]

Derrida's mobilization of the metaphors of seed, germ and sperm should not of course be interpreted as proposing an apriority of the biological. His inflection of the seed metaphor, via the atomist tradition, clearly does not essentialize life or vitalize phenomena. Such essentializing is in fact more typical of the idealist and logocentric tradition, which is predicated on the closed economy of what is proper to man, to life, to consciousness, and which achieves its most systematic expression in this century in the philosophy of phenomenology. Phenomenological analysis departs from the given of a living continuum of individual intentionality or consciousness. This living consciousness is taken to be separate from those artefacts that supplement its functions: it is independent, self-sufficient, automobile. Quite literally, this philosophy is a 'life' science or a science of 'man'. The atomist tradition, in contrast, through which Derrida appears increasingly to speak, necessarily sees a certain continuity between nature, man and culture. One important consequence of the materialist premise that atoms are not endowed with intelligence or life, is that life itself is viewed as merely a property of organized matter. In their turn, the many possible extensions of life, the technology of writing for example, are similarly organized, that is, they depend upon a syntax of combination. At the basis of 'life', therefore, there is a certain death, or non-being, continued into 'life' through its extensions or articulations, and necessary to it. The example of writing is, of course, not entirely gratuitous as it is an indispensable model both in Derrida's philosophy and in atomist philosophy. I shall now examine in more detail the articulation in Derrida's work of the biological and the scriptural.

THE GENETIC SCRIPT

The germ (sperm) is also a term. Derrida makes this verbal play in *La dissémination*, and it is not an entirely random association. The atomists saw the atom as a kind of germ but also as a letter, as Derrida indicates in 'Mes chances'. The passage in *La dissémination* describing the dispersal of seed characteristic of dissemination, quoted earlier, goes on to make precisely this equation:

> Il n'y a pas de première insémination. La semence est d'abord essaimée. L'insémination 'première' est dissémination. Trace, greffe dont on perd la trace. Qu'il s'agisse de ce qu'on appelle 'langage' (discours, texte, etc.) ou d'ensemencement 'réel', chaque terme est bien un germe, chaque germe est bien un terme. Le terme, l'élément atomique, engendre en se divisant, en se greffant, en proliférant. (*D*1, p. 338)

> (There is no first insemination. The semen is already swarming. The 'primal' insemination is dissemination. A trace, a graft whose traces have been lost. Whether in the case of what is called 'language' (discourse, text, etc.) or in the case of some 'real' seed-sowing, each term is indeed a germ, and each germ a term. The term, the atomic element, engenders by division, grafting, proliferation.) (*D*2, p. 304)

Atom, germ, term. If the three are not exactly the same thing, then they are isomorphic, that is, they possess the same formal property or structure of division, proliferation and combination. Derrida's rhetorical *mise en scène* of language, biology and physics in this example should not however be ascribed solely to the intertext of the atomist-materialist theories. These theories are an important reference in *La dissémination*, especially in the chapter of the same name, and as is the case in *Glas*, Derrida's deployment of them would seem to be part of his continued deconstruction of idealist metaphysics – albeit in a more playful and performative register than in the earlier, more 'classical' texts. However, in addition to the atomist reference, or rather, juxtaposed upon it, there appears to be another, more contemporary point of reference, the subtext of modern biology.

During the decade preceding Derrida's first publications and the beginnings of structuralism in France, biological science was revolutionized with the discovery of the structure of DNA, a discovery whose repercussions ranged far beyond the immediate context of the scientific community. In 1965, the French biologists François Jacob, Jacques Monod and André Lwoff were awarded the Nobel Prize for their research into the role of RNA in the transmission of genetic information. In 1970, Jacob's *La logique du vivant* and Monod's *Le hasard et la nécessité* gave both a historical and a philosophical perspective to the discoveries in which they had participated. Monod's book emphasized the importance of the element of chance – random mutation – in the emergence of life, but stressed equally the necessity of invariant reproduction in the perpetuation of the random event. For Jacob, the logic of life was contained in what could metaphorically be described as the genetic 'script': 'Par analogie, on compare souvent cette séquence linéaire [the polynucleotide chain of DNA] à celle qui agence les signes d'un alphabet au long d'un texte. Qu'il s'agisse d'un livre ou d'un chromosome, la spécificité naît de l'ordre dans lequel sont disposés les unités, lettres ou radicaux nucléiques' ('By analogy, this linear sequence is often compared to the arrangement of the letters of the alphabet in a text. Whether in a book or a chromosome, the specificity comes from the order in which the sub-units, letters or organic bases, are arranged').[32] This scriptural metaphor dominates the final two chapters of Jacob's book, which deal with the most recent developments in molecular biology. A few years later, Jacob focuses in more detail on the heuristic role the linguistic model has played in the elaboration of genetic theory, and he sees the success of the model as residing in its ability to account for a number of facts we now know about hereditary processes: the formation of the

polynucleotide sequence through the combination and permutation of the four bases; the 'punctuation' of a given
sequence, determining where the reading of its encoded
information begins and ends; the 'translation' (via RNA
'messenger') of this information into the appropriate protein
structure, this structure being the 'expression' of a specific
sequence of nucleotides; the phenomenon of genetic mutation,
comparable to the errors (additions, deletions, transpositions)
introduced into a text during the process of copying or editing.[33]
Despite the immense heuristic value of this model, the possibility
of the linguistic analogy in biology is in Jacob's opinion not
proof of a kind of filiation between the genetic and the linguistic
– as Jakobson would have it – but is rather a question of similar
functions imposing similar constraints on the respective systems.[34]

In his published work, Derrida's engagements with the
modern biological paradigm, and its inevitable (Althusser
would say 'spontaneous') philosophical expression, are rare.
There are the rather cursory references in 'Spéculer – sur
"Freud"' to a previous critique of Jacob's conception of death
and sexuality (*CP*, pp. 377, 384, 386; *PC*, pp. 355, 361, 364), but
this particular study, which formed part of a series of seminars
on Jacob, remains unpublished. Despite this, the extent to
which Derrida's work is influenced by the transformation of the
life sciences during this period is evident, and this is above all
perceptible at the level of what one might call his 'bio-genetic'
metaphors. The systematic use of such metaphors is first
apparent in *La dissémination*, and the complex of associations
built up in that text is extended and developed in a number of
subsequent texts. The conceptual matrix of writing-trace-
difference-'différance', characteristic of Derrida's initial philosophy of inscription, is thus supplemented by the bio-genetic
figures of (for instance) dissemination-germ(ination)-'différance séminale'. This supplement is also an inflection: while
in *De la grammatologie*, for example, the concept of writing is
already being thought conjointly with the question of life, it is
only with the elaboration of the later, bio-genetic lexicon that
Derrida begins to explore in an overtly rhetorical manner the

questions of life and writing. Since I have been citing *La dissémination* as an important interchange or point of departure for this rhetorical turn in Derrida's work, I shall continue with this text, or more exactly with its 'preface', 'Hors d'œuvre'.

In this rather unconventional preface, it is a question of Hegel's distaste for prefaces. Hegel does not approve of prefaces because they are for him like discourses on method, or rules for the direction of reason, external to the argument proper. Ideally, reason should proceed without the assistance of a prefacing meta-discourse, the living concept should unfold under its own steam (*D*1, p. 21; *D*2, p. 15). Again, we are confronted with the teleologicality of Hegel's thinking: 'Le savoir absolu est *présent* au point zéro de l'exposition philosophique. Sa téléologie a déterminé la préface en post-face, le dernier chapitre de la *Phénoménologie de l'esprit* en avant-propos, la *Logique* en Introduction à la *Phénoménologie de l'esprit*' (*D*1, pp. 26–7) ('Absolute knowledge is *present* at the zero point of the philosophical exposition. Its teleology has determined the preface as postface, the last chapter of the *Phenomenology of Spirit* as a foreword, the *Logic* as an Introduction to the *Phenomenology of Spirit*' (*D*2, p. 20)). The preface is therefore for Hegel a mere supplement, it is absolutely superfluous to the relieving circle of Absolute Knowledge. In 'Hors d'œuvre', Derrida obviously differs from Hegel, but not in the sense that he sees the preface as a necessary protocol, integrally determinative of the text to come (which is simply another variant of teleological thought). On the contrary, the preface as Derrida views it would obey 'cette étrange stratégie sans finalité, cette défaillance organisatrice du *telos* ou de l'*eschaton* qui réinscrit l'économie restreinte dans l'économie générale' (*D*1, p. 13) ('that strange strategy without finality, the debility or failure that organizes the *telos* or the *eschaton*, which reinscribes restricted economy within general economy' (*D*2, p. 7)). What is interesting here is that the written preface is assimilated, in Derrida's argument, with the notion of the genetic code: 'On ne peut plus éluder la question du pro-gramme génétique ou de la préface textuelle' (*D*1, p. 58) ('The question of the genetic pro-gram or the textual preface can no longer be eluded' (*D*2, p. 50)). Shortly afterwards, in a note criticizing the Hegelian '*philosophie de la semence* conçue comme enrichissement dans le retour à soi' ('*philosophy of the seed*, conceived as an enrichment in the return-to-self'), he proposes that 'il s'agit au contraire d'amorcer une articulation avec le mouvement de la science génétique et avec le mouvement génétique de la science, partout où celle-ci doit compter, *plus que métaphoriquement* [my emphasis] avec les problèmes de l'écriture et de la différence, avec la différance séminale' (*D*1, p. 58, note 35) ('it is rather a question of broaching an articulation with the movement of genetic science and with the genetic movement of science, wherever science should take into account, *more than metaphorically*, the problems of writing and difference, of seminal [différance]' (*D*2, p. 50, note 50)). So the traditional philosophy of the seed or germ, as well as becoming atomist dissemination in Derrida's system, is also inflected towards the conceptual field of modern genetics. The crucial role of the scriptural metaphor in the history of modern biology has already been mentioned, but Derrida also reminds us that this metaphor is more than a metaphor. This does not mean that, like Jakobson, he believes there to be a direct filiation between the genetic and the linguistic, but rather perhaps, as Jacob suggests, that the two systems, genetic and linguistic, are both subject to similar constraints.

Derrida's collapsing of atom, term and germ into the genetic code does not imply a code that is executed strictly and without remainder. What he calls *différance séminale*, for example, is not formulable in any definite manner:

Hétérogenéité, extériorité absolue de la semence, la différance séminale se constitue en programme mais en programme non-formalisable. *Pour des raisons formalisables* [my emphasis]. L'infinité de son code, sa rupture, donc, n'a pas la forme saturée de la présence à soi dans le cercle encyclopédique. Elle tient, si l'on peut dire, à la chute incessante d'un *supplément de code*. (*D*1, p. 60)

(As the heterogeneity and absolute exteriority of the seed, seminal [différance] does constitute itself into a program, but it is a program that cannot be formalized. *For reasons that* can *be formalized*. The infinity of its code, its rift, then, does not take a form saturated with self-presence in the encyclopedic circle. It is attached, so to speak, to the incessant falling of a *supplement to the code*.) (*D*2, p. 52)

The code, as Derrida understands it, is therefore constituted *in process* rather than in anticipation. Despite the suggestion of precedence implied above in Derrida's articulation of the word programme (*pro-gramme*), the gram, the trace, the inscription are never absolutely primary. There is instead a kind of *precipitation* towards sense that is ignorant of its future, as was the case with the writing described in 'Force et signification': 'C'est parce qu'elle est *inaugurale*, au sens jeune de ce mot, que l'écriture est dangereuse et angoissante. Elle ne sait pas où elle va – aucune sagesse ne la garde de cette précipitation essentielle vers le sens qu'elle constitue et qui est d'abord son avenir' (*ED*, p. 22, quoted in chapter 1 above) ('It is because writing is *inaugural*, in the [primal] sense of the word, that it is dangerous and anguishing. It does not know where it is going, no knowledge can keep it from the essential precipitation toward the meaning that it constitutes, and that is, primarily, its future' (*WD*, p. 11)). To give a more specific example – which is also more general, but in the present context by no means arbitrary – one could say that the process of evolution is not an ascent of species towards some determinate apex of development, but the selection after the event of mutations most amenable to environmental constraints. By virtue of a feedback process (both positive and negative) the genetic code is therefore regulating (before) but also regulated (after) in the sense that its pro-gramme is executed in a context that is perpetually changing, hence perpetually modifying the conditions of possibility of the code. The *supplément de code* described by Derrida above is this continual differing-from-itself of the code as it descends the evolutionary slope. Of course, the process of selection that operates a posteriori (*après coup, nachträglich*) upon the unprogrammed drift of the code gives the *appearance* of the necessity of the forms it produces. Like all auto-mobile processes, it has something of the uncanny about it, and is therefore, in the idealist interpretation, attributed to a transcendent (anthropologized) instance of intentionality, that is, given a theological and teleological explanation. According to a certain materialist tradition, on the other hand, the *unheimlich* is for the unsuperstitious mind quite *heimisch*, it is already quite at home within the system. A good example of such non-teleological and non-theological thinking is Lucretius' refutation of the theory that sense-organs and bodily members are evolved for a specific, predestined function:

To interpret these or any other phenomena on these lines is perversely to turn the truth upside down. In fact, nothing in our bodies was born in order that we might be able to use it, but the thing born creates the use. There was no seeing before eyes were born, no talking before the tongue was created ... All the limbs, I am well assured, existed before their use. They cannot, therefore, have grown for the sake of being used.[35]

If, as Derrida proposed above, the code is not formulable, if, as Lucretius is arguing here, the *telos* of a structure exists only to the degree that it is constituted after the event, *nachträglich*, then there is no paradox in saying that this process in itself is a formulable law. As Derrida has already asserted, the (infinity of the) code is non-formulable 'pour des raisons formalisables'.

I have already cautioned that Derrida's use of biological metaphors is not in any way biologistic or organicist in orientation. His articulation of the genetic and the textual, described above, is visibly influenced by modern genetic theory which has given new perspectives on the nature of life, but he is not interested in the biological *per se*. Indeed, the present evolution, the present finality of 'man' ('Mais qui, nous?' ('But who, we?') Derrida asks at the end of 'Les fins de l'homme' in *Marges*), is no longer in the first instance biological. The descent of man, as told by Darwin, is now finished, at least on the biological plane, and the process of evolution, if it can be said to continue at all for humanity, has for millenia done so in the cultural sphere. Human culture is in a sense the relief, the *Aufhebung* of biological evolution, though obviously not its necessary accomplishment. As the biologist Henri Atlan explains, 'aujourd'hui, l'espèce humaine est considérée comme n'ayant pratiquement plus de potentiel évolutif, en dehors de nouveaux mécanismes, utilisant de nouvelles sortes de redondances et d'ambiguïtés, qui peuvent fonctionner dans ce qu'il est convenu d'appeler l'évolution culturelle, où le langage, parlé et écrit semble jouer un rôle déterminant' ('Today, the human species is considered as having practically no further potential for evolution, apart from the deployment of new mechanisms, involving new kinds of redundancy and ambiguity, working in the sphere of what is called cultural evolution, where language, both spoken and written, appears to play a determining role').[36] The externalization and mediation – what Derrida would call the delegation – of vital processes in the form of technology permits a certain detachment from the constraints of nature. In what is perhaps the most extreme example of delegating technology, the abstraction of symbolic systems, there is an unprecedented degree of manipulability or play, over and above the restricted economy of natural determinants. These systems, these dead articulations or extensions of the somatic and the psychic, which simulate life and mind are arguably *the* subject of Derrida's philosophical enquiry. This is not to say that he recognizes there to be a break between 'nature' and 'culture'. The relieving instance of (Western) alphabetic culture, for example, is not viewed by him to be in any sense foreign to human nature, as is the case with the onto-theological tradition (Plato, Rousseau, Husserl) that refuses or represses the supplement of technology and writing. Again, what Derrida is describing when he speaks of writing in the normal sense of the word is perhaps best represented by the structure of articulation: writing is both adherent to and detached from the psycho-somatic instance it relieves. Despite the articulating break of nature ('biology', 'ecology') with culture ('writing'), there is at the same time a profound continuity which closed-system, logocentric philosophy has been content to suppress.

When, therefore, Derrida aphoristically proposes that the term is a germ and the germ is a term, he is not simply proposing an appropriate, but ultimately arbitrary, metaphor. Derrida himself has said that metaphor is never innocent. The metaphor of writing, as it is articulated with the genetic and the biological in Derrida's texts, is not simply metaphor. As Derrida says in 'La pharmacie de Platon' apropos of Plato, 'dans toutes ces *comparaisons* avec l'écriture, il ne faut pas prendre les lettres à la lettre' (*D*1, p. 184) ('in all these *comparisons* with writing, we are not supposed to take the letters *literally*' (*D*2, p. 159)); and in the passage quoted earlier concerning the preface and the (genetic) pro-gramme, he insists that the use of the scriptural metaphor in genetic science is more than metaphor ('partout où [la science] doit compter, plus que métaphoriquement, avec les problèmes de l'écriture et de la différence' ('wherever science should take into account, more than metaphorically, the problems of writing and difference')). One could attempt here to employ a more discriminating vocabulary, to speak of isomorphism rather than metaphor. But even this is not a sufficient approximation of what Derrida is arguing, it merely displaces the problem which is that the similarity of form (isomorphism) of writing and genetic code is indicative of their *identity*. Quite literally, the term *is* a germ and the germ *is* a term. Viewed from within the context of evolution, which is a continuum, they are the *same thing*. Functionally, there is a genetic or genealogical continuity between the two, an unbroken line of descent from the one to the other.[37] Of course, formulated in this way, this genealogy would appear to be self-evident, but as Derrida's analyses of speech and writing show, the logocentric tradition has consistently denied and repressed such a continuity, drawing a limit to the 'human' at the frontier of speech, as if speech were not also a (communication) technology. As is demonstrated in the impressive reasoning of *De la grammatologie* and texts contemporary to it, speech is simply an instance of the generalized writing that is the structure of all systems. This general writing, like writing in the common sense of the word or, more precisely, of which writing is an extension, is the condition of possibility of the transmission of information (communication) within or between all complex systems. As Wilden reminds us, without the trace, the consigning of information to a memory or archive, there is no communication.[38] The genetic code which ensures the invariant reproduction of species is just an example (though for 'man' and 'life', the most important example) of such a writing.

It follows that Derrida's articulation of the biological and the textual ('the term is a germ') does not simply place writing proper in the wider, enveloping context of the genetic, but in turn presents the genetic as a subset or special case of the more abstract category of the trace. So the above formulation could be rephrased more clearly as 'the term (scriptural) is a germ (genetic) is a term (trace)', which expresses an ascending order of generality. If the continuity of species taught by Darwinian science in the nineteenth century prompted many to ask what is man?, the findings of genetics, cybernetics and information theory in the twentieth century inevitably lead to Schrödinger's question, what is life?

'Life', as Derrida knows or understands it, is carried over into our cultural space in the most exemplary fashion in the form of written codes. This explains the persistence of biological and genetic metaphors in his texts, metaphors which are neither idle nor innocent. Apart from the complex system of associations established in the 'sister' texts *Glas* and *La dissémination*, there is a series of other texts which continue to elaborate upon these biological and genealogical figures. In these texts, it becomes clearer that Derrida is not simply enunciating a law (the co-implication of the genetic and the textual and, ultimately, the primacy of the trace or equivalent 'concepts' as a structuring principle), but that in enunciating this law, the inflection he lends to established systems of knowledge amounts to an *active* management of our literal heritage, something like a bio-technology. But again, this is anticipation.

THE DESCENT OF (LOGOCENTRIC) MAN

Like the Darwinian descent of man, or the descent of atoms in the atomist theories, for Derrida texts, and the philosophical, scientific or ideological systems they support, *descend*. On the one hand, their descent is accidental, without an absolute origin or an absolute *telos*. On the other hand, the accident becomes necessary, chance constellates *après coup*, *nachträglich*, in the form of a code that is conserved, archived, reproduced from generation to generation. Like the prehistory of biological evolution, the history of Western thought is characterized by this descent (Hegel would say the ascent) of ever increasing constraints, resulting in the powerful logocentric tradition, whose implicit project is to contain any future evolution within its own reappropriating circle. Of course, the hierarchical constraints established during this history are not a necessary finality of the system, its *eschaton* or *telos*, but simply the result of 'frozen accidents'.[39] They are necessary only in the sense that they push the future development of the system *a tergo*, from behind, from the past. This *a tergo* structure (again, the sexual metaphor is not arbitrary) is described by Derrida in *La carte postale*. The twin fathers of Western philosophy, Plato and Socrates, as they are depicted in a postcard from the Bodleian Library in Oxford, with Plato standing *behind* Socrates and dictating to him, have handed down to us the most constraining of legacies. The genetic metaphors used here are significant: 'Plato veut émettre. Artificiellement, techniquement, de la semence. Ce démon de Socrates tient la seringue. Ensemencer la terre entière, envoyer la même carte fertile à *tout le monde*. Une pancarte que nous avons dans le dos et sur laquelle nous ne pourrons jamais vraiment nous retourner' (*CP*, p. 33) ('*Plato* wants to emit. Seed, artificially, technically. That devil of a *Socrates* holds the syringe. To sow the entire earth, to send the same fertile card to *everyone*. A *pancarte*, a pan-card, a billboard that we have on our backs and to which we can never really turn round' (*PC*, p. 28)). So we are all quite literally Plato's children. His artificial insemination, via Socrates' pen, coded 'like' the genetic code, reproduces itself invariantly, unilaterally ('la même carte fertile', 'une pancarte') from generation to generation, even down to 'poor' Freud, who inherits 'sans trop le savoir' ('without being too aware of it'), 'un ensemble de contraintes logiques' ('an ensemble of logical constraints') (*CP*, p. 60; *PC*, p. 53). In *Otobiographies*, Derrida describes this constraining heritage as a 'puissante machine programmatrice' ('powerful programming machine') or an 'implacable programme' which have governed our thinking for twenty-five centuries and more. Again, these metaphors, taken from the ambient culture of information technology and cybernetics, are more than simply metaphors, in the sense that the ideas of 'machine' and 'programme' are not for Derrida separable from 'life': 'Cette "machine" n'est évidemment plus une machine au sens classiquement philosophique, puisque la "vie" en est ou fait partie et qu'elle joue avec l'opposition vie/mort. Ce "programme" n'est pas davantage un programme au sens téléologique ou mécaniste du terme' (*OT*, p. 95) ('Obviously, this "machine" is no longer a machine in the classical philosophical sense, because there is "life" in it or "life" takes part in it, and because it plays with the opposition life/death. Nor would it be correct to say that this "program" is a program in the teleological or mechanistic sense of the term' (*EO*, p. 29)).

Following, with the necessary cautions, Derrida's genetic and cybernetic 'metaphors', the descent of Western metaphysics is therefore equivalent to the reproduction of a powerful and pervasive code. However, in the same way that the transmission of genetic or cybernetic information is not an entirely deterministic process, so the execution of the logocentric programme is not without complications. To begin with, there is the problem of reproduction (or repetition) which, as Derrida has shown, is never pure and simple. In Plato's closed shop (as in Hegel's circular economy), reproduction is ideally the return of the same, son is like father, the paternal seed always arrives at its destination. As Derrida remarks in 'Envois', Plato, through the written deposit of his dialogues and letters, through Socrates to whom he dictates, wants to send himself his own child (*CP*, p. 111; *PC*, p. 101). This is the mono-sexual (circular, restricted, ideal) economy of auto-insemination (see Derrida's remarks in *Glas* on the self-inseminating God, quoted above). The problem is that reproduction, the emission or transmission of seed, requires an exit from the homely economy of the same, which means a certain death. The seed or the sign is a consigning of 'life' in dead matter, the external delegation of its structure and function. Hegel saw the sign as a kind of tomb (*sôma/sêma*), as Derrida reminds us in 'Le puits et la pyramide': 'Le tombeau, c'est la vie du corps comme signe de mort, le corps comme autre de l'âme, de la psyché animée, du souffle vivant. Mais le tombeau, c'est aussi ce qui abrite, garde en réserve, thésaurise la vie en marquant qu'elle continue ailleurs ... De la vie, il consacre la disparition en attestant sa persévérance' (*M*1, p. 95) ('The tomb is the life of the body as the sign of death, the body as the other of the soul, the other of the animate psyche, of the living breath. But the tomb also shelters, maintains in reserve, capitalizes on life by marking that life continues elsewhere ... It consecrates the disappearance of life by attesting to the perseverance of life' (*M*2, p. 82)). The necessity of this passage through, or passion of, the other (the seed, the sign) exposes the living (Idea) to failure or contamination. This is neither accidental nor contingent, but is the fate of all communication (reproduction may be seen as a special case of communication). As one learns from information theory, communication requires a *channel* – here that of the term or germ – and the channel is never properly free from noise. The pure passage of the message is impossible, since the medium always affects the message. The phenomenological reactivation of the origin of geometry dreamt of by Husserl assumes an unbroken chain of Being, a continuity of living thought apart from and outside of the supplement of the dead archive. But as Derrida shows in his Introduction to Husserl's book, such reactivation necessarily entails the exteriorization and digitalization of the supposedly self-present consciousness, at both ends of the communicational process. The difference is the same as that between Hegel's *Erinnerung* and *Gedächtnis*, as examined by Derrida (commenting on de Man) in 'L'art des mémoires'. For Hegel, *Gedächtnis* is 'la mémoire qui pense ... *et* la mémoire volontaire, la faculté mécanique de mémorisation' ('both memory that thinks ... and voluntary memory, specifically the mechanical faculty of memorization'), while *Erinnerung* is 'la mémoire intériorisante, le souvenir "comme recueuillement intérieur et comme conservation de l'expérience"' ('interiorizing memory, "recollection as the inner gathering and preserving of experience"') (*ME*1, p. 64; *ME*2, p. 51). *Erinnerung* is therefore the re-membering, re-appropriating memory, it is in the Platonic–Husserlian tradition of anamnesis, Meno's slave intuitively reviving the chain of geometrical reasoning in spite of himself, without mediation, without loss, through and in spite of the sediment of generations. On the other hand, as Freud would doubtless confirm, we are all subject to disturbances of memory, a deficiency which we supplement with a note, a 'materialized portion', as Freud puts it, of our memnic apparatus. If one accepts, with this materialist tradition, which Freud does and does not inherit, that all memory (= reproduction = communication) requires a support or a channel, then de-legation, the dis-membering articulation of the psycho-somatic (Hegel's *Gedächtnis*) is inevitable. Such remote control, or communication at a distance, always carries with it the danger of interference by a 'third' party, a parasite who will intercept the message and inflect or divert it to his or her own ends, within and according to a specific context.[40] Expressed in the language of 'Envois', the letter never (necessarily) arrives at its destination, 'une lettre *peut* toujours *ne pas* arriver à destination' (*CP*, p. 135) ('a letter *can* always *not* arrive at its destination' (*PC*, p. 123)). The proviso of 'necessarily' is crucial here, because Derrida does not say that all communication is doomed to failure (which is as deterministic as the opposite proposition) but that the possibility of a failure in communication is inherent to all systems, is their very condition of possibility: 'Non que la lettre n'arrive jamais à destination, mais il appartient à sa structure de pouvoir, toujours, ne pas y arriver'; 'on peut dire qu'elle n'y arrive jamais vraiment, que quand elle arrive, son pouvoir-ne-pas-arriver la tourmente d'une dérive interne' (*CP*, pp. 472, 517) ('Not that the letter never arrives at its destination, but it belongs to the structure of the letter to be capable, always, of not arriving'; 'one can say that it never truly arrives, that when it does arrive its capacity not to arrive torments it with an internal drifting' (*PC*, pp. 444, 489)).

This notion of the undecidability of destination, a central theme of *La carte postale*, is in many ways similar to what is argued in cybernetic and communication theory, where the reliability of a system, paradoxically it would seem (though the paradox exists only from the point of view of a traditional, deterministic science, restricted to the study of simple systems), depends upon the 'looseness' of its connections. This looseness is a defining feature of what Ashby calls the 'ultrastable' or 'multistable' system, a system which has a number of possible stable states. As Atlan puts it: 'Une caractéristique importante de tels systèmes ... est qu'ils ne peuvent exister sans une certaine quantité de bruit, sous la forme d'un certain degré d'aléatoire dans les connections, ou d'un certain nombre d'"erreurs" dans le fonctionnement de leurs composants' ('An important characteristic of such systems is that they cannot exist without a certain quantity of noise, in the form of a certain degree of randomness in their connections, or a certain amount of "error" in the functioning of their parts').[41] If all components or circuits of a system were finalized, the result would be a kind of paralysis: the system would be unable to adapt to a changing environment, it would hold no reserves of alternatives to draw upon.[42]

This idea of 'looseness' is similar to the concept of equifinality described earlier: while the overall goal of the open system is to persevere or to reproduce itself, there are a number of ways of getting there, and these alternative paths may, by a process of feedback with a changing environment, actually change the structure or programme of the system – the process of morphogenesis described by Bateson as characteristic of biological and ecological systems: the more such systems attempt to remain stable, the more they change, or, as Bateson expresses it, *'plus c'est la même chose, plus ça change'*.[43]

It is perhaps this structure of evolutionary drift that is being described in the footnote appended to Derrida's assertion in 'Envois' of the meaninglessness of proving a law of non-destination, quoted above:

'Une lettre *peut* toujours *ne pas* arriver à destination, etc.' C'est une chance*.

*La malchance (la mal-adresse) de cette chance, c'est que pour *pouvoir* ne pas arriver, cela doit comporter en soi une force et une structure telles, une *dérive de destination* [my emphasis], que cela *doit* aussi ne pas arriver de toute façon. Même en arrivant... la lettre se soustrait *à l'arrivée*. Elle arrive ailleurs, toujours plusieurs fois. Tu ne peux plus la prendre. C'est la structure de la lettre (comme carte postale, autrement dit la fatale partition qu'elle doit supporter) qui veut ça. (*CP*, p. 135)

('A letter *can* always *not* arrive at its destination, etc.' This is a chance.*

*The mischance (the mis-address) of this chance is that in order *to be able* not to arrive, it must bear within itself a force and a structure, a straying of the destination, such that it *must* also not arrive in any way. Even in arriving ... the letter takes itself away *from the arrival at arrival*. It arrives elsewhere, always several times. You can no longer take hold of it. It is the structure of the letter (as post card, in other words the fatal partition that it must support) which demands this.) (*PC*, pp. 123–4)

The endless division ('partition') of the letter, or in Derrida's bio-genetic language, the splitting and scattering of seed through dissemination, results in an inflected *telos* ('dérive de destination' ('a straying of the destination')), a pluralization of trajectories ('elle arrive ailleurs, toujours plusieurs fois' ('it arrives elsewhere, always several times')), comparable to the concept of multifinality explained above (evolution, it will be remembered, is a multifinal process). To return to the question of Plato's children, to the postcard he sends to Western science and metaphysics, it is difficult to see, given the logic of the letter or seed as Derrida describes it, how Plato's message ever arrives, how his legacy can be anything other than a bastard one. And so it is. Despite his efforts, like Freud, to manage and police his succession through the extended family of an institution (the Academy, the Psychoanalytical Institution) and through his writings, his descendants differentiate, proliferate and people the earth in Babelian confusion.[44] It is as if the very survival of the Platonic lineage is dependent upon its corruption, the inflection of its destination, as soon as it is consigned to the archive, to the necessary death of (bisexual) reproduction.

All this is not to say that the (dead) letter or postcard sent by Plato did not arrive, and in the most momentous of fashions, in the logo- and phallocentric reflex that would now condition and programme all of our thinking. If we are the bastard children of Plato, then our reflex is nonetheless to establish a pure line of descent from father to son. Just as Plato is anxious to secure his succession, so his bastard progeny feel it necessary to legitimate their genealogy. Placed at the receiving end of the chain of communication, they attempt to purge the message of its noise. This is true, for example, of the scholars Derrida criticizes in 'Envois', who need either to authenticate or disown the more doubtful of Plato's letters (*CP*, p. 93; *PC*, p. 84). Derrida himself finds these contested letters the most interesting of all, because it is precisely their divergences from what is commonly known to be 'Plato' that present us with the possibility that he himself (like Derrida) is a 'bastard'. The source, the origin of the message is itself divided. As Derrida points out in 'Mes chances', Plato disowns the materialist side of his parentage by systematically eliminating references to Democritus from his texts:

La tradition démocritéene, dans laquelle s'inscrit le nom d'Épicure et de ses disciples, a été soumise, dès l'origine et d'abord sous l'autorité violente de Platon, à un puissant refoulement tout au long de l'histoire de la culture occidentale. On peut maintenant en suivre la symptomatologie, à commencer par l'effacement du nom de Démocrite dans les écrits de Platon alors même que Platon connaissait sa doctrine. Il redoutait probablement qu'on ne tire quelque conclusion quant à la proximité, voire à la filiation de certains de ses philosophèmes. (MC, p. 24)

(The Democritean tradition, in which the names of Epicurus and his disciples are recorded, has been submitted since its origin (and initially under the violent authority of Plato) to a powerful repression. One can now follow its symptomatology, which begins with the effacement of the name of Democritus in the writings of Plato , even though Plato was familiar with his doctrine. Plato probably feared that one would draw some conclusion with respect to the proximity, indeed to the filiation, of some of his philosophemes.) (*TC*, p. 18)

This scrubbing out of Democritus is equivalent to the two-handed movement of p-S described in 'Envois', a simultaneous inscription (of the onto-theological) and effacement (of the materialist). Such repression is possible precisely because of the testamentary nature of the reproduction of ideas, referred to above; at the same time, however, the bequeathed body of knowledge bears traces of its repressions. As we know, repression is not suppression; the materialist strand of Western philosophy subsists as a shadow of logocentric discourse, as one of its half-hidden virtualities. Derrida's analysis of the body of Western metaphysics – 'analysis' in its most literal sense, the loosening of constraints – is intended to reactivate such virtualities. Expressed in the bio-genetic idiom examined in this chapter, one could say that it is something like a *bio-technology*.

BIO-TECHNOLOGY AND 'NATURAL' SELECTION

The descent of logocentrism, it was learnt above, is not irrevocable. What returns from generation to generation is not necessarily the same. Derrida recognizes the power of the logocentric tradition, but not its absolute necessity. Its only necessity is an *a tergo* and a posteriori necessity, not an a priori or teleological one. It is a frozen accident rather than a divine law. The question is, how can one intervene practically, technically, so to speak, in order to break its vicious circle? Derrida appears to believe that one should be able not simply to describe its code, but also to transform it. In the passage of *Otobiographies* quoted above, Derrida referred to the co-implication of 'life' and 'machine' in the strictly programmed development of Western philosophy. He continues: 'La "machine programmatrice" qui m'intéresse ici n'appelle pas seulement au déchiffrement, mais aussi à la transformation, à la récriture pratique, selon un rapport théorie/pratique qui, si possible, ne fasse plus partie du programme' (*OT*, pp. 95–6) ('The "programming machine" that interests me here does not call only for decipherment but for transformation – that is, a practical rewriting according to a theory-practice relationship which, if possible, would no longer be part of the program' (*EO*, p. 30)). Given the appropriate technology, the 'oreille fine' (finely tuned ear) of deconstruction, as it is described in *Otobiographies* and *L'oreille de l'autre*, one can therefore tamper with the code. The specificity of the linguistic code, especially in its written form, is that by virtue of its semi-detached relation to 'vital' processes, it is reversible and time-independent: one can produce and present one's fathers. Like Plato in relation to Socrates, it is possible to be one's own grandfather. Freud, who as we have seen, has Plato pushing him in the back, does much the same thing to Plato, thus inverting the patri-unilinear sequence of father-son: 'c'est alors Platon l'héritier, pour Freud. Qui fait à Platon un peu le coup que celui-ci a fait à Socrate' (*CP*, p. 33) ('it is then Plato who is the inheritor, for Freud. Who pulls the same trick, somewhat on Plato that Plato pulls on Socrates' (*PC*, p. 28)). This 'rétroactivité fabuleuse', as Derrida terms it, is in effect a kind of feedback: the input (*a tergo*, from the past) is filtered, selected, inflected (compressed or amplified).

If Derrida's bio-genetic metaphor is followed to its logical conclusion, then his proposed rewriting of the logocentric programme could be expressed in terms of genetic manipulation. In genetic technology, alterations in the DNA of a cell are obtained by means of the splicing and grafting of sequences of the genetic code, and this recombination of sequences can serve to modify aspects of metabolism or anatomical structure. In Derrida's system, not only is the term (like) a germ, but the atomic germ-term also agglutinates into what might be described as a *molecular* formation, words or concepts combine to form specific 'sequences'. The metaphor of the sequence is a consistent one in Derrida's work, extending across a whole range of texts from *De la grammatologie* onwards, and normally refers to the conceptual complexes, the 'chains' of reasoning or 'philosophemes', which constitute the body of our philosophical tradition. This is the image conveyed in the extremely suggestive first page of 'Economimesis', where Derrida describes the crossing and interference of philosophemes or textual sequences over time in the following manner:

Pliées à un nouveau système, les grandes séquences se déplacent, changent de sens et de fonction. Une fois introduit dans un autre réseau, le 'même' philosophème n'est plus le même, et il n'a d'ailleurs jamais eu d'identité hors de son fonctionnement. Simultanément, les philosophèmes 'inédits', s'il en est, dès lors qu'ils entrent en composition articulée avec des philosophèmes hérités, s'en trouvent affectés sur toute leur surface et sous tous leurs plis. (*E*1, p. 57)

(Folded into a new system, the long sequences are displaced; their sense and their function change. Once inserted into another network, the 'same' philosopheme is no longer the same, and besides it never had an identity external to its functioning. Simultaneously 'unique and original' philosophemes, if there are any, as soon as they enter into articulated composition with inherited philosophemes, are affected by that composition over the whole of their surface and under every angle.) (*E*2, p. 3)

This contextual and adaptational interpretation of the evolution of philosophical systems is similar to Derrida's argument regarding the *insignifiance marquante* of the *stoikheia*, quoted in the previous chapter: they are motivated and meaningful only in that they are located within a particular series of terms; without such association or intersection, they are nothing. The difference here is that it is no longer simply a question of the random collisions of atoms, the motivating 'glu' of the aleatory encounter, but of another level of combination and organization, the 'molecular' sequences which fold and combine at specific points or angles of their surfaces in what can only be described, by analogy with the terminology of molecular biology, as *stereospecific* conjunction.

When, therefore, it is a question of practical intervention, of the rewriting of the logocentric code, Derrida's model or metaphor is the cutting and transplanting of the 'sequences' or 'chains' (philosophemes) one finds embedded in the text of Western philosophy, that is, something approaching a biotechnology. The first systematic use of this analogy is to be found in 'La dissémination', which is an extended commentary or 'cooperative reading' (*P*1, p, 61; *P*2, p. 44) of Philippe Sollers' *Nombres*.[45] Sollers' book is not conventional narrative fiction, rather it is an extreme parody of what all narrative, 'literary' or otherwise, is about. In *Nombres*, Sollers quotes, paraphrases and juxtaposes material from the most heterogeneous sources, from literature to philosophy, from science to politics, in the process calling into question the reality or validity of such generic divisions. Derrida calls this citational practice the 'prélèvement', as in the taking of a blood sample or the removal of an organ, or the 'greffe' (graft, transplant). His account of the 'prélèvement' recalls the passional or violent character of inscription, discussed in previous chapters: 'Violence appuyée et discrète d'une incision inapparente dans l'épaisseur du texte, insémination calculée de l'allogène en prolifération par laquelle les deux textes se transforment, se déforment l'un par l'autre, se contaminent dans leur contenu, tendent parfois à se rejeter, passent elliptiquement l'un dans l'autre et s'y régénèrent dans la répétition' (*D*1, p. 395) ('It is the sustained, discrete violence of an incision that is not apparent in the thickness of the text, a calculated insemination of the

proliferating allogene through which the two texts are transformed, deform each other, contaminate each other's content,
tend at times to reject each other, or pass elliptically one into the
other and become regenerated in the repetition' (*D*2, p. 355)).[46]
Though Derrida is firstly describing Sollers' text in this passage,
with a peculiar reflexive or torsional gesture he is also describing
his own strategy of transformation, a key instrument of which is
citation, equivalent to a kind of genetic manipulation of
sequences. In 'Limited Inc.' he argues that quotation, or a
certain kind of quotation, *alters* that which it supposedly
reproduces: 'une certaine pratique de la citation, de l'itération
aussi ... travaille, *altère* toujours, aussitôt, aussi sec, ce qu'elle
paraît reproduire ... L'itération altère, quelque chose de nouveau a lieu' (LI1, p. 12) ('a certain practice of citation, and also
of iteration ... is at work, constantly *altering*, at once and without
delay ... whatever it seems to reproduce. Iteration alters,
something new takes place' (LI2, p. 40)). In the contaminating
and contaminated context of its new environment, the trans-
planted sequence repeats its origin *elliptically*. It is important
here to note the reciprocal nature of this citational practice: it
does not maintain the fiction of objective detachment from the
incorporated sequence – the techno-logocentric distinction between subject and object, user and instrument. The discrete-
continuous articulation of the cited and the citing instance
results in a kind of circular (elliptical) causality or feedback:
each instance is affected by the other ('les deux textes se
transforment, se déforment l'un par l'autre, se contaminent
dans leur contenu' ('the two texts are transformed, deform each
other, contaminate each other's content')). This feedback is not
the same as that described earlier, in the case of a certain Freud
and a certain Plato, who retroactively and selectively repress
elements of their forebears. In this latter case, the process could
be compared to *negative* feedback, where the input is measured
against an 'ideal' state and its effects on the system kept within
the limits prescribed by that ideal, that is, the kind of feedback
one finds in the homeostatic system. In contrast, the feedback
described here is *positive* feedback, in the sense that the
incorporated sequence is not restricted to the *telos* of the

incorporating milieu, but through its contaminating influence on that milieu sets in train an exponential amplification of differences. Unlike the controlled, restricted economy of citation practised by positivistic discourse (which attempts to maintain an aseptic distance between itself and its 'sources'), the process does not end with the instrumental quoting of an example illustrating a truth – as is the case with Freud's narrowly didactic use of literature described in *La carte postale*. With Derrida's citational grafts, the sequence generated from the finite implant is literally infinite, its trajectory incalculable, its analysis interminable. The surgical, bio-technological practice of the 'prélèvement' or the 'greffe citationnelle' is the narrow, finite window through which an infinite context is summoned forth.

At this point, it would be legitimate to ask how this philosophy or, more exactly, practice of the transplant actually brings about the rewriting of the logocentric programme proposed by Derrida above. Quite clearly, he does not propose to replace this code with a more powerful or a more adequate code, whatever that might mean. Indeed, such a manœuvre would depend upon knowledge of what was in the last instance the 'true', the 'adequate', in other words, upon a teleology of finished form. Derrida's selection of sequences is obviously not teleological: the immeasurable, exponential growth to which it gives rise has no single direction or meaning, it is dissemination and bifurcation rather than purpose or *telos*. At the same time, it is not a random process, whatever Derrida may say in 'Mes chances' about his 'falling upon' certain texts. In short, and somewhat tautologically, Derrida's selection of textual sequences is itself highly selective, with the difference that he selects not according to the fixed (teleological) form of truth, but the difference of *forces*, like Nietzsche, who is never able definitively to sign his work:

Nietzsche a le plus grand mal à signer, il veut signer mais il est obligé de différer sa signature, de la confier à quelque chose comme le retour éternel ... qui ne signera pas une fois en posant une identité mais qui indéfiniment signera le plus fort ... sélectionnera le plus fort et finalement ne signera que sous la forme de différences des forces et des qualités. (*OA*, p. 79)

(Nietzsche has great trouble signing. He wants to sign but he is obliged to defer his signature, to entrust it to something like the eternal return which will not sign just once by stating an identity. Rather, it will sign the strongest indefinitely, it will select the strongest, and finally it will sign only in the form of the difference of forces and qualities.) (*EO*, p. 57)

Derrida's own selection of forces is intended to keep the system moving, to ensure the continual transformation of the code, the continuous differentiation of the 'supplément de code', as it was described above. This means a process of selection that is no longer part of the code ('qui ne fasse plus partie du programme', *OT*, p. 96; *EO*, p. 30). A good ear is needed, like Nietzsche's 'oreille fine', an ear sensitive to the minimal difference, open to what Derrida calls the 'tout autre', the monstrous. This active selection of forces Derrida sometimes calls 'deconstruction'.[47]

What is strange is that deconstruction, the selection of more powerful forces, when considered in the context of the bio-genetic metaphors examined in this chapter, seems to approximate to a form of 'natural' selection. There is a lateral reference to this in Derrida's description of Nietzsche's 'sélection du plus fort', quoted above. Like evolution, deconstruction is blind to the extent that its essence, if such a word can be used, is precisely the impossibility of a project, the impossibility of the *telos*. While (inevitably) inhabiting our immemorial descendance, experiencing its implacable determination, it is at the same time the continuous sifting and transformation of this descendance, a turning back on itself in order to proceed, a continual, elliptical passage through the origin. Like evolution, and like Freud's analysis, this continuous sifting of the past is an interminable process; like Mallarmé's throw of the dice, its 'compte total en formation' can never be arrested in the form of one code and one finality. Like natural selection, it operates upon minimal differences, minimal displacements which become amplified into changes of the most monstrous character. 'L'avenir absolu ne peut s'annoncer que sous l'espèce de la monstruosité, au delà de toutes les formes ou les normes anticipables, au delà des genres' (*SCH*, p. 102) ('The absolute future can only announce itself under the species of the monstrous, beyond all anticipable forms or norms, beyond all genera').

In this assimilation of deconstruction and natural selection, the word 'like' should be used with caution. As has been pointed out, the bio-genetic metaphor in Derrida's work is both metaphor and more than metaphor. The conventional impulse when confronted with analogies of this kind is to attempt to insulate the two halves of the equation: analogy is simply analogy, more or less appropriate or adequate to its object, but nothing more than this. One might, using a more discriminating terminology, speak of 'model' or 'isomorphism', but the isolating gesture remains. For Derrida, on the other hand, language is an open system, it is open at the top to the infinite possibilities of semiotic freedom ('jeu'), and at the bottom to the biological instance it subsumes. The separation between the biological and the textual is fictional, rhetorical, discursive, a theoretical fiction, since the one is simply an articulated (adherent and detached) continuation of the other. One arrives therefore at the rather surprising conclusion that more than simply 'imitating' the march of evolution, more than being 'like' a form of natural selection, deconstruction *is* evolution. It is survival itself, the continual filtering of virtualities, of our infinite, immemorial descent, the *Über-leben* that perseveres over and above the economy of 'life'. This recognition – and enactment – of the continuum of the 'natural' world is profoundly materialist. If there is any truth in deconstruction, it is in this mundane truth of common descent rather than in the ascendent (idealist) truth of the teleological horizon. Perhaps it is to this that Henry Staten was alluding, with his intriguing assertion: 'My own view is that deconstruction and everything else are ultimately contained by Darwin's tale – but that is another story and will wait for another day.'[48]

Conclusion
Metaphor and more than metaphor

L'inéluctable, c'est la pré-impression et cela marque la désistance du sujet ... Mais cela n'entraîne pas encore que l'inéluctable se laisse concevoir comme un programme génétique ou une prédestination historique. Ce sont là des déterminations supplémentaires et tardives.

(*PS*, p. 598)

(Ineluctability is pre-impression, and this marks the desistance of the subject ... But this does not imply that the ineluctable might be conceived of as a genetic program or a historical predestination; rather, the latter are supplemental and late determinations of it.)

(DE, p. 2)

The analysis of the categories of system and writing attempted in this book might ultimately have followed any of a number of possible paths through Derrida's texts. The rhetorical coherence and continuity of Derrida's work makes it possible to depart from different sets of linguistic associations and still arrive at what would basically be the same formal structure. Expressed in system-cybernetic language, Derrida's discursive system is itself highly overdetermined or equifinal. Despite this 'looseness' or 'play' in Derrida's system, and hence the difficulty in reducing it to a set of isolable concepts, the formal rigour of his argument remains undiminished; and despite the differences in style and subject matter that characterize his published work of the past thirty years, his theory of system and writing remains re- remarkably consistent. The following description recapitulates some of the main elements of this theory. It follows the general schema (infinity, inscription, the economy) set forth in the second chapter, but adds to it the qualification and amplification provided in subsequent chapters.

1 There is a certain infinity that is the precondition of the system as such, its possibility or virtuality. However, this infinity is nothing in itself. It is not 'before' the system in the simple sense of the word, nor is it transcendent in the classically metaphysical or theological sense. Indeed it is arguably more materialist than idealist, and could be seen as something like the total ecology, the total context (spatial and temporal) – that which, when one is considering any system in isolation, always exceeds the determination of its frontiers.

2 Infinity is only presentable (the system is only possible) through the narrow, finite window of determination. Determination requires a minimal departure ('écart') from infinity, a minimal difference, that constitutes the location, the actualization of the infinite within the finite. The minimal difference is of maximal consequence.

3 Determination is not predetermination. Though structure, stricture and coding are the necessary conditions of the system, and contain its tendency to exponential 'démesure', they are not the sufficient conditions for its persistence or survival. If determination were simply the intentioned appropriation and containment of the infinite, the pre-established harmony of sense (meaning, direction, *telos*), then the system would become paralysed in a circular repetition of the same, which is death. On the contrary, determination, as Derrida sees it, is a blind precipitation towards sense, through which becoming is, so to speak, stamped with the authority of being only after the event (*après coup*, *nachträglich*). Furthermore, the undecidability of the inaugural instance, the danger and violence of such precipitation or descent is not abolished in one sweep. The inaugural is also percurrent, chance inhabits necessity (in this connection, Derrida frequently quotes Mallarmé's 'Un coup de dés jamais n'abolira le hasard'). The reappropriation or containment (the reproduction) of the inaugural difference can never be absolute, and the closure of the system is only possible through its continued (repeated) opening. It is not a question of standing or falling, but of continuously standing *and* falling, walking *and*

limping. The possibility of this failure of destination is a constitutional weakness of the system, but it is also its strength. The system works because it does not work. This double bind of divergent tendencies, of force and form, destination and detour, constraint and excess, treads the thin line between the restricted and the general economy. The element of play or non-finalization in the system is the condition of its survival; given the openness of the system to environmental change, to the unanticipated and incalculable intrusion of the event, it offers the possibility of new structures, in short, of evolution. As in Heidegger's dramatic reversal of Aristotle, 'higher than actuality stands *possibility*'.[1]

Such would be the logic of the systems described in Derrida's texts, a logic that is dependent upon the model or metaphor of writing. Thus the equivocal moment of determination, upon which the system turns, can be translated as the moment of inscription. The metaphor of inscription points to and makes evident the necessity of the localization of difference or determination, its passage through (but not its presence in) the space of this world. Difference, or the repetition of difference, is the condition of the system, but it requires a support, it must be written (violently, in Derrida's estimation) into some structure. Difference is impossible without the trace, and the consistent recourse in the history of Western philosophical thought to the scriptural model, when it is a question of describing the differential structure of systems, is no accident. In Plato, for example, 'la "métaphore" scripturale intervient donc chaque fois que la différence et la relation sont irréductibles, chaque fois que l'altérité introduit la détermination et met un système en circulation' (*D1*, p. 189) ('the scriptural "metaphor" thus [comes into play] every time difference and relation are irreducible, every time otherness introduces determination and puts a system in circulation' (*D2*, p. 163)).

But as the quotation marks around the word 'métaphore' indicate, writing is both metaphor and more than metaphor. This is because for Derrida writing in its common sense is not only a useful model for the differential structure of systems, it is also in its general sense the fundamental structure of systems.

This emphasis on the fundamental nature of writing has often exposed Derrida to the charge of practising the 'onto-theology' he so readily criticizes in others.[2] Apart from Derrida's own strenuous efforts to demarcate himself from such positions, one possible response to such criticisms would be to underline the similarity of Derrida's reference to writing with other, wider configurations of contemporary thought, none of which could be said to be 'onto-theological'. The similarity of Derrida's formulation of writing, trace and other afferent concepts to some of the central concepts of information, cybernetic and systems theory would tend to invalidate or at least relativize the somewhat precipitate conclusion that he is simply restating a classically transcendental position with respect to writing and difference. The homology between Bateson's definition of difference[3] and Derrida's numerous qualifications of the non-substantiality and non-localizability of the trace is just one example of this.

Derrida himself situates his philosophy of the trace at least partly within this wider context. From his earliest texts he is aware of, and makes clear, the fact that the logocentric repression of writing is to an extent only now visible and understandable in the light of recent developments in contemporary science. While Derrida's work itself remains within what might conventionally be defined as philosophy (though it also questions the reality or purpose of such generic demarcations), his conception of system and writing nevertheless has some remarkable affinities with the entirely different field of systems theory. The following table summarizes the possible correlations between Derrida's work and some of the main concepts of system-cybernetic thought as they emerged in the previous chapter. Despite the different idioms involved, and, to an extent, the differing points of departure, a case could be made that Derrida's philosophy of writing and systems theory belong to the same major shift of perspective which characterizes late twentieth-century thought. Within this new perspective, of particular significance is the influence of information and cybernetic theory and modern biology (historically, systems theory can be said to have developed out of and generalized the

Derrida	systems theory
'ouverture', double-bound figures of inclusion-exclusion, general economy	open systems
stratification, instance, 'scène'	level, hierarchy
'décision', 'critique'	punctuation of context
inscription, writing, trace	code
'rétroactivité (fabuleuse)'	feedback
'différance', 'après-coup'	teleonomy, 'goalseeking'[4]
'jeu', percurrence of the 'écart' (infinity), failure of destination	equifinality, ultrastability
dissemination	multifinality

findings of these disciplines). While Derrida's primary response to this paradigm is the scriptural model elaborated in the earlier texts, a second response, articulated on the first, and developing from it, is the proliferation of biological, genetic and genealogical metaphors in and after *La dissémination*. This 'turn' in Derrida's writing to the bio-genetic should not be seen as an inflection of his theory of writing towards a kind of organicism or biologism, quite the contrary. Just as systems theory is not simply a variant of previous organicist philosophies, so Derrida is not suggesting the transcendence of the biological. In the closing stages of the last chapter, certain of Derrida's texts appeared to gesture towards a kind of ecology of systems, contained within the wider context of evolution. This does not, however, mean that evolution, at least not in its bio-anthropological sense, is being posited as a possible last instance. In the most empirically limited of senses, that is, considered at the level of the survival of the living system plus its environment, this is quite evidently the case, but Derrida's articulation of the genetic and the textual is not reducible merely to this. The co-implication of biology and technology described in some of Derrida's later texts points to a conception of system and writing before and beyond the instance of 'life'. This point is particularly well articulated in his reading of Benjamin's thoughts on translation in 'Des tours de Babel' (*PS*, pp. 203–35). In the preface to his translation of Baudelaire's

Tableaux parisiens, Die Aufgabe des Übersetzers (*The Task of the Translator*), Benjamin uses a series of familial, genealogical and genetic metaphors to describe the process of translation from one language to another. Benjamin's use of these metaphors is neither innocent nor arbitrary, and Derrida shows Benjamin to be quite aware of this. According to Derrida, the theory behind Benjamin's metaphorical correlation of the textual and the genetic is not simply that we as living beings produce texts, use them, translate the vital into the textual, but that the translation of a text in general is a more fundamental process than life itself. Derrida insists therefore that Benjamin's use of the metaphor of the maturation of a seed, for example (again, it is a question of the seed), in his discussion of the difficulties of translating Mallarmé, is not vitalistic:

L'allusion à la maturation d'une semence pourrait ressembler à une métaphore vitaliste ou génétiste; elle viendrait alors soutenir le code généalogiste et parental qui semble dominer ce texte. En fait, il paraît ici nécessaire d'inverser cet ordre et de reconnaître ce que j'ai ailleurs proposé d'appeler la 'catastrophe métaphorique': loin que nous sachions d'abord ce que veut dire 'vie' ou 'famille' au moment où nous nous servons de ces valeurs familières pour parler de langage et de traduction, c'est au contraire à partir d'une pensée de la langue et de sa 'survie' en traduction que nous accéderions à la pensée de ce que 'vie' et 'famille' veulent dire. (*PS*, p. 213)

(The allusion to the maturation of a seed could resemble a vitalist or geneticist metaphor; it would come, then, in support of the genealogical and parental code which seems to dominate this text. In fact it seems necessary here to invert this order and recognize what I have elsewhere proposed to call the 'metaphoric catastrophe': far from knowing first what 'life' or 'family' mean whenever we use these familiar values to talk about language and translation, it is rather starting from the notion of a language and its 'sur-vival' in translation that we could have access to the notion of what life and family mean.) (TB, p. 178)

This 'catastrophe métaphorique', first referred to in *La carte postale* (*CP*, p. 52; *PC*, p. 46), is equivalent to the 'more than metaphor' ('plus que métaphoriquement') discussed in the preceding chapter: not only is the term a germ, but the germ is, in the most general sense, a term. So the continuous chain that extends from writing (technology) to the biological to evolution is a subset of the more general category of the trace. The enveloping context or condition of possibility is therefore something much wider than the bio-social or the bio-anthropological, the essentializing alliance of 'life' and (at the apex of evolutionary ascent) 'man' being a central tenet of logocentric thinking. Similarly, systems theory, though indebted to modern neo-Darwinian biology with its use of concepts such as teleonomy and equifinality, goes on to formulate a theory of self-organizing and self-regulating systems of which 'life' is but a special case, a regional instance. One arrives therefore at a non-biological theory of evolution in which the testamentary structure of survival (in the delegation and translation of the trace), the supplementary *Über-leben* over and above (before and after) the economy of life, is the organizing principle. It is striking to read Bateson practising what is basically the same metaphorical inversion as Derrida and Benjamin when he describes the adjusted hierarchy system-cybernetic theory has obliged us to adopt: 'Formerly we thought of a hierarchy of taxa – individual, family line, sub-species, species, etc. – as units of survival. We now see a different hierarchy of units – gene-in-organism, organism in environment, ecosystem, etc. Ecology, in the widest sense, turns out to be the study of the interaction and survival of ideas and programs (*i.e.*, differences, complexes of differences, etc.) in circuits'.[5] Again, the terminology differs, but the basic idea, that symbolic systems, or more precisely, the translations between symbolic systems, are the condition of possibility of life, rather than the reverse, remains the same.

Derrida's commentary on Benjamin shows quite clearly that this metaphorical inversion, which is more than simply metaphorical, is consciously articulated in Benjamin's text: the fact that mind, history, art have a 'life' of their own, survive over and above their biological support, leads us to think natural life in terms of the wider life that is history, and not vice versa (*PS*, p. 214; TB, pp. 178–9). At the same time, while Derrida is faithful to the letter of Benjamin's text, his chosen focus ('Suivons le fil de vie ou de survie', *PS*, p. 215 ('Let us follow the thread of life or sur-vival', TB, p. 180)) indicates a selective inflection of Benjamin towards a conceptual and rhetorical field (*Über-leben*, sur-vival, etc.) operative in a series of texts contemporary to 'Des Tours de Babel', most notably in 'Survivre' (*Parages*), *Otobiographies* and *L'oreille de l'autre*.[6] Benjamin speaks of translation as surviving the original, as giving it a second life. It is not simply the reconstitution or reproduction of the sense or content of the original. Derrida extends this argument, and pushes it to its logical limit, by proposing that it is the structure of translation, the structure of survival which is fundamental: 'En ce sens la dimension *survivante* est un *a priori* – et la mort n'y changerait rien' (*PS*, p. 217) ('In this sense the *surviving* dimension is an a priori – and death would not change it at all' (TB, p. 182)). Derrida is thus proposing, via Benjamin, a form of pure translation that is logically prior to the 'original'. This is expressed in more ample terms in the context of the parallel reading of Blanchot and Shelley in 'Survivre':

> La traduction triomphante n'est donc ni la vie ni la mort du texte, seulement ou déjà sa survie. On en dira de même de ce que j'appelle écriture, marque, trace, etc. ça ne vit ni ne meurt, ça survit. Et ça ne 'commence' que par la survie (testament, itérabilité, restance, crypte, détachement déstructurant par rapport à la rection ou direction 'vivante' d'un 'auteur'). (*PA*, pp. 148–9b)

> (Thus triumphant translation is neither the life nor the death of the text, only or already its living *on* ... The same thing will be said of what I call writing, mark, trace, and so on. It neither lives nor dies; it lives *on*. And it 'starts' only with living on (testament, iterability, remaining, crypt, detachment that lifts the strictures of the 'living' *rectio* or direction of an 'author'.) (LO, pp. 102–3b)

If survival for any system is delegation in the trace, the consigning to a 'memory' whose principles are more general than human or even biological (genetic) memory, this memory, which is the 'history' of the system (or more exactly, its future, its future anterior), is therefore not a static script. In an 'evolutionary' situation, reproduction is never reproduction of the same, which is ultimately counter-adaptive. Delegation is also translation. The *Überleben* is the supplementary *Übersetzen* described in Derrida's reading of Benjamin which displaces or transplants what it translates. Survival is only ensured by the alteration (translation) of the original, the differing from itself of the code (the 'supplément de code'), the perpetual rewriting of its history, the percurrence of its infinite, immemorial descendance. If one follows the logic of Derrida's word-play, then the anagram 'trace-écart' examined in chapter 4 provides a suitably condensed definition of this double-bound structure: the trace is both 'reste' and 'restance', deposit and movement. Within this structure, the 'écart' of the trace is more fundamental than its remainder, since it is only through such spacing that new structures and new possibilities are produced. The chance or risk of the 'écart' is percurrent, which means that the system is maintained in an ultrastable (non-finalized) state, open to possibility and change, to the promise of the new.

Derrida's insistence on the primacy of the 'écart' within the 'trace' (of survival over life, of translation over text) again bears a striking resemblance to current thinking on life processes. Whereas biologists have traditionally taken reproduction to be the defining feature of living systems, the category of fluctuation is now considered to be logically prior to that of reproduction. In *L'organisation biologique*, for example, Henri Atlan takes issue with François Jacob's proposition, put forward in *La logique du vivant*, that the 'dream' of the cell is to become two cells, and argues for the logical primacy of perturbation (what he calls the 'écart d'équilibre') as opposed to reproduction in biology:

Un tel principe spinoziste de persévérance dans l'être ne pourrait être admis que s'il s'agissait d'êtres en équilibre. Mais dès qu'on a affaire à des systèmes en état de non équilibre, la reproduction ne peut être première, ni logiquement, ni chronologiquement. Ce qui est premier, c'est la perturbation qui écarte et maintient loin de l'équilibre. La reproduction est alors un mécanisme surajouté grâce à quoi cet écart est maintenu de façon plus efficace et plus économique…

Les algorithmes du monde vivant ne peuvent pas être d'abord des algorithmes de reproduction d'états d'équilibre, mais plutôt d'écarts par rapport à l'équilibre et de retours à cet état par des voies détournées, pendant lesquelles, de façon dynamique, les caractères d'une organisation intégrée peuvent se constituer et se manifester.[7]

(Such a Spinozist principle of the perseverance of being could only be accepted if we were dealing with beings in a state of equilibrium. But as soon as it is a question of systems in a state of non-equilibrium, reproduction cannot be primary, neither logically, nor chronologically. What is primary is the perturbation which diverts the system from the equilibrium state and maintains it in a state far from equilibrium. Reproduction would then be a superadded mechanism by virtue of which this divergence is maintained more efficiently and more economically ...

The algorithms of the living world cannot be primarily algorithms for the reproduction of equilibrium states, but rather algorithms describing departure from equilibrium and the return to this state by roundabout paths, in the course of which the typical features of integrated organization can be dynamically constituted and made apparent.)

The type of systems Atlan is describing here is what the physicist Ilya Prigogine terms 'dissipative structures', or 'systems far from equilibrium', of which life is only one, albeit one significant, example. In contrast to the classical deterministic description of the static system, the defining characteristic of dissipative structures is non-linearity, instability and fluctuation. The dissipative structure is the product of a minimal fluctuation or departure from equilibrium. It is maintained in an ultrastable state only through the continual dissipation of energy, and it is the effort of the system to return to a state of equilibrium which is constitutive of its structure. Structure is therefore the result of an entropic process, order emerges from noise.[8]

A significant philosophical mediation of the model of the dissipative structure is to be found in Michel Serres' reading of Lucretius' *De rerum natura* in his book *La naissance de la physique dans le texte de Lucrèce*.[9] Against traditional interpretations of Lucretius, Serres argues that the concept of the *clinamen*, the corner-stone of Lucretian cosmology, is not an absurdity, but on the contrary provides a powerful analogy for how complex systems, systems far from equilibrium, work. As a random departure or deviation from a state of global equilibrium, represented in the infinitely laminar stream of atoms, the *clinamen* causes the atoms to collide and combine, producing order and structure; but it is also the continuously perturbing force that maintains the system far from equilibrium. Each time the system attains a certain level of stability (homeostasis), each time the random fluctuation has been frozen into a structure (a history, a memory), the structure or system remains open to further destabilization, leading to either its destruction or its passage to a different level of organization. What emerges from Serres' reading of Lucretius' text is a theory of the *clinamen* as a fundamental principle, operating at all levels of organization, before, in and beyond life. He shows how the model of the *clinamen* applies not only at the cosmological level, but equally structures Lucretius' descriptions of other complex states, biological, psychological, social.

What is of particular interest for the present discussion is that in *La naissance de la physique*, the theory of the *clinamen* is consistently articulated upon a concept of writing or inscription. Though logically prior and constitutively percurrent, the 'écart d'équilibre' is nothing if it is not conserved in a code, written into a structure. Lucretian physics proposes therefore a co-implication of chance and necessity, conservation and dissipation, and the metaphor of writing provides the conceptual bridge between these two domains. However, in the Lucretian system, and in Serres' contemporary reappraisal of it, writing is both metaphor and more than metaphor, it is part of the continuum of nature: 'Que les atomes soient des lettres n'est pas une thèse arbitraire ou une décision ou une métaphore. C'est une nécessité de ce que Lucrèce et ses prédécesseurs appelaient la nature' ('That these atoms are also letters is not an arbitrary hypothesis, nor a decision, nor a metaphor. It is a necessity of what Lucretius and his predecessors called nature').[10]

The atom and the letter as both metaphor and not metaphor inevitably returns us to Derrida and his 'chances', his *clinamen*, his own atomistic philosophy. The points of correspondence and intersection between the two thinkers, Serres and Derrida, are in fact numerous and fascinating, despite the differences of language and disciplinary specialization. Apart from the study of Lucretius, Serres' early analysis of the scriptural model in contemporary science, or his work on parasitic communication, spring immediately to mind as candidates for such comparison.[11] To follow the full implications and ramifications of these parallels would, however, be an entire subject in itself. Again, this is another story and will wait for another day.

My own inflection of Derrida towards contemporary scientific thought, or various philosophical mediations of it, is of course only one possibility and one dimension of his work. There also remains the task of defining the specificity or, following the metaphor of the subtitle of 'Mes chances' ('Au rendez-vous de quelques stéréophonies épicuriennes' ('A Rendezvous with some Epicurean Stereophonies')), the *stereospecificity* of his writing. It could be argued that for all the conceptual insight systems philosophy has provided, in its discursive practice and with respect to the phenomena it treats, it is still (necessarily) restricted to the subject–object dichotomies of traditional science. In a sense, for scientific discourse, this is the final frontier which cannot be crossed, only probed. Derrida, however, in a number of his texts which are neither 'philosophy' nor 'science' nor 'literature' initiates a step beyond this frontier by including his own discourse as an example, and more than an example, of the systems he describes. This co-implication of discourse and referent is more than metaphorical because the linguistic system is not separate from the world, but as technology, as an articulation of life, is a natural extension of it. As the most open of systems in a hierarchy of systems, above all in its scriptural form, it is an extreme case of the structure of coding and redundancy inherent in all open systems. The linguistic system is both highly determined (coded) and overdetermined (equifinal), and is therefore characterized by a high degree of semiotic freedom. Derrida's writing makes more than conventional use of this semiotic freedom: its sometimes (literally) exorbitant verbal play probes the dividing line between subject and object, discourse and referent. It is a deliberate confusion of levels that refuses to punctuate, that refuses to entertain the dichotomies of traditional closed-system thought. Though some may find this writing obscure, opaque, difficult, its paradox is only apparent: true paradox is generated by the punctuations of context that separate what is always

Notes

Translations are mine unless otherwise indicated. Modifications to standard translations of Derrida's works are indicated in square brackets.

INTRODUCTION. FROM LANGUAGE TO WRITING:
THE INTERDISCIPLINARY MATRIX

1 See the first three chapters of Vincent Descombes, *Le même et l'autre. Quarante-cinq ans de philosophie française (1933–1978)*, Editions de Minuit, Paris, 1979; chapters 3 and 9 of Michael S. Roth, *Knowing and History: Appropriations of Hegel in Twentieth-Century France*, Cornell University Press, Ithaca and London, 1988.

2 'The Letter on Humanism', in *Martin Heidegger: Basic Writings*, translated by F. Capuzzi, G. Gray and D. Krell, edited by D. Krell, Harper and Row, New York, 1977, p. 193.

3 Descombes, *Le même et l'autre*, p. 89.

4 Claude Lévi-Strauss, *Anthropologie structurale*, Plon, Paris, 1958; Jacques Lacan, *Ecrits*, Editions du Seuil, Paris, 1966.

5 Roth, *Knowing and History*, pp. 8–9.

6 *Le structuralisme*, Presses Universitaires de France, Paris, 1968.

7 *Hermès IV, La distribution*, Editions de Minuit, Paris, 1977, p. 275.

8 *Hermès III, La traduction*, Editions de Minuit, Paris, 1974, p. 17.

9 *Ibid.*, p. 21.

10 *Ibid.*, pp. 20–1.

11 *De la grammatologie*, Editions de Minuit, Paris, 1967, p. 19; *Of Grammatology*, translated by Gayatri Chakravorty Spivak, Johns Hopkins University Press, Baltimore and London, 1976, p. 9. Page references for Derrida's works will henceforth be cited in the body of the text, titles abbreviated in accordance with the list of abbreviations.

12 *The Languages of Criticism and the Sciences of Man*, edited by R. Macksey and E. Donato, Johns Hopkins University Press, Balti-

more, 1970, p. 266. Hyppolite is an interesting transitional figure, whose own intellectual development is in certain respects emblematic of the evolution of French thought during the period in question. For much of his career he was a distinguished and influential commentator of Hegel and a major force in the revival of Hegelian studies in France. In the 1950s, however, via his reading of Heidegger, he began to abandon the humanist-historical perspective for a conception of Being logically prior to the subjective and the historical (see Roth, *Knowing and History*, chapter 3). In his reading of Hegel, this reorientation involved a change in emphasis from the *Phenomenology* to the *Logic*, but was also accompanied by an increasing preoccupation with three problems, distinct but interrelated: (i) the essence of life as complex and reticulate organization; (ii) the question of language as structure and combination; (iii) more generally than (i) and (ii), the reprise of the Leibnizian project of the *mathesis universalis* – the possibility of translation between disciplines and therefore the breaking-down of traditional disciplinary divisions (see François Dagognet, 'Vie et théorie de vie selon Jean Hyppolite', in S. Bachelard, G. Canguilhem, F. Dagognet *et al.*, *Hommage à Jean Hyppolite*, Presses Universitaires de France, Paris, 1971, pp. 181–2).

13 'Du graphème au chromosome', *Les lettres françaises*, 1429, 29 March 1972, p. 7.

14 In *Mémoires*, for example, Derrida speaks of 'l'immense question de la mémoire artificielle et des modalités modernes de l'archivation qui affecte aujourd'hui, à un rythme et dans des dimensions sans commune mesure avec celles du passé, la totalité de notre rapport au monde (en deçà ou au-delà de sa détermination anthropologique)' (*ME1*, p. 109) ('the immense question of artificial memory and of the modern modalities of archivation which today affects, according to a rhythm and with dimensions that have no common measure with those of the past, the totality of our relation to the world (on this side of or beyond its anthropological determination)' (*ME2*, p. 107)).

15 Cf. Wilden's critique of Piagetian and Lévi-Straussian structuralism in chapter 11 of *System and Structure: Essays in Communication and Exchange*, Tavistock Publications, London, second edition, 1980.

16 On the influence of systems theory in France, see Jean-Pierre Dupuy's article 'La pensée systémique', in *Magazine littéraire*, 218, April 1985, pp. 28–31. See also the chapter entitled 'La systémique', in Jean-Marie Domenach's *Enquête sur les idées contemporaines*, Editions du Seuil, Paris, 1981, pp. 89–99, which, however,

rather crudely polemicizes the difference between structuralism and systems theory.

17 This frequent misinterpretation of 'play' probably stems initially from 'polysemic' glosses of 'Le système, le signe et le jeu dans le discours des sciences humaines', the paper read at Johns Hopkins University in 1966, and later published as a chapter of *L'écriture et la différence* (1967). It is significant that at this stage Derrida was already defining 'play' not as unlimited polysemy, but as a kind of 'looseness' in the relations between the elements of a given structure: answering a question during the discussion following the paper, he refers to '"free play" in the sense in which one speaks of the "jeu dans la machine", of the "jeu des pièces"' (*The Languages of Criticism*, p. 268).

18 Irene H. Harvey, *Derrida and the Economy of Différance*, Indiana University Press, Bloomington, 1986, p. xi. For similar evaluations, see Henry Staten, *Derrida and Wittgenstein*, Blackwell, Oxford, 1985; Rodolphe Gasché, *The Tain of the Mirror: Derrida and the Philosophy of Reflection*, Harvard University Press, Cambridge, Massachusetts, 1986; Christopher Norris, *Derrida*, Fontana, London, 1987.

19 Norris, *Derrida*, p. 46. In an earlier book, *The Contest of Faculties*, Norris argues that the tendency towards 'limitless hermeneutic freedom' in texts like 'La structure, le signe et le jeu' represents 'one side of Derrida's strategy, and the side he has shown most often of late in writing (via translation) for a largely American readership. What it always *presupposes* – by way of enabling background – is the rigorous work of deconstruction as practised in other, more scrupulous texts like *Of Grammatology*' (*The Contest of Faculties*, Methuen, London, 1985, p. 219). Again, while Norris' polemical intentions here are understandable and to an extent defensible, it is not clear that the implicit separation between a 'playful' Derrida and a 'serious' or 'rigorous' Derrida is necessarily the most effective approach to a fuller understanding of his texts.

20 The text in which this philosophical affiliation is particularly apparent is 'Mes chances', where the tradition represented by Democritus, Epicurus and Lucretius participates in a complex *mise en scène* involving Freud, psychoanalysis and literature. In his contribution to *Taking Chances*, a volume which includes an English version of the text, William Kerrigan notes the significance of Derrida's reference to the atomists: 'Writing for this volume, he associates his project of deconstruction with the wayward and oppressed tradition of classical atomism. While not, as we will see,

inconsistent with the usual genealogy that derives his themes from
Marx, Nietzsche, Freud, Husserl and Heidegger, this new linkage
betrays a notable swerve in his historical self-regard' (*Taking
Chances: Derrida, Psychoanalysis and Literature*, edited by Joseph H.
Smith and William Kerrigan, Johns Hopkins University Press,
Baltimore and London, 1984, p. 87).

I THE PASSION OF INSCRIPTION

1 *Forme et Signification: Essais sur les structures littéraires de Corneille à
Claudel*, José Corti, Paris, 1962.

2 Rousset's 'geometrical' analysis does in fact include a third
dimension: the loop-shaped movement Rousset isolates in Corneille's *La Galerie du Palais* becomes in *Le Cid* a spiral, the added
vertical dimension thereby accounting for the 'quality' and
'intensity' (Derrida's terms) of experience in *Le Cid* (*ED*, pp. 31–2;
WD, p. 18). Rousset's method is therefore not powerless when
confronted with such a text ('Ce serait sous-estimer la ressource du
critique', *ED*, p. 31 ('one would underestimate the resources of the
critic', *WD*, p. 18)). But what Derrida appears to object to is
Rousset's assumption that the addition of the dimension of height
accommodates what he calls the 'mouvement cornélien' (more
'Roussetian' than 'Cornelian' says Derrida, *ED*, p. 33; *WD*,
p. 19), what he sees as the progressive 'ascension' from play to
play, towards the perfection of *Polyeucte*. This movement has
nothing dynamic about it, according to Derrida, who compares its
pseudo-dynamics to the Aristotelian *energeia* which is orientated by
the *telos* of a final equilibrium of perfectly achieved form (*ED*,
p. 36; *WD*, p. 21).

3 'Dem Werden den Charakter des Seins *aufzuprägen* – das ist der
höchste Wille zur Macht!' (*Werke in drei Bänden*, edited by Karl
Schlechta, Carl Hanser, Munich, 1965, vol. III, p. 895). Heidegger
considers these words to represent 'the summit of the completion of
Western philosophy' (*Early Greek Thinking*, translated by D. F.
Krell and F. A. Capuzzi, Harper and Row, London, 1975, p. 22).

4 These correspond to the original form of 'Force et signification'
which appeared in two separate instalments in successive numbers
of *Critique* (193–194, June–July, 1963).

5 As Herman Rapaport points out in his book *Heidegger and Derrida*,
Blanchot is perhaps the first commentator of Heidegger in France
to locate and explicate the linguistic turn in his work, and
Blanchot's writing on writing in the 1950s itself anticipates
Derrida's 'grammatological' texts of the 1960s. According to

Rapaport, Derrida's reading of Blanchot led him to a reconsideration of Heidegger in the early 1970s, and it is also at this point that the interactive relationship between the writings of Blanchot and Derrida begins (*Heidegger and Derrida. Reflections on Time and Language*, University of Nebraska Press, Lincoln and London, 1989, chapter 3).

6 Compare what Walter Ong says on writing in his book *Interfaces of the Word*: 'As contrasted with speech, writing is associated with death because it is never "natural" the way speech is ... Writing requires special reflexive training, and terrifying restraints. Moreover, the concepts and vocabulary connected with writing often associate the activity itself with activities which are, or can be, lethal, such as cutting and dismembering. The word can be "incised" or cut into a surface ... the "stylus" originally means a stake, a spearlike instrument, etc.' (Walter J. Ong, *Interfaces of the Word: Studies in the Evolution of Consciousness and Culture*, Cornell University Press, London, 1977, p. 240).

7 The opposition of 'air' and 'terre' proposed in this passage also figures in Derrida's commentary of Hegel in *Glas*: 'Homogène et fluide, l'air laisse transparaître et résonner, voir et entendre. Milieu théorico-phonique. La première puissance de la conscience est "la pure existence théorique". Elle se détermine et se retient comme telle dans la mémoire, c'est-à-dire sans secours solide. Il s'agit évidemment de la mémoire pure et vivante. Elle serait purement évanescente sans le langage qui lui fournit des produits stables mais encore tout intérieurs et spontanés. Mais à cause de cette intériorité et de cette spontanéité, le langage est un produit qui s'efface lui-même dans le temps. En lui la conscience théorique disparaît aussi. Elle ne peut *se poser*, exister comme conscience théorique. Pour le faire, elle doit donc sortir d'elle-même, passer encore dans son opposé, nier sa propre théoricité, son *air*. Elle ne peut se poser comme conscience théorique qu'en devenant conscience pratique, à travers l'élément terreux. A la mémoire s'enchaîne alors le travail, au produit linguistique de la mémoire l'instrument et le produit du travail. De même que le langage était à la fois l'effet et l'organe de la mémoire, l'instrument (*Werkzeug*) sert le travail dont il procède. Dans les deux cas, une activité donne lieu à la production d'une permanence, d'un élément de subsistance relative' (*GL1*, p. 136a) ('Homogeneous and fluid, air allows showing through and resonating, seeing and hearing. Theoretico-phonic [medium]. The first power of consciousness is "pure theoretical existence". It determines and holds itself back as such in memory, that is, without solid assistance. The question is

evidently of the pure and living memory, a memory that would be purely evanescent without language, which furnishes it stable but still completely interior and spontaneous products. But because of this interiority and this spontaneity, language is a product that effaces itself in time. In time theoretical consciousness also disappears. It cannot *posit itself*, exist as theoretical consciousness. To do that, it must then go out of itself, pass yet into its opposite, deny its own proper theoreticity, its *air*. Theoretical consciousness cannot posit itself as theoretical consciousness except by becoming practical consciousness, through the earthly element. To the memory then is chained labor, to the linguistic product of memory the tool and the product of labor. Just as language was at once the effect and the organ of memory, the tool (*Werkzeug*) serves the labor from which it proceeds. In both cases, an activity gives rise to the production of a permanence, of an element of relative subsistence (*GL2*, p. 119a)).

8 On the subject of creation, poetic and cosmological, Derrida quotes Canguilhem: 'Consciemment ou non, l'idée que l'homme se fait de son pouvoir poétique répond à l'idée qu'il se fait de la création du monde et à la solution qu'il donne au problème de l'origine radicale des choses' (*ED*, p. 21) ('Consciously or not, the idea that man has of his poetic power corresponds to the idea he has about the creation of the world, and the solution he gives to the problem of the radical origin of things' (*WD*, p. 10)). Like the cosmogony, Derrida's enquiry is concerned with the conditions of inauguration of a system, its genesis, whereas the structuralist method he criticizes is interested only in the static synchrony of an already constituted system. See also 'La pharmacie de Platon', in *La dissémination*, pp. 184–7 (*Dissemination*, pp. 159–61), for writing and inscription as essential metaphors of creation (human and cosmological) in Plato.

9 Later in the text, Derrida quotes a passage from Rousset's *Forme et Signification* which is distinctly Leibnizian in tenor: 'Tout obéit à la loi de *composition*, c'est la loi de l'artiste comme c'est la loi du Créateur. Car l'univers est une simultanéité, par laquelle les choses mènent une existence concertante et forment une solidarité harmonique' (*ED*, p. 40, note 1) ('Everything obeys the law of composition, which is the law of the artist as it is of the Creator. For the universe is a simultaneity, by virtue of which things at a remove from each other lead a concerted existence and form a harmonic solidarity' (*WD*, p. 24, note 51)).

10 As was seen beforehand, it is impossible entirely to separate Derrida's argument from the language in which it is expressed, a

language that appears to operate on a number of levels. With the formulation 'la pointe du style', for example, the possibilities of interpretation are several. The word 'style' may firstly be translated as the stylus which writes. Its tip is pointed and the act of writing therefore scratches or incises the receiving surface. The 'pointe' at the same time suggests a taper, a narrowing passage through which ink might flow, with force, one assumes. (Both of these images relate to the passional aspect of inscription already discussed.) Alternatively, one may translate 'style' in its general and abstract sense of 'manner'. Style differentiates; it is an idiolect which distinguishes not only writer from writer, but possibly also a writer from him- or herself (the structuralist tendency being to regard the corpus of a writer's work as a coherent whole). This idiolectical nature of writing means that the text is, to an extent, solitary, isolated, as Derrida suggests shortly afterwards (*ED*, p. 21; *WD*, p. 11). It is not simply a monad without doors or windows, but is also deaf to the harmony of the Leibnizian (and structuralist) concert.

11 *La voix et le phénomène*, 1967.

12 For a very similar argument concerning the order of precedence (or lack of it) between the signifier and signified, see *De la grammatologie*, p. 32, note 9 (*Of Grammatology*, p. 19, note 9).

13 For example, 'ce redoublement étrange' (*ED*, p. 22) ('the strange redoubling' (*WD*, p. 11)), 'étrange labeur de conversion et d'aventure' (*ED*, p. 23) ('The strange labour of conversion and adventure' (*WD*, p. 11)). This idea of strangeness is closely related to the anguish of the inaugural instant (Derrida says in the same passage that writing is dangerous and distressing), as distinct from the serene and reassuring totalities of structuralism. Derrida's dramatization of the strange, the bizarre, is reminiscent of the existential mood of the *unheimlich* in Heidegger's *Being and Time*.

14 See 'Genèse et structure', where a certain kind of *telos* is deemed 'le plus puissant *apriori* structural de l'historicité' (*ED*, p. 250) ('The most powerful structural a priori of historicity' (*WD*, p. 167)). On the other hand, the classical *telos* 'a toujours eu la forme de la présence, fût-ce d'une présence future' (*ED*, p. 172) ('has always had the form of presence, be it a future presence' (*WD*, p. 117)).

15 The translation in the English edition, *Writing and Difference* (translated by A. Bass, Routledge and Kegan Paul, London, 1978, p. 26), is 'the meaning of meaning'. While the translation is an excellent one, it falls prey in this instance to the misfortune of all translation, that is, the difficulty of accurately rendering verbal

ambiguity without the loss of clarity and coherence. Bass in fact cites this example when discussing such difficulties (*WD*, p. xvii).

16 The metaphor of light and the privilege of sight in the history of metaphysics is also examined in 'Violence et métaphysique', Derrida's extended commentary of Levinas (*ED*, pp. 125ff; *WD*, pp. 84ff).

17 It could be advanced that, if from Plato to Husserl and beyond, the photology preconditions our understanding of form and being, then from Heraclitus to Derrida (via Lucretius and Nietzsche), a *hydraulics* underlies our conception of force and becoming.

18 This is clearly reminiscent of the Bergsonian 'élan'. Bergson has already been quoted by Derrida on the subject of duration and simultaneity (*ED*, p. 42; *WD*, p. 25), and the word 'élan' itself appears a few pages after this: 'la différence entre Dionysos et Apollon, entre l'élan et la structure' (*ED*, p. 47) ('the difference between Dionysus and Apollo, between [élan] and structure' (*WD*, p. 28)).

19 *Thus Spoke Zarathustra*, part 3, 'Of Old and New Law-Tables'.

20 For example: 'Elle [l'écriture] crée le sens en le consignant, en le confiant à une *gravure*, à un *sillon*, à un *relief*, à une surface que l'on veut transmissible à l'infini' (*ED*, p. 24, my emphasis) ('[Writing] creates meaning by enregistering it, by entrusting it to an *engraving*, a *groove*, a *relief*, to a surface whose essential characteristic is to be infinitely transmissible' (*WD*, p. 12)).

21 The figure of the 'fraternal other' also recalls the example of the brothers Dionysus and Apollo, both sons of Zeus.

22 Hence Derrida's frequent verbalization of nouns which imparts a certain 'movement' to their conceptual fixity. The word 'différance' is a good example of this. In *Positions*, he points out that the 'a' of 'différance' renders the indefinite sense of activity-passivity, beyond any opposition between active and passive (*P1*, pp. 38–9; *P2*, p. 27).

2 INFINITY, INSCRIPTION, THE ECONOMY

1 The exact context is Derrida's commentary of Levinas in 'Violence et métaphysique', where he indicates that the classical idea of the positive infinity can only be expressed in negative fashion, for the very word 'infini' ('in-fini') explains the infinite only in terms of what it is not (the finite) (*ED*, pp. 167, 168; *WD*, pp. 113, 114). My interpretation is an extension of this.

2 This metonymic sliding or 'slippage' from term to term, a frequent rhetorical device in Derrida's writing, is akin to what Schöfer

terms Heidegger's 'paranomasia', 'a stringing of words of different word types which, however, belong to the same word stem', which gives a kind of perspectival variation or negotiation of 'intellectual objects' (Rapaport, *Heidegger and Derrida*, p. 108).

3 Unfortunately, the picture is not quite as simple as it may seem. Typically, Derrida is presenting *two* Foucaults, just as elsewhere he will propose two Saussures, two Lévi-Strausses, two Freuds. Foucault does not simply privilege the single 'coup de force' of the *cogito* and the classical age. At the same time, he does in fact recognize the structural necessity of the 'décision', of which the movement of the 'grand renfermement' is but a particular manifestation. On this, Derrida quotes Foucault's *Histoire de la folie*: '*La nécessité de la folie*, tout au long de l'histoire de l'Occident est liée à ce geste de décision qui détache du bruit du fond et de sa monotonie continue un langage significatif qui se transmet et s'achève dans le temps; bref, elle est liée à *la possibilité de l'histoire*' (*ED*, p. 67) ('*The necessity of madness*, throughout the history of the West, is linked to the deciding gesture which detaches from the background noise, and from its continuous monotony, a meaningful language that is transmitted and consummated in time; briefly, it is linked to the *possibility of history*' (*WD*, p. 42)). And yet, Foucault does accord special privilege to the 'coup de force' of the classical age. This is the first, the second, or the 'other' of the two Foucaults, the Foucault Derrida criticizes in 'Cogito et histoire de la folie'.

4 This codification or encipherment of the theatrical process, as Derrida shows, runs counter to Artaud's desire that each performance of the theatre of cruelty should be a singular event, should take place only once, and should not be repeated. There are therefore *two* Artauds: the Artaud who desires a certain singularity of the theatrical event; and the Artaud who recognizes the necessity of the inscription – and therefore the contained repetition – of that event, without which (Derrida argues) it simply would not exist.

5 For a detailed discussion of 'différance', see the chapter 'La différance' in *Marges – de la philosophie*, pp. 1–29 (*Margins of Philosophy*, pp. 1–27).

6 Compare Girard, who sees the violent decision of sacrifice as a necessary containment of the infinite violence of mimetic desire: 'Pour renoncer complètement à l'ancrage objectal du désir, pour admettre l'infini de la *mimesis* violente, il faut comprendre, simultanément, que le sans mesure potentiel de cette violence peut et doit être maîtrisé dans le mécanisme de la victime émissaire' (*La violence et le sacré*, Pluriel, Grasset, Paris, 1972, p. 320) ('In order to

abandon entirely the anchorage of desire in the object, and to recognize the infinity of mimetic violence, we must at the same time realize that the potential excess of this violence can and must be mastered through the scapegoat mechanism'). 'Jean souligne que toute *décision* véritable dans la culture a un caractère sacrificiel (*decidere*, je le redis, c'est couper la gorge à la victime)' (*Le bouc émissaire*, Pluriel, Grasset, Paris, 1982, p. 169) ('John stresses that all real *decisions* in culture are of a sacrificial character (*decidere*, I repeat, means to cut the victim's throat)').

3 BEYOND THE SEEN OF WRITING

1 Gregory Bateson, *Steps to an Ecology of Mind*, Ballantine Books, New York, 1972, p. 459.

2 These terms are used rarely in *L'écriture et la différence*, and figure far more frequently in *De la grammatologie*. The same is true of the term 'logocentrism'.

3 This double articulation of Derrida's argument was suggested in the Introduction above, with the distinction made between Derrida's 'special' and 'general' theory of writing.

4 *Project for a Scientific Psychology*, in *The Origins of Psycho-Analysis. Letters to Wilhelm Fliess, Drafts and Notes: 1887–1902*, translated by Eric Mosbacher and James Strachey, edited by Marie Bonaparte, Anna Freud and Ernst Kris, Imago, London, 1954, pp. 349–445; page references to Freud's *Project* will henceforth be given in the text.

5 See also the discussion of Condillac, Warburton and Rousseau's theories of writing in *De la grammatologie*: 'Il s'agit de *l'écriture par sillons*. Le sillon, c'est la ligne, telle que la trace le laboureur: la route – *via rupta* – fendue par le soc de la charrue' (*GR*1, p. 407) ('It is a matter of *writing by furrows*. The furrow is the line, as the ploughman traces it: the road – *via rupta* – broken by the plough-share' (*GR*2, p. 287)).

6 A few pages later, Derrida makes the distinction between three levels of violence: the primary level of 'archi-écriture'; the violence of the law; the tertiary, conditional and 'empirical' level of the transgression of law, as observed by Lévi-Strauss in the writing lesson and the 'guerre des noms propres' (*GR*1, p. 165; *GR*2, p. 112). On empiricism, see note 7 below.

7 Empiricism, or a *certain* empiricism, is frequently criticized by Derrida (see especially, 'Violence et métaphysique', *ED*, pp. 224–6; *WD*, pp. 151–2). He associates the philosophical presuppositions of empiricism with the metaphysics of presence

which commands the logocentric tradition. Such an empiricism, according to Derrida, makes the erroneous supposition that direct experience of phenomena is possible, that the phenomenon experienced is somehow present to our intuition, immediately intelligible (*GR*1, p. 89; *GR*2, pp. 60–1), that it is possible and legitimate to enquire of its essence in the interrogative voice of the *Qu'est-ce que* (*GR*1, p. 110; *GR*2, p. 75). On the other hand, Derrida appears to advocate a certain other form of empiricism, an 'errant' thought that attempts to step (elliptically) outside the constraining circle of traditional metaphysical discourse (*GR*1, pp. 231–2; *GR*2, p. 162).

8 *System and Structure*, p. 398.

9 *Ibid.*, p. 138.

10 *Ibid.*, p. 399; see also Serres: 'Tout se passe comme si Freud, parti de modèles énergétiques issus de la thermodynamique, avait intuitionné, par une dynamique du langage, le développement prochain de celle-ci en théorie de l'information' (*Hermès IV, La distribution*, p. 271) ('It all seems as if starting from energetical models derived from thermodynamics, Freud had with his dynamic conception of language anticipated the subsequent development of the former into information theory').

11 Compare Bateson's definition of information: 'The technical term "information" may be succinctly defined as *any difference which makes a difference in some later event*. This definition is fundamental for all analysis of cybernetic systems and organization' (*Steps to an Ecology of Mind*, p. 381).

12 Cf. Wilden: 'Unlike energy, information is not a substance. Although memory retains "LOCATABLE" information in patterns, the information cannot be "LOCALIZED", because it involves a relationship between patterns' (*System and Structure*, pp. 137–8).

13 On hieroglyphs in particular, see also 'Scribble', Derrida's preface to Warburton's *Essai sur les hiéroglyphes*, translated by Léonard Des Malpeines, edited by Patrick Tort, Aubier-Flammarion, Paris, 1977, pp. 7–43.

14 In *The Interpretation of Dreams* (chapter 6, section D) Freud himself stresses the importance of 'considerations of representability' (*Rücksicht auf Darstellbarkeit*) in dreams, over and above the determination of their latent content. The already theatrical overtones of Freud's use of the word *Darstellbarkeit* are emphasized and extended by Derrida's play on the terms 'représentation' (performance) and 'répétition [générale]' (rehearsal). Such play is also apparent in the two chapters of *L'écriture et la différence* on

Artaud, 'La parole soufflée' and 'La clôture de la représentation'. Both chapters include references to Freud and the hieroglyph.

15 I will be referring to the translation by James Strachey published in the Pelican Freud Library, Harmondsworth, 1984, vol. XI, pp. 427–34; page references will be given in the text.

16 This is doubtless a reference to the optical model Freud used in *The Interpretation of Dreams* and elsewhere to describe the psychical system. Derrida's interpretation of the refraction of light in this model is again coloured by the supposition of a certain violence: he translates the German word *Strahlenbrechung* (refraction) literally, as 'brisure du rayon' ('breaking of the ray') (*ED*, p. 319; *WD*, p. 215).

17 Most notably in 'La pharmacie de Platon', already cited, and the commentary of Rousseau in chapters 2, 3 and 4 of the second part of *De la grammatologie*.

18 In *Mémoires*, some twenty years after 'La scène de l'écriture', Derrida draws attention to the effects of the increasingly rapid developments in information technology upon our relationship with the world: 'Cette prodigieuse mutation n'accroît pas seulement la taille, l'économie quantitative de la mémoire dite artificielle mais sa structure qualitative. Elle oblige à repenser ce qui la rapporte à la mémoire dite psychique et intérieure de l'homme, à la vérité, au simulacre et à la simulation, etc.' (*ME1*, p. 109) ('This prodigious mutation not only heightens the stature, the quantitative economy of so-called artificial memory, but also its qualitative structure – and in doing so it obliges us to rethink what relates this artificial memory to man's so-called psychical and interior memory, to truth, to the simulacrum and the simulation of truth, etc.' (*ME2*, pp. 107–8)).

4 THE ELEMENT OF PLAY

1 This idea of the small cause and the large effect is in fact a common topos of eighteenth-century thought, explaining the existence of the random in the universe and becoming a standard account of historical causality. Cf. Voltaire's 'Les petites causes et les grands événements'. I thank Marian Jeanneret for drawing my attention to this.

2 For a discussion of this tendency to external projection of internal contradictions, see Wilden's criticisms of equilibrium and gradualist models of socio-economic change, in his chapter on Piaget: 'in equilibrium models of "consensus", all tensions, problems, deviations, conflicts, and so on are necessarily defined as DEVIANT

INTRUSIONS into the system ... any sudden change must therefore, by definition, come from outside the system. It must, by definition, be NOISE – and therefore, again by definition, it must be VIOLENCE' (*System and Structure*, p. 332).

3 Hegel's genealogy of the family and the State, as it is read by Derrida in *Glas*, similarly depends upon a kind of theoretical fiction: 'Comme Condillac, comme Rousseau, Kant et quelques autres, Hegel recourt à une sorte de fiction théorique: le récit d'un événement catastrophique reconstitue l'origine de la société humaine. Et il réinscrit la narration biblique les yeux fixés sur un réseau de philosophèmes ... Le déluge, c'est la perte de la nature. Avant le déluge, l'homme vivait en harmonie naturelle avec la nature. Le déluge déchire l'homme, l'arrache à la nature, détruit la belle unité' (*GL*1, p. 46a) ('Like Condillac, like Rousseau, Kant and some others, Hegel resorts to a kind of theoretical fiction: the recital of a catastrophic event reconstitutes the ideal-historic origin of human society. And this recital reinscribes the Biblical narration with eyes fixed on a network of philosophemes ... The flood is the loss of the state of nature. Before the flood man lived in natural harmony with nature. The flood tears man, uproots him from nature, destroys the beautiful unity' (*GL*2, p. 37a)).

4 'Il faut que le pas le plus normal comporte le déséquilibre, en lui-même, pour se porter en avant, pour se faire suivre d'un autre, le même encore, qui soit pas, et que l'autre revienne, au même, mais comme autre. Il faut que le boitement soit avant tout le rythme même de la marche, *unterwegs*' (*CP*, p. 433) ('The most normal step has to bear disequilibrium, in order to carry itself forward, in order to have itself followed by another one, the same again, that is a step, and so that the other comes back, amounts to the same, but as other. Before all else limping has to be the very rhythm of the march, *unterwegs*' (*PC*, p. 406)). This is a reference not simply to the rhythm of walking, but to the rhythm and operation ('marche') of life and the psychical system, as they are described in Freud's *Beyond the Pleasure Principle*, and indeed to the hesitant, limping gait of Freud's (and in the event, Derrida's) own discourse.

5 The translators use this now obsolete spelling of 'size' to render the dual sense of the French 'taille' (connoting both dimension and incision). See *TP*, p. 120, note 32.

6 On the structure and function of the 'ni ... ni' in Derrida's texts, see Marian Hobson's 'Les négations de Derrida', in *Cross-References: Modern French Theory and the Practice of Criticism*, edited by David Kelley and Isabelle Llasera, Society for French Studies, Leeds, 1986, pp. 57–64.

7 Note the coherence of this description with previous descriptions of other systems: the infinite precondition ('l'unité infinie'), the narrowness of the inaugurational passage ('l'écart étroit') from infinity to system, the use of the verb 'surgir' to describe the emergence of the system.

8 *Steps to an Ecology of Mind*, pp. 206–8.

9 'Double posture. Double postulation. Contradiction en soi de deux désirs inconciliables. Je lui donne ici, accusé dans ma langue, le titre de DOUBLE BANDE, le (la, les) mettant pratiquement en forme et en jeu. Un texte sangle en deux sens. Deux fois ceint. Bande contre bande' (*GL*1, p. 77bi) ('Double posture. Double postulation. Contradiction in (it)self of two irreconcilable desires. Here I give it, accused in my own tongue, the title DOUBLE BAND(S), putting it (them) into form and into play practically. A text laces in two senses, in two directions. Twice girt. Band contra band' (*GL*2, p. 66bi)).

10 In addition, it should be noted that Titus Carmel's paintings often depict objects (spheres, boxes, etc.), whose surfaces or extremities appear tarnished or corroded. A number of Carmel's paintings illustrated in *La vérité en peinture* could be seen as graphical equivalents of Derrida's ideas of 'entame' and 'altération' (see, for example, 'Variations sur l'idée de détérioration', 'Exemples d'altération d'une sphère', *VP*, p. 287; *TP*, p. 250).

11 The term 'économie bindinale' is probably a parodic allusion to Lyotard's *Economie libidinale*, and possibly also a compression of Lyotard's term 'bande libidinale'. With its emphasis on the necessary restriction of energies in the psychic economy, the concept of 'économie bindinale' could be interpreted as a lateral interrogation of the celebration of libidinal excess in Lyotard's text.

12 Lucretius, *On the Nature of the Universe*, Penguin, Harmondsworth, 1982, p. 66.

13 *Ibid.*, pp. 66, 67.

14 Robert Strozier also draws attention to this parallel, and suggests that there is a strong analogy between the Lucretian *clinamen* and the notions of 'différance' and 'archi-trace' in Derrida's texts (Robert M. Strozier, *Saussure, Derrida, and the Metaphysics of Subjectivity*, Mouton de Gruyter, Berlin, New York, Amsterdam, 1988, pp. 180–3).

15 In *Human, All Too Human*, Nietzsche similarly argues for motion as opposed to materiality, rejecting the mechanistic idea of atoms as solid objects: 'Here [in atomic theory] we continue to feel ourselves compelled to assume the existence of a "thing" or a material "substratum" which is moved, while the whole procedure of

science has pursued the task of resolving everything thing-like (material) into motions' (*Human, All Too Human*, translated by R.J. Hollingdale, Cambridge University Press, Cambridge, 1986, p. 22).

16 Another visible intertext here, in parallel with the reference to atomist theory, is of course Mallarmé's 'Coup de dés', with its aleatory throw of the dice, its descent or declension of letters and their uncertain constellation.

5 EVOLUTION AND THE 'LIFE' SCIENCES

1 Wilden, *System and Structure*, p. 203.

2 Heidegger, *Being and Time*, Blackwell, Oxford, 1962, p. 30.

3 Staten, *Derrida and Wittgenstein*, p. xvi.

4 *General Systems Theory: Foundation, Development, Applications*, Allen Lane, The Penguin Press, London, 1971, p. 16.

5 *Steps to an Ecology of Mind*, p. 454.

6 *Ibid.*, p. 483.

7 'Voice and Opening Closed Systems', in *Interfaces of the Word*, p. 324.

8 *General Systems Theory*, pp. 76–7.

9 *Ibid.*, p. 79.

10 *Ibid.*, p. 39.

11 *System and Structure*, p. 35.

12 This correlates with Wilden's understanding of the difference between system and structure: structure (homeostasis, reproduction) is preponderant at lower levels of organization, while system (process, evolution) predominates at more complex levels (*ibid.*, pp. 204, 406).

13 'The digital system has greater "semiotic freedom", but it is ultimately governed by the rules of the analog relationship between systems, subsystems, and supersystems in nature. The analog (continuum) is a set which includes the digital (discontinuum) as a subset' (*ibid.*, p.189).

14 See Wilden, *ibid.*, p. 331; also Bateson: 'All that is not information, not redundancy, not form and not restraints – is noise, the only possible source of *new* patterns' (*Steps to an Ecology of Mind*, p. 410).

15 'Since the survival of the error [in the reproduction of DNA] involves a mutually interdependent and equally unpredictable set of variables – the internal and external environment – it is difficult to see how any probability equations could possibly be applied to its potential to survive' (*System and Structure*, p. 331).

16 *General Systems Theory*, p. 37.

17 *System and Structure*, p. 308. This criticism of Bertalanffy's 'organicism' is made by Piaget in *Le structuralisme*. Wilden goes on to criticize what he calls Piaget's own 'bioenergetic organicism' (*System and Structure*, p. 308).

18 *Derrida and the Economy of Différance*, p. 179; see also pp. 166–7.

19 From the long-term perspective of human evolution, André Leroi-Gourhan demonstrates in his book *Le geste et la parole* the crucial role of manual technology in the development of human intelligence. According to Leroi-Gourhan, such development was only possible through the close and mutually reinforcing interaction of hand and brain over the millenia. The importance of his natural historical account of the evolution of symbolic systems for Derrida's understanding of writing cannot be overestimated, though it is not normally acknowledged (one exception is Christian Descamps, *Les Idées philosophiques contemporaines en France, 1960–1985*, Bordas, Paris, 1986, p. 119). Leroi-Gourhan's book was one of the three works reviewed in the original article 'De la grammatologie', published in *Critique* in 1965 and 1966, and can therefore be seen to contribute directly to what Derrida calls the 'theoretical matrix' (*GR*1, p. 7; *GR*2, p. lxxxix) elaborated in the first part of *De la grammatologie*, 'L'écriture avant la lettre', which is a development of that article.

20 *The Dimensionality of Signs, Tools and Models*, Indiana University Press, Bloomington, 1981, p. 73.

21 See, for example, *Parts of Animals* I.1, 641b.

22 *Lectures on the Philosophy of Religion*, vol. I, translated by R. F. Brown, P. C. Hodgson and J. M. Stewart, Berkeley, California, 1984, pp. 175, 393, quoted in J. P. Leavey, *Glassary*, University of Nebraska Press, Lincoln and London, 1986, p. 48a.

23 Derrida also associates 'annulaire' with 'annuler', the annulment of all contradictions in the satisfaction or accomplishment of absolute relief.

24 In *Glas*, the *Sa* is Derrida's cursive manner of referring to Hegel's Absolute Knowledge ('savoir absolu'), also implying the possessive sense of self-(re)appropriation, the circular return to the (self)-same.

25 *On the Nature of the Universe*, p. 57.

26 *Ibid.*

27 *Ibid.*, pp. 80–1; this follows Aristotle, *Parts of Animals* I.1, 641b.

28 *On the Nature of the Universe*, pp. 196–8.

29 *Ibid.*, p. 168.

30 In her paper 'Le tout premier écart', Sylviane Agacinski examines

the continuity between Aristotle and Hegel in their conception of biological reproduction. In Aristotle, as is later the case with Hegel, the sperm is transmitted linearly from male to male, father to son, male engenders male in a closed economy. For Aristotle, woman is the monster, the deviation ('écart') that perverts this reappropriating circle of patri-linear descent (*Les fins de l'homme – Colloque de Cérisy*, edited by Philippe Lacoue-Labarthe and Jean-Luc Nancy, Editions Galilée, Paris, 1981, pp. 117–32). See also Aristotle, *Generation of Animals* II.1, 732a; II.3, 737a27; IV.3, 767b8.

31 In contrast to this, the tradition of 'dynamic Platonism' extending from Aristotle down to Hegel and beyond is non-evolutionary. Despite his avowed 'Heracliteanism', his philosophy of becoming, Hegel is a true descendant of the Eleatic tradition in his denial, against the scientific evidence of his time, of biological evolution, according to Milič Čapek: 'Nature is devoid of history; history begins with historians. When Hegel speaks of the hierarchy of nature, he means by it the system of gradations without any evolutionary significance, the static *scala naturae* of the pre-evolutionary thought... His opposition to [evolution] stemmed from the Eleatic strain in his thought, that is, from the characteristically idealistic contempt for time and change' ('Hegel and the Organic View of Nature', in *Boston Studies on the Philosophy of Science*, vol. 64, *Hegel and the Sciences*, edited by R. S. Cohen and M. W. Wartofsky, D. Reidel, Dordrecht, 1984, pp. 112, 114).

32 *La logique du vivant: une histoire de l'hérédité*, Gallimard, Paris, 1970, p. 294. *The Logic of Life*, translated by Betty E. Spillman, Pantheon Books, New York, 1973, p. 274.

33 'Le modèle linguistique en biologie', *Critique*, 322, March 1974, pp. 198, 204.

34 *Ibid.*, pp. 199, 203.

35 *On the Nature of the Universe*, p. 156.

36 *L'organisation biologique et la théorie de l'information*, Hermann, Paris, 1972, p. 276.

37 This is not equivalent to the 'filiation' between the genetic and the linguistic proposed by Jakobson, and rejected by Jacob, above. Jakobson speculates that 'the foundations of the overt linguistic patterns superimposed upon molecular communication have been modeled directly upon its structural principles' (quoted by Jacob, 'Le modèle linguistique en biologie', p. 199), whereas I would see Derrida's understanding of the term-germ to be closer to Jacob: the structural homology between the genetic and the linguistic is

due to similar functional constraints, in other words, Derrida appears to be saying that they are both (ultimately) *for* the same thing.

38 'In communication theory, the trace is the condition of both message and code'; 'MEMORY: The *sine qua non* of communication, dependent on the TRACE' (*System and Structure*, pp. 446, 374).

39 'Hierarchical constraints or rules are embodied in structures that are to some extent "frozen accidents"' (Howard H. Pattee, *Hierarchy Theory: The Challenge of Complex Systems*, edited by Howard H. Pattee, George Braziller, New York, 1973, p. 74).

40 The parasite is an important figure in 'Signature événement contexte' and 'Limited Inc.'. See also Michel Serres' *Le parasite* (Grasset, Paris, 1980), where Serres' descriptions of the structure of the parasite (inclusion-exclusion, its systemic necessity, etc.) are very similar to Derrida's remarks on the subject. Serres' own philosophy is very much influenced by information theory and modern biology.

41 *L'organisation biologique*, p. 170. Derrida expressed something very close to this in his definition of 'play' in a recent interview: 'Play, not in the sense of gambling or playing games, but what in French we call *jouer*, which means that the structure of the machine, or the springs, are not so tight, so that you can just try to dislocate: that's what I meant by play' (Imre Salusinszky, *Criticism in Society*, Methuen, New York and London, 1987, p. 20).

42 See Wilden on the necessity of ambiguity in human communication: 'In any highly complex system, the function of levels and thresholds, the function of unavoidable error, and that of unpredictable contextual relations, are such that no message of any complexity can be completely and unambiguously understood at all times and in all places. And when the relationship is that between subjects and signifiers in the human world, no true dialogue is possible. The really important aspect of this last point is that a full dialogue is not possible because such a situation has no survival value. It would amount to an overload of information and thus to death. So much for the romantic, utopian illusions of the *parole pleine*' (*System and Structure*, p. 433).

43 *Steps to an Ecology of Mind*, p. 441.

44 'Je risque cette énormité: ils [Plato–Socrates] n'auront eu aucune progéniture (rien, zéro, malentendu absolu, erreur sur les noms, pas le moindre héritage socratico-platonicien qui tienne vraiment) bien qu'ils aient eu tous les descendants de la terre' (*CP*, p. 144) ('I venture this enormity: they will have had no progeniture (nothing, zero, absolute misunderstanding, error over the names, not the

slightest socratico-platonic heritage that really holds) although they have had all the descendants in the world' (*PC*, p. 132)).

45 *Nombres*, Editions du Seuil, Paris, 1968. A central point of reference in the novel is atomist philosophy: as Derrida reminds us, the epigraph to *Nombres* is taken from Lucretius' *On the Nature of the Universe*, which is 'quoted' throughout the book (*D*1, p. 376; *D*2, p. 338).

46 The correlation of this violence with that of inscription is not surprising given that Derrida associates the graphical and the graft by way of their etymological kinship. In 'La double séance', for example: 'Il faudrait explorer systématiquement ce qui se donne comme simple unité étymologique de la greffe et du graphe (du *graphion*: poinçon à écrire)' (*D*1, p. 230) ('One ought to explore systematically ... what appears to be a simple etymological coincidence uniting the graph and the graft (both from *graphion*: writing implement, stylus)' (*D*2, p. 202)).

47 In an interview given in 1980, Derrida insisted that deconstruction is not a pluralist or random interpretation of texts, and compared it to Nietzsche's selection of forces described above ('An Interview with Jacques Derrida', *The Literary Review*, 14, 1980, p. 21).

48 See note 3 above.

CONCLUSION. METAPHOR AND MORE THAN METAPHOR

1 *Being and Time*, p. 63.

2 Rorty, for example, while praising the deconstructive force of Derrida's texts, regrets the 'unfortunately constructive' side of his thought represented in what he considers to be Derrida's essentializing of trace and writing: 'But in developing this alternative [of the trace, etc.] Derrida comes perilously close to giving us a philosophy of language and thereby perilously close to slipping back into what he and Heidegger call "the tradition of onto-theology"' ('Philosophy as a Kind of Writing', in *Consequences of Pragmatism. Essays: 1972–1980*, Harvester Press, Sussex, 1982, pp. 99, 100).

3 'But what is a difference? A difference is a very peculiar and obscure concept. It is certainly not a thing or an event' (*Steps to an Ecology of Mind*, pp. 451–2).

4 'The "essence" of life (which is no essence, but rather no-thing) is *différance*. This I translate here as "goalseeking" in the sense that both origins and goals are Imaginary illusions: it is the SEEKING and not the goal which is at the origin of human affairs' (Wilden, *System and Structure*, p. 399).

5 *Steps to an Ecology of Mind*, p. 483. It should be noted that the

context of this passage is a critique of the Western 'epistemological fallacy' that separates the 'self' from object, instrument, environment, others. The 'ecology of mind' Bateson proposes attempts to correct these fundamental – and he believes, ultimately counter-adaptive – mispunctuations of context. The parallels between this critique and readjustment of hierarchies and deconstruction are evident.

6 Again, this selective inflection is an example of the self-reflexivity of Derrida's text, which includes itself as an example of the law it enunciates. Derrida quite consciously and conspicuously advances his own theory of translation and survival as a supplementary layer or translation of Benjamin's text on translation. In a phrase recalling his interpretive inflection of Lucretius in 'Mes chances' ('Mon *clinamen*, ma chance ou mes chances', MC, p. 22 ('My *clinamen*, my luck or my chances' (*TC*, p. 16)), he reflexively underlines his own torsion of Benjamin's text: 'Telle est du moins mon interprétation – ma traduction, ma "tâche du traducteur"' (*PS*, p. 224) ('Such at least is my interpretation – my translation, my "task of the translator"' (TB, p. 191)).

7 *L'organisation biologique et la théorie de l'information*, p. 224.

8 Compare Rousseau's ultrastable systems, natural and social, examined in chapter 4 above.

9 *La naissance de la physique dans le texte de Lucrèce. Fleuves et turbulences*, Editions de Minuit, Paris, 1977.

10 *Ibid.*, p. 182.

11 See, for example, *Le parasite*; 'L'interférence objective: ce qui est écrit sur la table rase', in *Hermès II, L'interférence*, Editions de Minuit, Paris, 1972, pp. 67–125.

Bibliography

WORKS BY DERRIDA

Edmund Husserl, *L'origine de la géométrie*, translation and introduction, Presses Universitaires de France, Paris, 1962.

L'écriture et la différence, Editions du Seuil, Paris, 1967.

De la grammatologie, Editions de Minuit, Paris, 1967.

La voix et le phénomène, Presses Universitaires de France, Paris, 1967.

La dissémination, Editions du Seuil, Paris, 1972.

Marges – de la philosophie, Editions de Minuit, Paris, 1972.

Positions, Editions de Minuit, Paris, 1972.

L'archéologie du frivole. Lire Condillac, introduction to Condillac's *Essai sur l'origine des connaissances humaines*, Editions Galilée, Paris, 1973.

Glas, Editions Galilée, Paris, 1974.

'Economimesis', in Sylviane Agacinski, Jacques Derrida *et al.*, *Mimesis. Désarticulations*, Aubier-Flammarion, Paris, 1975, pp. 55–93.

'Fors. Les mots anglés de Nicolas Abraham et Maria Torok', preface to Nicolas Abraham and Maria Torok, *Cryptonymie. Le verbier de l'homme aux loups*, Aubier-Flammarion, Paris, 1976, pp. 7–73.

'Entre Crochets' and 'Ja, ou le faux bond', two interviews with Derrida, *Digraphe*, 8 and 11, April 1976 and March 1977, pp. 97–114 and 83–121.

'Limited Inc., a, b, c', in *Glyph*, 2 (supplement), Johns Hopkins University Press, Baltimore, 1977.

'Scribble', preface to Warburton, *Essai sur les hiéroglyphes*, translated by Léonard Des Malpeines, edited by Patrick Tort, Aubier-Flammarion, Paris, 1977, pp. 7–43.

Éperons. Les styles de Nietzsche, Flammarion, Paris, 1978.

La vérité en peinture, Flammarion, Paris, 1978.

La carte postale, de Socrate à Freud et au-delà, Flammarion, Paris, 1979.

'An Interview with Jacques Derrida', *The Literary Review*, 14, 1980, pp. 21–2.

'Ocelle comme pas un', preface to Jos Joliet, *L'enfant au chien-assis*, Editions Galilée, Paris, 1980, pp. 9–43.

L'oreille de l'autre. *Textes et débats avec Jacques Derrida*, edited by Claude Lévesque and Christie V. McDonald, VLB Editeur, Montreal, 1982.

'Mes chances. Au rendez-vous de quelques stéréophonies épicuriennes', *Tidjschrift voor filosofie*, 45 (1), 1983, pp. 3–40.

D'un ton apocalyptique adopté naguère en philosophie, Editions Galilée, Paris, 1983.

An interview with Christian Descamps in *Entretiens avec le Monde*, vol. I, *Philosophies*, Editions la Découverte, Paris, 1984, pp. 78–90.

Otobiographies. *L'enseignement de Nietzsche et la politique du nom propre*, Editions Galilée, Paris, 1984.

'Préjugés – devant la loi', in Jacques Derrida *et al.*, *La faculté de juger*, Editions de Minuit, Paris, 1985, pp. 87–139.

Parages, Editions Galilée, Paris, 1986.

Schibboleth. *Pour Paul Celan*, Editions Galilée, Paris, 1986.

De l'esprit. *Heidegger et la question*, Editions Galilée, Paris, 1987.

An interview with Imre Salusinszky in Imre Salusinszky, *Criticism in Society*, Methuen, New York and London, 1987, pp. 8–24.

Psyché. *Inventions de l'autre*, Editions Galilée, Paris, 1987.

Ulysse gramophone. *Deux mots pour Joyce*, Editions Galilée, Paris, 1987.

Mémoires – pour Paul de Man, Editions Galilée, Paris, 1988.

Du droit à la philosophie, Editions Galilée, Paris, 1990.

Le problème de la genèse dans la phénoménologie de Husserl, Presses Universitaires de France, Paris, 1990.

'Circonfession', in Geoffrey Bennington and Jacques Derrida, *Jacques Derrida*, Editions du Seuil, Paris, 1991.

TRANSLATIONS

Of Grammatology, translated by Gayatri Chakravorty Spivak, Johns Hopkins University Press, Baltimore and London, 1976.

Writing and Difference, translated by Alan Bass, Routledge and Kegan Paul, London, 1978.

'Living On', translated by James Hulbert, in Harold Bloom *et al.*, *Deconstruction and Criticism*, Continuum, New York, 1979, pp. 75–176.

Dissemination, translated by Barbara Johnson, University of Chicago Press, Chicago, 1981.

'Economimesis', translated by Richard Klein, in *Diacritics*, 11 (2), summer 1981, pp. 3–25.

Positions, translated by Alan Bass, University of Chicago Press, Chicago, 1981.

Margins of Philosophy, translated by Alan Bass, University of Chicago Press, Chicago, 1982.

Glas, translated by John P. Leavey Jr and Richard Rand, University of Nebraska Press, Lincoln and London, 1984.

'My Chances/*Mes Chances*: A Rendezvous with some Epicurean Stereophonies', translated by Irene Harvey and Avital Ronell, in *Taking Chances: Derrida, Psychoanalysis and Literature*, edited by Joseph H. Smith and William Kerrigan, Johns Hopkins University Press, Baltimore and London, 1984.

'Des Tours de Babel', translated by Joseph F. Graham, in *Difference in Translation*, edited by Joseph F. Graham, Cornell University Press, Ithaca and London, 1985.

The Ear of the Other: Otobiography, Transference, Translation, edited by Christie V. McDonald, translated by Peggy Kamuf and Avital Ronell, Schoken Books, New York, 1985.

'*Fors*: The Anglish Words of Nicolas Abraham and Maria Torok', foreword to *The Wolf Man's Magic Word: A Cryptonymy*, translated by Barbara Johnson, University of Minnesota Press, Minneapolis, 1986.

Memoires for Paul de Man, translated by Cecile Lindsay, Jonathan Culler, and Eduardo Cadava, translations edited by Avital Ronell and Eduardo Cadava, Columbia University Press, New York and Guildford, 1986.

The Post Card. From Socrates to Freud and Beyond, translated by Alan Bass, University of Chicago Press, Chicago and London, 1987.

The Truth in Painting, translated by Geoffrey Bennington and Ian McLeod, University of Chicago Press, Chicago and London, 1987.

Limited Inc., translated by Samuel Weber and Jeffrey Mehlman, Northwestern University Press, Evanston, 1988.

'Desistance', translated by Christopher Fynsk, introduction to Philippe Lacoue-Labarthe, *Typography: Mimesis, Philosophy, Politics*, Harvard University Press, Cambridge, Massachusetts and London, 1989.

CRITICAL WORKS ON DERRIDA

Bennington, Geoffrey, 'Derridabase', in Geoffrey Bennington and Jacques Derrida, *Jacques Derrida*, Editions du Seuil, Paris, 1991.

Carroll, David, *Paraesthetics: Foucault, Lyotard, Derrida*, Methuen, New York and London, 1987.

Culler, Jonathan, 'Jacques Derrida', in *Structuralism and Since: From Lévi-Strauss to Derrida*, edited by John Sturrock, Oxford University Press, London, 1979.

On Deconstruction: Theory and Criticism after Structuralism, Routledge and Kegan Paul, London, 1982.

Finas, Lucette *et al.*, *Ecarts: Quatre essais à propos de Jacques Derrida*, Fayard, Paris, 1973.

Garver, Newton, preface to Jacques Derrida, *Speech and Phenomena and Other Essays on Husserl's Theory of Signs*, translated with an introduction by David B. Allison, Northwestern University Press, Evanston, 1973, pp. ix–xxix.

Gasché, Rodolphe, *The Tain of the Mirror: Derrida and the Philosophy of Reflection*, Harvard University Press, Cambridge, Massachusetts, 1986.

Goux, Jean-Joseph, 'Du graphème au chromosome', *Les Lettres françaises*, 1429, 29 March 1972, pp. 6–7.

'La dissémination de Jacques Derrida', *Les Lettres françaises*, 1455, 11–17 October 1972, p. 15.

Guibal, Francis, and Stanislas Breton, editors, *Altérités – Jacques Derrida et Pierre-Jean Labarrière*, Editions Osiris, Paris, 1986.

Hartman, Geoffrey H., *Saving the Text: Literature/Deconstruction/Philosophy*, Johns Hopkins University Press, Baltimore and London, 1981.

Harvey, Irene H., *Derrida and the Economy of Différance*, Indiana University Press, Bloomington, 1986.

Hobson, Marian, 'Deconstruction, Empiricism and the Postal Services', *French Studies*, 34 (3), July 1982, pp. 290–314.

'Les négations de Derrida', in *Cross-References: Modern French Theory and the Practice of Criticism*, edited by David Kelley and Isabelle Llasera, Society for French Studies, Leeds, 1986, pp. 57–64.

'History Traces', in *Post-structuralism and the Question of History*, edited by D. Attridge, G. Bennington and R. Young, Cambridge University Press, Cambridge, 1987, pp. 101–15.

Krupnik, Mark (editor), *Displacement: Derrida and After*, Indiana University Press, Bloomington, 1983.

Lacoue-Labarthe, Philippe, and Jean-Luc Nancy, editors, *Les fins de l'homme – Colloque de Cérisy*, Editions Galilée, Paris, 1981.

Leavey Jr, John P., 'This (then), will not have been a book', in *Glassary*, University of Nebraska Press, Lincoln and London, 1986, pp. 2–128.

Lévesque, Claude, *L'étrangeté du texte: Essais sur Nietzsche, Freud, Blanchot et Derrida*, VLB Editeur, Montreal, 1976.

Llewelyn, John, *Derrida on the Threshold of Sense*, Macmillan, London, 1986.

Macann, Christopher, 'Jacques Derrida's Theory of Writing and the Concept of Trace', *Journal of the British Society for Phenomenology*, 2, May 1972, pp. 197–200.

Megill, Allan, *Prophets of Extremity: Nietzsche, Heidegger, Foucault, Derrida*, University of California Press, Berkeley, 1985.

Norris, Christopher, *Deconstruction: Theory and Practice*, Methuen, London, 1982.

 The Deconstructive Turn: Essays in the Rhetoric of Philosophy, Methuen, London, 1984.

 The Contest of Faculties: Philosophy and Theory after Deconstruction, Methuen, London, 1985.

 Derrida, Fontana, London, 1987.

Rapaport, Herman, *Heidegger and Derrida. Reflections on Time and Language*, University of Nebraska Press, Lincoln and London, 1989.

Rorty, Richard, 'Philosophy as a Kind of Writing', in *Consequences of Pragmatism. Essays: 1972–1980*, Harvester Press, Sussex, 1982.

Sallis, John, *Spacings – of Reason and Imagination in the Texts of Kant, Fichte, Hegel*, University of Chicago Press, Chicago and London, 1987.

Sallis, John, editor, *Deconstruction and Philosophy: the Texts of Jacques Derrida*, University of Chicago Press, Chicago and London, 1987.

Smith, Joseph H., and William Kerrigan, editors, *Taking Chances: Derrida, Psychoanalysis and Literature*, Johns Hopkins University Press, Baltimore and London, 1984.

Spivak, Gayatri C., translator's preface to *Of Grammatology*, Johns Hopkins University Press, Baltimore and London, 1976, pp. lx–lxxxvii.

Staten, Henry, *Derrida and Wittgenstein*, Blackwell, Oxford, 1985.

Strozier, Robert M., *Saussure, Derrida, and the Metaphysics of Subjectivity*, Mouton de Gruyter, Berlin, New York, Amsterdam, 1988. ✓

Taylor, Mark C., *Deconstructing Theology*, Scholars Press, New York, 1982.

 Erring(s): a Postmodern(ist) a/theology, University of Chicago Press, Chicago and London, 1984.

Taylor, Mark C., editor, *Deconstruction in Context: Literature and Philosophy*, University of Chicago Press, Chicago and London, 1986.

Ulmer, Gregory L., *Applied Grammatology: Post(e)-pedagogy from Jacques Derrida to Joseph Beuys*, Johns Hopkins University Press, Baltimore and London, 1985.

 'Sounding the Unconscious', in *Glassary*, edited by John P. Leavey Jr, University of Nebraska Press, Lincoln and London, 1986, pp. 23–129.

Wahl, François, 'La structure, le sujet, la trace' in François Wahl, *Qu'est-ce que le structuralisme?*, vol. V, Editions du Seuil, Paris, 1968.

Wood, David, 'Beyond Deconstruction?', in *Contemporary French Philosophy*, edited by A. Phillips Griffiths, Royal Institute of Philosophy Lecture Series: 21 (Supplement to *Philosophy*, 1987), Cambridge University Press, Cambridge, 1987.

OTHER WORKS CONSULTED

Aristotle, *Parts of Animals*, translated by A. L. Peck, Loeb Classical Library, Heinemann, London, 1961.
    Generation of Animals, translated by A. L. Peck, Loeb Classical Library, Heinemann, London, 1990.
Artaud, Antonin, *Le théâtre et son double*, Gallimard, Paris, 1964.
Atlan, Henri, *L'organisation biologique et la théorie de l'information*, Hermann, Paris, 1972.
    Entre le cristal et la fumée: essai sur l'organisation du vivant, Editions du Seuil, Paris, 1979.
Bataille, Georges, *Œuvres complètes*, 12 vols., Gallimard, Paris, 1970–88.
Bateson, Gregory, *Steps to an Ecology of Mind*, Ballantine Books, New York, 1972.
Benoist, Jean-Marie, *La révolution structurale*, Grasset, Paris, 1975.
Bertalanffy, Ludwig von, *General Systems Theory: Foundation, Development, Applications*, Allen Lane The Penguin Press, London, 1971.
    'Chance or Law', in *Beyond Reductionism: New Perspectives in the Life Sciences*, edited by Arthur Koestler and J. R. Smythies, Radius Books/Hutchinson, London, second edition, 1972, pp. 56–84.
    Perspectives on General System Theory. Scientific-Philosophical Studies, edited by Edgar Taschdjian, George Braziller, New York, 1975.
Blanchot, Maurice, *Le livre à venir*, Gallimard, Collection Idées, Paris, 1959.
Bunn, James H., *The Dimensionality of Signs, Tools and Models*, Indiana University Press, Bloomington, 1981.
Clarke, Simon, *The Foundations of Structuralism. A Critique of Lévi-Strauss and the Structuralist Movement*, Harvester Press, Sussex, 1981.
Cohen, R. S., and M. W. Wartofsky, editors, *Boston Studies in the Philosophy of Science*, vol. LXIV, *Hegel and the Sciences*, D. Reidel, Dordrecht, 1984.
Dagognet, François, 'Vie et théorie de vie selon Jean Hyppolite', in S. Bachelard, G. Canguilhem, F. Dagognet *et al.*, *Hommage à Jean Hyppolite*, Presses Universitaires de France, Paris, 1971.
Descamps, Christian, *Les idées philosophiques contemporaines en France, 1960–1985*, Bordas, Paris, 1986.
Descartes, René, *Méditations métaphysiques*, Nouveaux Classiques Larousse, Paris, 1973.

Descombes, Vincent, *Le même et l'autre. Quarante-cinq ans de philosophie française (1933–1978)*, Editions de Minuit, Paris, 1979.

Domenach, Jean-Marie, *Enquête sur les idées contemporaines*, Editions du Seuil, Paris, 1981.

Dupuy, Jean-Pierre, 'La pensée systémique', *Magazine littéraire*, 218, April 1985, pp. 28–31.

Foucault, Michel, *Histoire de la folie à l'âge classique*, Gallimard, Paris, 1972.

Freud, Sigmund, *Project for a Scientific Psychology*, in *The Origins of Psycho-Analysis. Letters to Wilhelm Fliess, Drafts and Notes: 1887–1902*, translated by Eric Mosbacher and James Strachey, edited by Marie Bonaparte, Anna Freud and Ernst Kris, Imago, London, 1954.

The Interpretation of Dreams, translated and edited by James Strachey, Pelican Freud Library, vol. IV, Harmondsworth, 1980.

Beyond the Pleasure Principle; 'A Note upon the "Mystic Writing-Pad"', in Pelican Freud Library, vol. XI, Harmondsworth, 1984, pp. 269–338 and 427–34.

Moses and Monotheism, in Pelican Freud Library, vol. XIII, Harmondsworth, 1985, pp. 237–386.

'The "Uncanny"', in Pelican Freud Library, vol. XIV, Harmondsworth, 1985, pp. 335–76.

Girard, René, *La violence et le sacré*, Pluriel, Grasset, Paris, 1972.

Le bouc émissaire, Pluriel, Grasset, Paris, 1982.

Hegel, G. W. F., *Phenomenology of Spirit*, translated by A. V. Miller, Oxford University Press, Oxford, 1977.

Lectures on the Philosophy of Religion, vol. I, translated by R. F. Brown, P. C. Hodgson and J. M. Stewart, University of California Press, Berkeley, 1984.

Heidegger, Martin, *Being and Time*, Blackwell, Oxford, 1962.

Early Greek Thinking, translated by D. F. Krell and F. A. Capuzzi, Harper and Row, London, 1975.

Basic Writings, translated by F. Capuzzi, G. Gray and D. Krell, edited by D. Krell, Harper and Row, New York, 1977.

Hyppolite, Jean, *Figures de la pensée philosophique*, 2 vols., Presses Universitaires de France, Paris, 1971.

Jacob, François, *La logique du vivant: une histoire de l'hérédité*, Gallimard, Paris, 1970; translated by Betty E. Spillman as *The Logic of Life*, Pantheon Books, New York, 1973.

'Le modèle linguistique en biologie', *Critique*, 322, March 1974, pp. 195–205.

Kant, Immanuel, *The Critique of Judgement*, translated by James Creed Meredith, Oxford University Press, Oxford, 1973.

Kojève, Alexandre, *Introduction à la lecture de Hegel*, Gallimard, Paris, 1947.

Lacan, Jacques, *Ecrits*, Editions du Seuil, Paris, 1966.

The Language of the Self: the Function of Language in Psychoanalysis, translated with notes and commentary by Anthony Wilden, Johns Hopkins University Press, Baltimore and London, 1968.

Leroi-Gourhan, André, *Le geste et la parole*, 2 vols., Albin Michel, Paris, 1964 and 1965.

Levinas, Emmanuel, *Totalité et Infini: essai sur l'extériorité*, *Phænomenologia* 8, Martinus Nijhoff, The Hague, 1961.

Lévi-Strauss, Claude, *Tristes tropiques*, Plon, Paris, 1955.

Introduction à l'œuvre de Marcel Mauss, in Marcel Mauss, *Sociologie et Anthropologie*, Presses Universitaires de France, Paris, 1973.

Anthropologie structurale, Plon, Paris, 1958, second edition 1974.

Lucretius, *On the Nature of the Universe*, translated with an introduction by R. E. Latham, Penguin, Harmondsworth, 1982.

Lyotard, Jean-François, *Economie libidinale*, Editions de Minuit, Paris, 1974.

Macksey, Richard, and Eugenio Donato, *The Languages of Criticism and the Sciences of Man*, Johns Hopkins University Press, Baltimore, 1970.

Mallarmé, Stéphane, *Œuvres complètes*, edited by Henri Mondor and G. Jean-Aubry, Gallimard, Paris, 1945.

Merrell, Floyd, 'Structuralism and Beyond: a Critique of Presuppositions', *Diogenes*, 92, winter 1975, pp. 67–103.

Monod, Jacques, *Le hasard et la nécessité*, Editions du Seuil, Paris, 1970.

Morin, Edgar, *La méthode: I. La Nature de la Nature*, Points-Seuil, Paris, 1977.

Nietzsche, Friedrich, *Werke in drei Bänden*, edited by Karl Schlechta, 3 vols., Carl Hanser, Munich, 1954–65.

Human, All Too Human, translated by R. J. Hollingdale, Cambridge University Press, Cambridge, 1986.

Ong Walter J., *Interfaces of the Word: Studies in the Evolution of Consciousness and Culture*, Cornell University Press, London, 1977.

✓ Pattee, Howard H., editor, *Hierarchy Theory: The Challenge of Complex Systems*, George Braziller, New York, 1973.

Piaget, Jean, *Le structuralisme*, Presses Universitaires de France, Paris, 1968.

Plato, *Phaedrus*, translated with an introduction by Walter Hamilton, Penguin, Harmondsworth, 1973.

The Republic, translated with an introduction by Desmond Lee, Penguin, Harmondsworth, second edition, 1974.

Prigogine, Ilya, and Isabelle Stengers, *La nouvelle alliance: métamorphose de la science*, Gallimard, Paris, 1979.

Roth, Michael S., *Knowing and History: Appropriations of Hegel in Twentieth-Century France*, Cornell University Press, Ithaca and London, 1988.

Rousseau, Jean-Jacques, *Essai sur l'origine des langues*, A. G. Nizet, Paris, 1970.

Rousset, Jean, *Forme et Signification: Essais sur les structures littéraires de Corneille à Claudel*, José Corti, Paris, 1962.

Saussure, Ferdinand de, *Cours de linguistique générale*, Payot, Paris, 1986.

Serres, Michel, *Hermès II, L'interférence*, Editions de Minuit, Paris, 1972.

Hermès III, La traduction, Editions de Minuit, Paris, 1974.

Hermès IV, La distribution, Editions de Minuit, Paris, 1977.

La naissance de la physique dans le texte de Lucrèce. Fleuves et turbulences, Editions de Minuit, Paris, 1977.

Le parasite, Grasset, Paris, 1980.

Sollers, Philippe, *Nombres*, Editions du Seuil, Paris, 1968.

Wiener, Norbert, *Cybernetics or Control and Communication in the Animal and the Machine*, MIT Press, Cambridge, Massachusetts, second edition, 1961.

Wilden, Anthony, *System and Structure: Essays in Communication and Exchange*, Tavistock Publications, London, 1972, second edition, 1980.

Index of names

Subject index

CAMBRIDGE STUDIES IN FRENCH

General editor: Malcolm Bowie (*All Souls College, Oxford*)
Editorial board: R. Howard Bloch (*University of California, Berkeley*),
Ross Chambers (*University of Michigan*), Antoine Compagnon
(*Columbia University*), Peter France (*University of Edinburgh*),
Toril Moi (*Duke University*), Naomi Schor (*Duke University*)